Studies in the Scope and Method of
"THE AUTHORITARIAN PERSONALITY"

Studies in the Scope and Method of

"THE AUTHORITARIAN PERSONALITY"

CONTINUITIES IN SOCIAL RESEARCH

Edited by

RICHARD CHRISTIE

and

MARIE JAHODA

THE FREE PRESS, GLENCOE, ILLINOIS

Copyright 1954 by the Free Press, a corporation

Printed in the United States of America

FORMAT BY SIDNEY SOLOMON

For
Gail and Lotte

New and Continued
Experiments in Continuity

CONTENTS

Marie Jahoda
INTRODUCTION
11

Edward A. Shils
AUTHORITARIANISM: "RIGHT" AND "LEFT"
24

Herbert H. Hyman and Paul B. Sheatsley
*"THE AUTHORITARIAN PERSONALITY"—
A METHODOLOGICAL CRITIQUE*
50

Richard Christie
AUTHORITARIANISM RE-EXAMINED
123

Harold D. Lasswell
*THE SELECTIVE EFFECT OF PERSONALITY
ON POLITICAL PARTICIPATION*
197

Else Frenkel-Brunswik
*FURTHER EXPLORATIONS BY A CONTRIBUTOR
TO "THE AUTHORITARIAN PERSONALITY"*
226

INDEX
276

Studies in the Scope and Method of
"THE AUTHORITARIAN PERSONALITY"

MARIE JAHODA

INTRODUCTION

THIS volume is the second in a series designed to promote continuity in social research. Like its predecessor[1], which was devoted to a discussion of *The American Soldier*, it deals with a work whose content matter has deeply affected the life experience of our generation. *The Authoritarian Personality*[2] began as a study of anti-Semitism; in the course of the five years which went into its production the scope of the undertaking widened into an exploration of a problem not less decisive for the understanding of our times: the relation between personality, social discrimination, and political ideology.

Although both *The American Soldier* and *The Authoritarian Personality* are socially and historically relevant, there is a significant difference between the types of content matter they treat. *The American Soldier* dealt with a new subject; for the first time a mass of data was presented concerning a wide range of attitudes and opinions of soldiers in the army of a democratic country; had the work done nothing else it would have arrested the attention of social scientists who—whether they want to be or not—are often the historians of the present. In contrast, there is nothing new about the subject matter of *The Authoritarian Personality*; anti-Semitism, social discrimination and political ideologies have been experienced and analyzed throughout the history of Western civilization. The work's claim to attention rests not in the newness of its subject matter but in its combination of content, method and theory which, taken together, form a new approach to an old topic.

---

[1] Merton, R. K. and Lazarsfeld, P. F., eds., *Studies in the Scope and Methods of "The American Soldier,"* The Free Press, Glencoe, Ill., 1950.

[2] *The Authoritarian Personality*, Adorno, T. W., Frenkel, Brunswik, Else, Levinson, D. J., Sanford, R. N., in collaboration with Aron, Betty, Levinson, Maria H., and Morrow, W., Harper & Brothers, New York, 1950. Sponsored by the American Jewish Committee, Social Studies Series: Publication No. III.

It is this special feature of *The Authoritarian Personality* which suggests that a search for continuity should not be limited to appraising its relation to the current status of the social sciences or to considerations about the avenues it opens for future research. Nor will it do justice to the historical dignity of the subject to trace its relations to earlier efforts during the few decades of a scientific psychology. For the philosophers of many past centuries already knew much of what we are now rediscovering in the painstaking efforts of our young science. To give but one example: Tertullian in his often-quoted exasperated outcry against the persecutions of the early Christians[3] already fully realized the functional nature of prejudice, a concept which is basic to the researches in *The Authoritarian Personality*. However, we social scientists are notoriously delinquent in acknowledging our debts to the past. Whether this is due to ingratitude, impatience or just ignorance, the fact remains that we have here neither the knowledge nor the space to link systematically the ideas which have entered into *The Authoritarian Personality* to the history of thought. Inevitably, then, the task of tracing continuities must be conceived on a rather modest scale. The focus of attention in this volume is largely on the present.

What we have called the new approach of *The Authoritarian Personality* became possible because its authors made converge on the age-old subject several recent trends in social theory and research. First, the entire work is permeated with the theoretical system of psychoanalysis. The basic questions are formulated and interpretations are performed in terms of psychoanalytic theory. What is perhaps even more telling for the place of psychoanalytic theory in the authors' thoughts is the fact that their methods of data collection and analysis are geared to this theoretical orientation. In that respect the authors have followed a practice which has become more and more accepted in much of current clinical psychology. Their use of projective techniques such as the Thematic Apperception Test, of projective questions, and of the "clinical interview" illustrates a second trend in *The Authoritarian Personality*, which is, of course, closely related to the first. To use the methods of clinical psychology in conjunction with psychoanalytic theory is, of course, now a frequent procedure. To use this combination for

---

[3] "If the Tiber overflows into the city, if the Nile does not flow into the countryside, if the heavens remain unmoved, if the earth quakes, if there is famine or pestilence, at once the cry goes up: to the lions with the Christians!"

other than clinical purposes, however, that is, for the exploration of political ideologies and its relation to personality structure is a relatively rare and new approach. For the study of social attitudes and opinions had previously been conducted on a different basis. In the development of the methods applied to attitude measurement the basic unit of analysis was the attitude; and though types of attitudes have frequently been correlated with other attributes of persons, these correlations as a rule concerned such social characteristics as age, income, education, religion, etc., and not the whole person in the psychodynamic sense. Clinical psychology, on the other hand, is predicated on the assumption of unity of personality. Every form of human behavior, such as an attitude, for instance, is regarded as a manifestation of the whole person and is analyzed in terms of total personality structure.

Before the appearance of *The Authoritarian Personality* the study of social attitudes as functional from a personality point of view was a rare phenomenon. Fromm[4] and Maslow[5] were lonely pioneers in this respect. The entire conception of *The Authoritarian Personality* obviously owes a great debt which its authors acknowledge to their thinking. Particularly in his earlier study Fromm comes very close to the general approach of *The Authoritarian Personality*. This is hardly surprising since Fromm was at that time a member of the *Institut für Sozialforschung*, whose director, Max Horkheimer, played an important role in formulating both the *Institut's* earlier concern with the problems of authority and the plan and conception of *The Authoritarian Personality*. The early inquiries of the *Institut*, published (like Fromm's contribution in *Autorität und Familie*, used a questionnaire which is remarkable both for its similarities and differences with that developed in the California studies. As far as content is concerned it contains more than thirty questions which come close to what we have now learned to call the PEC scale (political and economic conservatism); and some forty questions about *Weltanschauung* which correspond to F scale (fascism) items. In addition, it contains many questions on actual family relations designed to elicit patterns of domination and submission, i. e., the

---

[4] Fromm, E., *Escape from Freedom*, Farrar & Rhinehart, Inc., New York, 1941. See also his contribution to *Autorität und Familie*, Studien aus dem Institut für Sozialforschung, Librairie Felix Alcan, Paris, 1936.

[5] Maslow, A. H., "The authoritarian character structure," *Journal of Social Psychology*, 1943, 18, 401-411.

authority structure of the family, and a much more detailed account of the respondent's actual life situation in all aspects, than the data in *The Authoritarian Personality* reveal. Questions concerning anti-Semitism and other attitudes toward groups are, however, conspicuous by their absence.[6]

As for the art of asking questions and the method of interpreting answers, these two studies are as different as possible. In that respect the German studies are naive to an extent that recalls Whitehead's statement: "But to come very near to a true theory, and to grasp its precise application, are two very different things, as the history of science teaches us. Everything of importance has been said before by somebody who did not discover it." The *Institut* studies strove after a concept similar to that of *The Authoritarian Personality;* their relatively crude methods did not permit them to clinch the point. One or two of the contributions to this volume are devoted to a discussion of how close *The Authoritarian Personality* comes in its methods to establish its theory. The reader of this volume and of the work to which it refers must make up his own mind on this question. Whatever the answer, it is clear that *The Authoritarian Personality* has benefited considerably by taking advantage of another trend in American social science: the methodological development of opinion and attitude measurement and the corresponding techniques of statistical analysis.

Within the last two or three decades publications in this area have swollen to such proportions that it is virtually impossible to survey here adequately the vast array of preceding studies on whose cumulative contribution the attitude measurement in *The Authoritarian Personality* is based. A few selected references must suffice to indicate the links with the past. Bogardus was, of course, one of the first to concern himself with the standardization of an attitude scale[7], which led to the establishment of his familiar social distance scale. Notwithstanding its predictive value, the Bogardus scale has been criticized for ignoring the problem of equality of intervals between the various steps on the scale. For instance, is the degree of difference in attitude which distinguishes one who would marry a person

---

[6] The inquiry was, of course, conducted before the victory of National Socialism. As is well known, however, anti-Semitism was by no means an unknown phenomenon in Germany, even before 1933.

[7] Bogardus, E. S., "Measuring social distances," *Journal of Applied Sociology*, 1925; and Bogardus, E. S., "A social distance scale," *Sociology and Social Research*, 1933.

of different ethnic origin from another who would not do so though he would admit that person to his club as a personal "chum," similar to that which distinguishes the latter from those who would go no farther than admitting the foreigner to their residential neighborhood? It was Thurstone and his collaborators who developed attitude scales designed to insure equal step-intervals. The Thurstone method, based on paired comparison and the utilization of judges, proved rather cumbersome in its application, notwithstanding its logical sophistication. And though his basic approach has led to the most advanced mathematical scaling techniques as developed by Guttmann and Lazarsfeld, the need for more easily applicable attitude measures has also led to Likert's revision of the Thurstone scale which put the equal distance problem back where Bogardus had left it. Likert's simplified version consists in eliciting the degree of agreement or disagreement with an attitudinal statement (agree very much, pretty much, a little; undecided; disagree a little, pretty much, very much). While this may at first sight appear as a regression, there is an important empirical justification for Likert's approach: when the attitudes of students were scored both by Thurstone and Likert scales, the correlation between the two scores was .88 and their reliability coefficients exactly alike.[8]

The Authoritarian Personality actually used the Likert technique. This was an appropriate choice in view of another advantage which the Likert technique offers: in the Likert scale, items can be included which need not be related in an overt and logical manner to the attitude to be tested. What is finally included in a Likert scale is determined by an item's correlation with the entire scale score. In contrast, the judges in the Thurstone technique are restricted, of course, to a rational judgment about an item's relation to others; underlying psychological relationships of items are by that method excluded. The entire approach in *The Authoritarian Personality* is served much better by the greater psychological flexibility of the Likert technique. The concomitant disadvantage is this method's lack of "objectivity."

In the application of attitude scales, political and ideological items similar in many respects to those used in the California project have long dominated the scene. As early as 1927, for instance, M.

---

[8] For a more detailed discussion of this point see Murphy, Murphy and Newcomb, *Experimental Social Psychology*, Harper & Brothers, New York and London, 1937.

H. Harper[9] developed an instrument to measure the political attitudes of American educators. His categories ranged from extremely conservative over a liberal position to extremely radical. In discussing Harper's study Murphy, Murphy and Newcomb take care to point out that terms such as 'conservative,' 'liberal' or 'radical' must be interpreted in their proper "space-time context." In other words, the measurement of liberalism, conservatism and radicalism is always dependent on some more or less explicit assumptions about political concepts and movements. This terminological point is of no small importance here.[10] Shils' and Christie's contributions to this volume suggest that the related terminology used in *The Authoritarian Personality* impedes rather than advances the full interpretation of the data.

Harper's items were originally classified along the conservatism-radicalism dimension by the use of judges. It would be of considerable interest to repeat the procedure with the same items now, 25 years after their first use. In any case, at that earlier period, a whole host of studies used Harper's or similar scales to investigate the frequency distribution of these political attitudes among various groups and to establish their correlation with other attitudes, and with social and economic characteristics of their proponents.

Stagner's[11] study of fascist attitudes conducted a decade later is of special interest to us because of his clear realization that fascist views are more than just political opinions. He describes them as part of an integrated system of outlook, beliefs, and attitudes (including group prejudices), a thought which is clearly in agreement with the approach in *The Authoritarian Personality*. Stagner's study actually influenced Edwards'[12] work from whom, in turn, the California investigation borrowed several items for the E scale (Ethno-

---

[9] Quoted from Murphy, Murphy and Newcomb; op. cit.

[10] That terminological matters can, on occasion, seriously impede the vision of a scientist is illustrated by an episode out of Freud's life. Freud records that his early observations of hysteria in men were disbelieved by his colleagues. Consequently he wanted to demonstrate such patients at the Viennese Society of Medicine. But the senior physicians in whose department he discovered them refused permission for the demonstration. The basis of their refusal was epitomized by one surgeon who protested: "But my dear Sir, how can you talk such nonsense? Hysteron means the uterus. So how can a man be hysterical?" Quoted from Lasswell, H. D., *Psychopathology and Politics*, Univ. of Chicago Press, 1930.

[11] Stagner, R., "Fascist attitudes: an exploratory study," *Journal of Social Psychology*, 1936, 7.

[12] Edwards, A. L., "Unlabeled fascist attitudes," *Journal of Abnormal and Social Psychology*, 1941, 36.

centrism). *The Authoritarian Personality* acknowledges in several places its indebtedness to these and earlier workers in the field and points out striking similarities in some results.

In the full knowledge of the arbitrariness of selection two other early forerunners of the California investigation should be mentioned because some of their techniques and approaches foreshadow work which has followed the publication of *The Authoritarian Personality*:[13] T. H. Howells[14] conducted a number of experiments with 51 extreme radicals and 50 extreme conservatives with regard to religion, selected from an original group of 542 students. The experiments concerned muscle co-ordination, endurance of pain, persistence of effort, suggestibility, etc. In several instances highly significant differences were found. While not all of his results were replicated by subsequent studies, the idea nevertheless emerges that radicals and conservatives are entirely different types of persons as measured in personality manifestations which are not ego-controlled and which have no apparent bearing on their convictions and attitudes.

Even more striking, perhaps, are Moore's[15] findings that radicals excel in the ability to break long-established habits as measured by the degree of success in mirror-drawing, and that they surpass conservatives in their ability to think in unusual terms as judged by responses to the Kent-Rosanoff word association test.

With all this, Murphy, Murphy and Newcomb could say in 1937 that "American psychologists have not, until recently perhaps, been hospitable even to the more objective methods of 'total personality' study. At any rate, there are few investigations, in which data concerning both attitudes and 'total personality' are to be found—except those, useless for our purposes, in which each has been inferred in circular fashion from the other." That this statement, true in 1937, is so palpably untrue for 1953 is in no small measure due to *The Authoritarian Personality*.

[13] See, e. g., Rokeach's study on mental rigidity in ethnocentrism, and Frenkel-Brunswik's article on intolerance of ambiguity. Both are discussed in Frenkel-Brunswik's contribution to this volume.

[14] Howells, T. H., "A comparative study of those who accept as against those who reject religious authority," *Univ. of Iowa Studies*, 1930, 2, No. 3; and "An experimental study of persistence," *Journal of Abnormal and Social Psychology*, 1933, 28.

[15] Moore, H. T., "Innate factors in radicalism and conservatism," *Journal of Abnormal and Social Psychology*, 1929, 35.

There is yet another trend in American social science which has undoubtedly influenced the authors of the California studies. It is most easily, though perhaps not most accurately, identified by the growing concern with the relation between culture and personality. This relationship is in itself a topic of long standing in the history of thought, going back at least to the classical thinkers of ancient Greece. In the twentieth century Freud's genius has given new impetus to the study of culture and personality. Social anthropologists and political scientists have been stimulated to regard their respective subjects not as above and beyond the individual personality, but actually as inextricably interwoven with it. To the extent that these branches of the behavioral sciences have increased their interest in psychological phenomena they have begun to borrow methods and concepts from psychology for the advancement of their own fields. Harold Lasswell,[16] e. g., used the case study method in his *Psychopathology and Politics;* he collected his data largely through prolonged clinical interviews with patients in mental hospitals. The study was a radically new departure in political science. Conceptually and to some extent even methodologically *The Authoritarian Personality* follows much along the lines of Lasswell's earlier work, and, as he explains in his contribution to this volume, opens the way for further collaboration between psychology and political science.

In discussing past and present trends in the social sciences as they are reflected in *The Authoritarian Personality* one would like to be able to place the work with regard to the manner in which it handles the relationship between empirical data and theory. For this relationship determines more than anything else what might be called the *style* of a scientific effort. This is, however, a complicated task for two reasons. First, it is not easy to discern a definite trend in this respect in contemporary social psychology; and second, *The Authoritarian Personality* does not express explicitly a preference with regard to this question of style; implicit indications are open to various interpretations.

There are with regard to scientific style several contrasting trends noticeable in current publications. On the lip service level, to be sure, there is widespread agreement: blind empiricism is rejected as much as empty theorizing (though recent examples of the one as well as the other could easily be cited). Even if we take this re-

---

[16] op. cit.

Introduction

jection of extreme positions at face value, it does not yet indicate the precise manner in which data and theory are actually related to each other in current research. With some studies the impression is conveyed that the collection of data is arranged in such a manner that it cannot but bear out an established theory. With other studies the impression is equally strong that a concern for theoretical matters has not influenced at all the gathering of evidence; whatever theoretical considerations enter into such publications appear to be imposed upon the data *post factum*. At very rare occasions have these two constituent parts of science been handled in continuous interplay so that theoretical concerns govern the collection of empirical data which, in turn, are used to modify the theory so that it can better lead to new discoveries; and so on, in a continuous shift of emphases. Durkheim's *Suicide*, produced fifty years ago, is still an unrivalled model for this latter style.

At first glance *The Authoritarian Personality* with its many tables and verbatim quotations from clinical interviews and projective tests gives the impression of an overwhelmingly empirical emphasis, an impression which is strengthened by the absence of a concise formulation of its theoretical position in the almost one thousand pages of the book. A more thorough study, however, makes it possible to glean the theory from statements interspersed throughout the text. And under the critical eyes of some experts the empirical emphasis dissolves altogether[17]; they suggest that here, too, empirical evidence is obtained and used only to bear out the researchers' theoretical position assumed before they started the study and not modified after the effort. All that can be said, then, is that with regard to the handling of the relationship between empirical data and theory, *The Authoritarian Personality* has not clarified a generally confused picture.

Notwithstanding the foregoing comment, this brief survey of the various trends of thought and research which have converged in *The Authoritarian Personality* underlines its achievement. There is in social psychology and in the social sciences in general, too much work going on based on the foolish and arrogant assumption that no one else has ever given thought and effort to the problem under investigation. *The Authoritarian Personality* is free from that sin. The vast number of current studies which take the work as a starting point, and the acclaim it has found in many branches of social

---

[17] See, especially, Hyman's and Sheatsley's contribution in this volume.

science are the rewarding result of incorporating into a major work, the concepts, content and methods which concern many highly specialized students of human behavior.

The effect which *The Authoritarian Personality* has had on the social sciences presents one justification for this volume. There is another of no less importance. The book is influencing not only research workers but also other intellectuals, and many thousands of students. This wider influence is indeed one of the high hopes for the work which Max Horkheimer expressed in his Preface to *The Authoritarian Personality*:

> "The present work, we hope, will find a place in this history of the interdependence between science and the cultural climate. Its ultimate goal is to open new avenues in a research area which can become of immediate practical significance. It seeks to develop and promote an understanding of social psychological factors which have made it possible for the authoritarian type of man to threaten to replace the individualistic and democratic type prevalent in the past century and a half of our civilization. . . ."

That Horkheimer's hope for the work's influence on the current climate of thought appears to be realistic, is another justification for this volume. If the work is actually influencing various branches of the social sciences and, beyond it, a wider circle of intellectuals, it is in the interest of all to re-examine dispassionately the assumptions on which the book rests, the methods it uses, and the guides it contains for further research. The five contributions to this volume aim at performing such a re-examination.

Shils' critical contribution is concerned with a clarification of concepts. *Authoritarianism of the Right and Left* is an analysis of some of the political assumptions tacitly underlying the studies in *The Authoritarian Personality*. He does not take exception to what the work reveals about the personality of the extremist on the right. But as a student of political thought and political movement he questions the sharp dichotomy between personality predispositions for the extreme "right" and the extreme "left" which *The Authoritarian Personality* suggests. This dichotomy was appropriate for the political life of the 19th century. In the middle of the 20th century it is inappropriate notwithstanding its strong tendency for survival. The development of this thought leads Shils to point up a neglect in *The Authoritarian Personality*, namely the lack of dis-

Introduction

tinctions between all those who disagree with the views of the extreme right: they can be communists or democrats.

Actually, the original volume contains some treatment of the distinction between these two groups which are opposed to each other as well as to the extreme right (p. 771 ff. in *The Authoritarian Personality*). The "rigid" low scorer on items of prejudice has not integrated his view on minorities within his personality, but it "is derived from some general, external, ideological pattern." In contrast to the genuine low scorers, (the democrats), the "rigid" low scorers, (the communists), "are definitely disposed toward totalitarianism in their thinking." Whether the much less thorough discussion of the "rigid" low in *The Authoritarian Personality* is the inevitable result of a scarcity of such cases (as the authors think) or of a shortsightedness in the analysis (as Shils thinks) the reader of both will have to decide for himself.

The importance of Shils' contribution for an understanding of the current political climate in this country need hardly be pointed out. The chapter should stimulate sociologists and social psychologists to greater political sophistication in their reality-oriented research on the crucial questions of our times.

Hyman's and Sheatsley's *Methodological Critique* reviews each of the major research steps taken in the California studies and compares them with the best knowledge available on the methods under discussion. This contribution by two acknowledged experts in survey research raises a series of pertinent questions about the relation of data and theory in the original volume. It presents a concrete demonstration of the need for methodological rigor in asking and interpreting questions and in the analysis of qualitative material from clinical interviews. Its usefulness goes beyond the purpose it serves here; it may well become an indispensable reading assignment in all advanced courses on research methods. The critical nature of this chapter does, of course, not disprove the theories advanced in *The Authoritarian Personality*, as the authors of the chapter take care to point out. Their type of criticism is probably equally appropriate for other social psychological studies. It cannot always be made because few publications contain as much detail about procedures as *The Authoritarian Personality*. If other research followed this example, the raising of methodological standards in the field would be an easier task.

The main function of Christie's contribution consists in reviewing those studies which have taken off from *The Authoritarian Personality* and which have yielded results clarifying or modifying the original findings. It is a symbol for the impact of the work, that a comprehensive review of all research to some extent stimulated by it, is beyond the space he had at his disposal. The selection of studies for his chapter was largely guided by the wish to produce additional research evidence on some of the moot points in the book. To do so required another critical examination of its concepts and procedures. In comparing what *The Authoritarian Personality* left doubtful with research conducted since its publication, he indirectly points to the large unchartered field in which our present knowledge is still inadequate.

The two following contributions concentrate on ideas arising from the original volume and pointing to further work. In this context Lasswell's article occupies a special place, which reflects his position in American social science. There is hardly anyone who equals him as a living symbol for continuity and interdisciplinary integration in social research. His early work must be regarded as an antecedent to *The Authoritarian Personality;* here he appears again as one ready to take off from it into new and original research. In essence, he elaborates a set of hypotheses whose testing will depend on the cooperation of psychologists and political scientists. The subject in which he is interested—*homo politicus,* and especially the political leader of democratic and authoritarian parties and movements—clearly stems from political science; the nature of the hypotheses from psychology. His article should do much to bridge the gap between the two disciplines, in the interest of both.

Finally, Frenkel-Brunswik, one of the authors of the original work, discusses some of her current studies, stemming from her continued concern with the problems raised by *The Authoritarian Personality*. In doing so she elaborates some of the ideas in the original volume and brings striking confirmation from unexpected quarters for the psychological validity of the personality syndrome it established: the typology of the Nazi psychologist Jaensch.

Neither she nor any of the other authors of *The Authoritarian Personality* have been asked to reply to the criticisms raised in some of the following pages. This is a deliberate omission. A work of the scope and size of *The Authoritarian Personality* must speak for itself, as it most assuredly does. The extent to which what it says and

Introduction 23

how it is said needs clarification and revision is perhaps better judged by other experts in the field. For it need hardly be pointed out that it is not the purpose of this volume to praise or blame, to accuse or defend. The conceptual and methodological problems raised by *The Authoritarian Personality* are discussed but not resolved in the following pages. Some of them are, perhaps, taken a step further than where they were left by the original authors. To the extent that other research workers will benefit from the discussion here presented, this publication will have achieved its goal: to facilitate in some small measure the continuous flow of thoughts and studies which is required for the development of a solid body of knowledge in the social sciences.

EDWARD A. SHILS

AUTHORITARIANISM: "RIGHT" AND "LEFT"

*B*Y the end of the nineteenth century, it was widely believed in Continental Europe and in the United States that political institutions and activities could be described as either "radical" or "conservative." Each term had its synonyms and each admitted of variations in both directions. Radicalism moved off in one direction towards socialism, evolutionary and revolutionary, and ultimately towards anarchism, and in the other direction towards liberalism and the moderate position. On the other side, conservatism by accentuating its peculiar characteristics became reactionary, or it could modify itself in the opposite direction and move towards the "center." Radicalism was "left" and conservatism was "right." Continental and later British and American political intellectuals came to accept the validity of the dichotomy of right and left in political life even where it did not use the terminology which flourished particularly in radical and socialist circles. Every political programme could, it was thought, be placed on this scale and be fairly judged.

The view rested, especially among socialists, on the belief that fundamentally each of the main political positions formed a coherent and indissoluble unity. Thus, for example, conservatism, according to this notion, was characterized by attachment to private property, hostility towards universal male or adult suffrage, rejection of freedom of association and assembly for working men, an acknowledgment of the rightfulness of self-enrichment by individual exertion, a repugnance for humanitarian and social welfare legislation, devotion to economic and social inequality derived from a belief in the inequality of human qualities and achievements, disapproval of state regulation of private economic activity, etc. This was called the point of view of the Right. And each element in it was thought to be peculiar and necessary to the Right Wing outlook.

Authoritarianism: "Right" and "Left"

In contrast to it stood the point of view of the Left. This entailed a general derogation of private property, a preference for political democracy including the universal enjoyment of all civil liberties, a rejection of pecuniary goals and standards, the espousal of humanitarian goals to be achieved through social legislation, the aspiration towards economic and social equality based on a sense of the fundamentally equal dignity of all men and preference for the collective organization or regulation of economic life. The Left also believed in progress and therefore welcomed change. It was antagonistic towards religious institutions and beliefs and it had great faith in science as the liberator and benefactor of humanity. It believed that man's individual merit and not family connections should determine his position in life. The Right was opposed to the Left in all these respects and in all others. The opposition on every point was accentuated by the fact that the mere contention of the value of some institution or practice by the Right made it into a target of Leftist criticism. For example, patriotism or loyalty to the national state found its counterpart in the Marxist claim that the workingman has no fatherland. The seating arrangements in legislative chambers, ranging from extreme Left to extreme Right, seemed to confirm the inevitable nature of this continuum of political outlooks.

Nor can there be any doubt that in the decades surrounding the turn of the century in Continental political life this simplification did have a certain descriptive truth. There are good reasons for it. Continental domestic politics through much of the 19th century, centered to a large extent around the ideals of the Liberal Enlightenment and the "ideas of 1789." Particularly to the Radical or Liberal parties or movements, which were usually in opposition and therefore remote from the complex of fine and overlapping differences which separate those political parties which are in the actual arena of political power, did it appear as if all parties were located along the continuum of Right and Left. "Leftist" parties in opposition tended often to define their own position on an issue simply by taking what they thought was the diametrically opposite position to that of their ruling opponents. This strengthened the conviction that Right and Left were the two basic directions of political life which pervaded the entire outlook of every party and group and it gave to each the appearance of necessary and unavoidable unity.

The Bolshevik Revolution did not seem at first to constitute an infringement on this classification. It was obviously the achievement of a group which stood at the extreme left and which refused to admit that any other group could be more left than it. Demands for more revolutionary action from within its own ranks were labelled as "infantile leftism." More revolutionary demands emanating from outside its ranks were derogated as petit-bourgeois romanticism or adventurism and therewith transferred "rightward" on the continuum. To observers among the Western intellectuals, the Bolshevik claims recommended themselves as wholly just. The Bolsheviks were seeming to realize the most extreme Leftist program by equally Leftist methods. Many liberal and socialist intellectuals in the decade after the first world war did not see anything fundamental to censure in the Bolshevik regime. Even though to some of them a few actions seemed regrettable, such as the terror and the suppression of all opposition parties, that seemed to them to be only a tactical necessity which an obnoxious *ancien regime* and a ruthless counter-revolution justified and made expedient. Bolshevism seemed to be on the road to the realization of the classical programme of the socialist Left and the Stalin Constitution of 1935 seemed to give veracity to this interpretation.

The appearance of Fascism in Italy and Germany caused little embarrassment to those whose political *Weltanschauung* was built within the framework of the Right-Left continuum. The Marxist interpretation of Fascism as the penultimate stage in the polarization of all political life into the extreme Right and the extreme Left prevailed almost universally in the 1930's in many intellectual circles. Fascism was seen as an accentuation of bourgeois conservatism, a conservatism driven to desperation by the inevitable crisis of capitalism. It was devoted to private property, opposed to political democracy and humanitarianism, it was inegalitarian and antiscientific and it sought to stabilize the existing social order. The fact that it sought to introduce fundamental changes in the *status quo* which it was alleged to be stabilizing was less of an embarrassment than the fact that its elite did not consist for the most part of big business men or that it instituted a far reaching scheme of regulations of private business enterprise.

This was not the first time that Marxists were embarrassed by the insufficiency of the Right-Left scheme. Tory Radicalism in 19th century Great Britain and the social legislation of Bismarckian Germany had both created difficulties for the Marxist viewpoint. The former had been dismissed as an amalgam of romanticism and hypocrisy, the latter as *State* Socialism and hence fraudulent.

Authoritarianism: "Right" and "Left"

Georges Sorel's ideas which contained elements conventionally associated with both Right and Left were written off by Marxists as Fascist.

Ingenious and erudite Marxist writers in the late 30's and early 40's sought to overcome the embarrassment for their system of thought by the argument that Nazism was the servant of German Capitalism. Through resourceful arguments they sought to demonstrate the capitalistic nature of Nazism while at the very same time rendering the interpretation insecure by the impressive body of data which they presented.

During this time, however, events in the Soviet Union, particularly the "purges," the abortion laws, the introduction of school fees, the restriction of progressive education, the persistence and growth of pronounced inequalities in income and status, the re-emergence of patriotism as an official policy—these and many other backslidings from the purest ideals of Leftist extremism placed a further burden upon the now rickety structure of Right and Left as a scheme for political analysis.

What had been looked upon as a seamless unity was turning out to be a constellation of diverse elements which could be recombined in constellations which had not for many years been imagined. Hostility towards private property was now seen to be capable of combination with anti-Semitism, inequality, the repression of civil liberties, etc. Welfare legislation was seen to enter into combination with political oligarchy, the elimination of civil liberties was combined with an increase in equalitarianism. In short, what had once appeared to be a simple unidimensional scheme now turned out to be a complicated multidimensional pattern in which there were many different political positions. The attachment to private property was now perceived as compatible both with sympathy with humanitarianism and with a disapproval of welfare legislation, the respect for civil liberties could fit with either socialism or capitalism, equalitarianism could go with either democracy or oligarchy. But above all, the two poles of the continuum Right and Left which were once deemed incompatible and mutually antagonistic were discovered to overlap in many very striking respects.

Fascism and Bolshevism, only a few decades ago thought of as worlds apart, have now been recognized increasingly as sharing many very important features. Their common hostility towards civil liberties, political democracy, their common antipathy for parliamentary institutions, individualism, private enterprise, their image the political world as a struggle between morally irreconcilable forces, their belief that all their opponents are secretly leagued against them and their own predilection for secrecy, their conviction that all forms of power are in a hostile world concentrated in a few hands and their own aspirations for concentrated and total power—all of these showed that the two extremes had much in common.

The prejudice however dies very hard. Even those of us who have seen the spurious nature of the polarity of 'Right' and 'Left' still find it hard to dispense with it. There has been no re-coalescence or regrouping of the constituent ideas of our political outlook which is at once sufficiently simple and convenient for our use. In general conversation we still use these terms although we know that they are at most a shorthand which will have to be replaced by particulars as soon as the discussion is joined.

The obsolete belief that all political, social and economic philosophies can be classified on the Right-Left continuum however dies very hard. A recent and very instructive instance of this steadfast adherence to the Right-Left polarity is the monumental investigation into *The Authoritarian Personality*. An examination of the manner in which political preconceptions enter into one of the most elaborate social-psychological investigations hitherto undertaken illuminates important problems of procedure in social research and offers opportunities for the further interpretation of a body of rich data. The left-right dichotomy is present not only in the general interpretive chapters written by Professor Adorno but even in the severely empirical chapters written by Professor Levinson and Dr. Sanford. The entire team of investigators proceeds as if there were an unilinear scale of political and social attitudes at the extreme right of which stands the Fascist—the product and proponent of monopoly-capitalism and at the other end what the authors call the complete democrat who—as I shall presently demonstrate—actually holds the views of the non Stalinist Leninist.[1]

The anti-democrat or proto-fascist—the authoritarian personality—is distinguished by anti-Semitism, ethnocentrism and political-

---

[1] The authors themselves occasionally sense the difficulties of their position and seek to remedy them by the introduction of *ad hoc* concepts such as "pseudo-conservative" and "pseudo-democrat." These categories are not however introduced in a systematic way into either their quantitative or their clinical analyses. [See, in this connection the passage on the "rigid" low scorer in the Introduction to this volume, p. 21. eds.]

economic conservatism. He is rigid in his beliefs—although no evidence for this is presented—he makes frequent use of stereotypes in his political perceptions and judgments, he is sympathetic with the use of violence against his enemies, he distinguishes sharply between his "ingroup" and the "outgroups" which he interprets as menacing his security. More concretely he shares the most commonplace of the vulgar cliches about Jews, foreigners, reformers, homosexuals, intellectuals, and he admires strong men, business men, successful men, manly men who have no tender side or who allow it no play in their lives.

At the other extreme is the democrat who is sympathetic with the outcasts, the under-privileged, the discriminated against ethnic minorities, who sees through the hollowness of patriotism, who is alert to the defects of politicians and the selfishness of business men; governmental control of economic life appears to him necessary and just. He thinks wealth is not a great good, science the source of truth and progress. Indeed according to the expectations of Professor Levinson, he rejects every tenet of the anti-democrat's faith and *by implication* believes the opposite. I stress the denotative nature of the democratic beliefs as this study views them because the positive beliefs of the "democrat" are seldom presented in the questionnaire (only the "politico-economic conservatism" scale contains positive items). For the most part "democrats" are distinguished from "anti-democrats" through their rejection of a considerable series of illiberal opinions which are the stock in trade of the xenophobic fundamentalist, the lunatic fringe of the detractors of the late President Roosevelt. The more extreme opinions, in great measure, are those expressed before the war by the fanatical publishers of periodicals of tiny circulation and short lives, by the would-be leaders of the small conventicles of nativist saviors of the United States from Jewish and foreign influences and by American Legionnaires when on a campaign of righteousness. Those who reject these opinions are residually defined as "democrats"; the positive opinions they are expected to approve in the Politico-economic conservatism questionnaire are most often the commonplaces of the "left" intelligentsia—of those who approved the New Deal and more particularly those who in the late 40's sympathized with Mr. Henry Wallace and the Progressive Party. The positive items on the P.E.C. questionnaire are Wallaceite cliches to which at the time Communists and fellow travellers gave their assent as well as persons of humane sentiments who did not share the more elaborate ideology of the Stalinoid and fellow-travelling followers of the Progressive "line."[2] The questionnaire, concerned as it legitimately was to distinguish nativists and fundamentalists from others, put all those rejecting the nativistic-fundamentalist view expressed in each questionnaire item into the same category—distinguishing them only with respect to the strength of their disagreement. This failure to discriminate the substantially different types of outlook which could be called liberal, liberal collectivist, radical, Marxist, etc., is not just the outcome of the deficiency of the questionnaire technique in general nor does it arise from carelessness. It flows from the authors' failure to perceive the distinctions between totalitarian Leninism (particularly in a period of Peoples Front maneuvers), humanitarianism and New Deal interventionism.[3]

---

[2] Some of the positive items in the P.E.C. questionnaire are cited herewith:
First form 36: "It is the responsibility of the entire society, through its government, to guarantee everyone adequate housing, income and leisure." (p. 158)
44: "The only way to provide adequate medical care is through some programme of socialized medicine." (p. 158)
52: "It is essential after the war to maintain or increase the income taxes on corporations and private individuals." (p. 158)
53: "Labor unions should become stronger by being politically active and by publishing labor newspapers to be read by the general public." (p. 158)
Second form 9: "Most government controls over business should continue after the war." (p. 163)
15: "If America had more men like Henry Wallace in office we would get along much better." (p. 163)
43: "The government should own and operate all public utilities (transportation, gas, and electric, railroads, etc.)." (p. 163)
84: "Poverty could be almost entirely done away with if we made certain basic changes in our social and economic system." (p. 163)

[3] It might be pointed out that the investigators' failure to analyze in a differentiated manner the fundamentally heterogeneous outlooks which they group in the leftward sector of their continuum leads them into the same error as their antagonists, the Authoritarians of the Right, Senator McCarthy, the leading spirit of the House Un-American Affairs Committee, the Senatorial Committee on Internal Security, and their likeminded colleagues and supporters.

II

Opinion surveys are in themselves of no great importance in increasing our understanding of human behavior and the failure to measure the distribution of authoritarian attitudes would not of itself be especially interesting apart from the striking text which it provides for observations concerning the influence of political ideas and preferences on the categories of empirical analysis in the social sciences. In *The Authoritarian Personality*, however, this narrowness of political imagination, this holding fast to a deforming intellectual tradition, has greater significance. *The Authoritarian Personality* in its two major sections—in the sections by Levinson, Sanford and Dr. Else Frenkel-Brunswik—follows a quite highly integrated plan of analysis. The extreme cases of democratic and anti-democratic outlook (the High and Low Scorers on the various scales) which Dr. Frenkel-Brunswik analyzed more intensively were selected by virtue of their performance on the questionnaires. As a result it is highly probable that a number of authoritarians of the "Left" have been included among those who scored "low" in Anti-Semitism, Ethnocentrism, Political-Economic-Conservatism or Fascism. In her analysis Dr. Frenkel-Brunswik concentrated on the interpretation of the major differences between the deeper dispositions of the High Scorers and the Low Scorers and paid practically no attention to the Low Scorers in the questionnaire who in clinical interviews showed the traits of the High Scorers.[4]

Among the 35 low scorers, there were at least five "Leftists." In most of the categories of deeper cognitive and emotional disposition

---

[4] We shall not discuss Frenkel-Brunswik's interpretation of the major differences between High and Low scorers except to say that we regard them on the whole as in the right direction and as a valuable extension of the work done on German Nazi Prisoners of War.

As in Dr. Sanford's interpretation of the cases of Mack and Larry, two typical high and low scorers, there is a tendency in Dr. Frenkel-Brunswik's analysis to overinterpret the material. The exceptionally sensitive and subtle mind at work in these interpretations tends to widen differences more than seems necessary for any except rhetorical purposes. The two young men chosen to illustrate the extreme anti-democrats and extreme democrats are both quite moderate in their views as compared with Nativist fire-eaters one encountered before the war or even the ordinary supporters of the New and Fair Deals who were common in University classrooms over the past two decades. Likewise, in the case of Dr. Frenkel-Brunswik's interpretations, they make certain traits far more pronounced than they are likely to be in reality.

In a work of this sort it is however difficult to avoid this overstress. For one thing, our language for the description of small differences among human beings and social situations is far too crude—sociological and political concepts are too gross and the concepts of psychoanalytic derivation were developed in a field in which the symptoms to which the terms applied were much more fully developed than they were in these relatively run-of-the-mill subjects. Moreover, working with the doubtful hypothesis that the tests were selecting and analyzing potential fascists and anti-fascists, there is a readiness to interpret the rudimentary events of the present in categories more appropriate to the hypothetically more massive events which have not yet emerged but which the hypothesis predicts.

in which Low Scorers differ from High Scorers, there is almost always a significant number of Low Scorers whose deeper dispositions are closer to the High Scorer than to the Low Scorer. In conformity with the preconceived idea that authoritarianism is a charasteristic of the Right and the corresponding notion that there is no authoritarianism on the "left," there is no analysis of these deviant Low Scorers. It would be presumptuous to assert that it was always the same low scoring individuals who repeatedly received the high ratings in the clinical interviews and that these deviant low scorers were in the main the five "Leftists"[5] among the Low Scorers. It is however a reasonable interpretation, which would justify a reexamination of the original data.

Even if, however, these five "Leftists" were not the deviant "highs" among the Low Scorers, the investigators' belief that authoritarianism and its concomitants belongs to the Right and that the Right and Left, being at the two poles of the continuum, can never meet, has prevented them from seeing what appears to be very evident to a more detached eye.

The material gathered and the hypothesis employed by the Berkeley investigators provides a most valuable approach to the study of Bolshevism and to the re-evaluation of the idea of the political spectrum.

But the investigators accept the view that political opinions are located on a Right-Left continuum and because their political conceptions are exceedingly unsophisticated, they have described political, social and economic attitudes by sets of concrete cliches expressed in the phraseology of current usage.

Obviously a Fascist who says that the Jews have monopolized almost all the important posts in the Government is concretely different from the Bolshevik who asserts that the small circle of big business men control not only the economic life but the intellectual, political and religious life of the country. Concretely these two views are very different—one we know to be the usual paranoid anti-Semitism,—the other sounds like a somewhat crude social science proposition in which many intellectuals in the West believe. Yet looked at from another point of view, they are strikingly similar. Both aver that a small group has with doubtful legitimacy concentrated the power of the country in their hands.

---

[5] p. 300

Authoritarianism: "Right" and "Left"

The Berkeley group have emphasized, among others, the following deeper tendencies of the authoritarian of the Right:

a) Extreme hostility towards "outgroups;"
b) Extreme submissiveness towards the "ingroups;"
c) The establishment of sharp boundaries between the group of which one is a member and all other groups;
d) The tendency to categorize persons with respect to certain particular qualities and make "all or none" judgments;
e) A vision of the world as a realm of conflict;
f) Disdain for purely theoretical or contemplative activities;
g) A repugnance for the expression of sentiments, particularly sentiments of affection;
h) Belief that oneself and one's group are the objects of manipulative designs and that oneself and one's group can survive only by the manipulation of others;
i) The ideal of a conflictless wholly harmonious society in contrast with an environing or antecedent conflictful chaos.

There are other properties as well but these will serve for illustrative purposes.

Anyone well acquainted with the works of Lenin and Stalin[6], or with European and American Communists of recent decades, will immediately recognize that the cognitive and emotional orientations enumerated above correspond very closely to the central features of the Bolshevik *Weltanschauung*. Let us examine briefly their Bolshevik form in the order in which we have listed them:

a) The demand for complete and unqualified loyalty to the Party.
b) The insistence on the necessary conflict of interests between the working class of which the Party is the leader and all other classes and the need for unrelenting conflict against these other classes, even in times of apparent truce and cooperation.
c) The continuous application of the criteria of Party interests in judging every person and situation and the need to avoid eclecticism in doctrine and opportunism and compromise in practice.
d) The stress on the class characteristics of individuals and the interpretation of their actions in the light of their class position exclusively.
e) The belief that all history is the history of class conflict.
f) The denial of the existence of pure truth and attack on those who espouse pure science or "art for art's sake."

---

[6] For a very useful collection of excerpts from the writings of Lenin and Stalin arranged in categories similar to those used in the present analysis, c.f. Leites, Nathan, *A Study of Bolshevism*, The Free Press, Glencoe, Ill., 1953.

g) The belief that the expression of sentiment is an expression of weakness and that it interferes with the correct interpretation of reality and the choice of the right course of action.
h) The belief in the ubiquitousness of the influence of "Wall Street," the "City," the "Big Banks," "Heavy Industry," "200 families,"etc. and their masked control over even the most remote spheres of life and the counter-belief in the necessity to penetrate organizations and achieve complete control over them.
i) The ideal of the classless society, without private property in the instruments of production and hence without conflict, the "realm of freedom" where man will cease his alienation and become truly human.

There are important differences between the two authoritarianisms and we shall deal with some of these below. But what is so impressive is their very far-reaching overlap. Let us take for example the specific items in the F (Fascism) scale employed for the discrimination of persons with Fascist potentialities from those who are free of such potentialities.

Let us begin with the statements indicative of "Authoritarian Submission"[7] which is defined as a "submissive, uncritical attitude towards idealized moral authorities of the ingroup."

"1. Obedience and respect for authority are the most important virtues children should learn.

"4. Science has a place but there are many important things that can never possibly be understood by the human mind.

"8. Every person should have complete faith in some supernatural power whose decisions he obeys without question.

"21. Young people sometimes get rebellious ideas but as they grow up they ought to get over them and settle down.

"23. What this country needs most, more than laws and political programmes is a few courageous, devoted, tireless leaders in whom the people can put their faith.

"42. No sane, normal, decent person could ever think of hurting a close friend or relative." (p. 242)

Agreement with these sentences is indicative of belief in the rightness of submission to familial, political and religious authorities. At first glance, they appear to have nothing to do with the Communist attitude. They counsel respect for the family, and a refusal of respect for the powers of science. Modern revolutionaries including

---

[7] Table 7 (VII) (p. 255)

Authoritarianism: "Right" and "Left"

the Communists, especially outside the Soviet Union, have long been inclined toward the denial of familial authority and a conviction of the potency of science. There is a very obvious similarity concerning faith in political leaders who serve their followers with an unresting devotion. The Communist adulation of Stalin and of the national Party leaders could certainly not be exceeded by the awe in which Hitler was held by fervent Nazis—and the attitudes towards these two leaders, which party functionaries in Nazi Germany and the Soviet Union have tried to arouse in their respective peoples, through propaganda, certainly have very much in common.

But even where there are genuine surface differences, as with regard to family and science, there are also some similarities in the deeper dispositions associated with these particular concrete beliefs. It is one of the Berkeley group's most valuable hypotheses, for which there is plausible evidence, that the loyalty and submissiveness of the authoritarian personality (the High Scorer) is a reaction-formation against his hostility towards his parents' and particularly towards his father's authority, which he experienced, whether correctly or not, as harshly repressive. The Low Scorers on the other hand either reject their parental authority openly and without fear or, as deviant Low Scorers, they respect parental authority in the same manner as the Rightist Authoritarian High Scorer. Thus at the level of the deeper depositions, the two types of authoritarians share the same attitude towards their familial authorities. Indeed, in the matter of alleged victimization by parents, an unusually large number of eight of the low scorers felt they had been victimized by their parents while none of the Low Scorers expressed contrary opinions. Likewise five of the Low Scorers were capricious rebels against their parents—an attitude selected by the investigators as indicative of an authoritarian disposition. We see then that as far as hostility towards parents is concerned, there are Low Scorers who have the same overt attitude as the High Scorers. More fundamentally, moreover, the refusal to acknowledge the sacredness of parental authority exists in both groups. The difference arises on the level of the conscious expression of sentiment in which there is a genuine difference—a difference which should not however obscure the equally genuine similarity.

Furthermore, is the difference as it bears on our main thesis, as wide as the interpretation presented in the preceding paragraph would allow? The concentration of loyalty and obedience in the relationship with the political leader, such as is demanded of and actually given by many Communists, is all encompassing. The "left" authoritarians would deny familial authority, not as the liberal tradition sought, on behalf of the freedom of the individual, but rather on behalf of the authority of the Party and of the Party leader. Communists in Western countries preach the relaxation of family loyalties where these interfere with loyalty to the Party and they exploit and manipulate them where they can for the benefit of the Party. This is not to say that in those circles, wittingly or unwittingly, permeated by the outlook of the Liberal enlightenment and which have furthermore experienced the relaxation of kinship ties produced by many developments in modern society, there is not a genuine belief that for the benefit of the individual's freedom and the development of his individuality, there should be a minimum of parental authority. All I wish to do here is to point out that the anti-familistic sentiments which find freer expression in the Leftists authoritarian personality than they do in the Rightists authoritarian are different in their nature from the preference for looser family ties sought by moderate liberalism. The latter is what mainly engages Dr. Frenkel-Brunswik's attention and it is an error to confuse it with the rebellious type of antifamilism which is found among the Low Scorers.

We must also examine the difference between the High and Low Scorers concerning their attitudes towards science. There is a clear difference between these two groups in this explicit approval of science. The High Scorers are more superstitious and are more sympathetic to the claims of religious authority while practically none of the Low Scorers are antagonistic towards science. Is this not also a real difference between the two authoritarianisms? It might be. We should however recall that for the Communist who vigorously proclaims the "scientific" basis of his convictions, science is not the discovery of truths hitherto unknown by an individual scientist working freely within the framework of a scientific tradition; it is rather the corroboration of the truth of the writings of Marx, Engels, Lenin, and more recently, Stalin. The tradition of liberalism and revolutionism are both "scientistic" but the science to which Western Communists give their allegiance today is as authoritarian as their other beliefs. Once more, therefore, the affinity between "Right" and "Left" emerges and here too it could probably have been perceived by the Berkeley group were they themselves not so enmeshed in their doctrine.

Authoritarianism: "Right" and "Left"

The preoccupation with power is another feature of the "antidemocratic" outlook according to the findings of *The Authoritarian Personality*. They define this as a "preoccupation with the dominance-subordination, strong-weak, leader-follower dimension; identification with power figures; over-emphasis upon the conventionalized attributes of the ego; exaggerated assertion of strength and toughness."[8] The presence or absence of this syndrome is tested by agreement with the following assertions:

"2. No weakness or difficulty can hold us back if we have enough will power.

"13. What the youth needs most is strict discipline, rugged determination, and the will to work and fight for family and country.

"19. An insult to our honour should always be punished.

"22. It is best to use some pre-war authorities in Germany to keep order and prevent chaos.

"23. What this country needs most, more than laws and political programmes, is a few courageous, tireless, devoted leaders in whom the people can put their faith.

"26. People can be divided into two distinct classes: the weak and the strong.

"28. Most people don't realize how much our laws are controlled by plots hatched in secret places."[9]

For the most part, these items are quite discriminating between High and Low Scorers. Here too, however, the concrete content of the assertions—mainly cliches abominated by "progressive intellectuals"—blurs the distinction between Leftists authoritarians and reasonable persons of humanitarian, equalitarian dispositions. In any case, careful examination of the deeper elements in the test sentences reveal numerous points of affinity with Leftist authoritarianism. The stress on the value of persistence and determination is always present in the Communist image of the true Bolshevik, of the effective Party member who works on, even against great odds, sustained by confidence in the final victory. The importance accorded to discipline likewise figures centrally in the Communist doctrine of the good party member. The difference here is that the Right totalitarian whose reaction-formations are very strong, represses his rebellious sentiments towards family and country and instead gives them his loyalty; the Communist whose hostility

---

[8] p. 256
[9] p. 256

against these collectivities is unrepressed, subjects himself to the discipline of the Party.

The dichotomy between the weak and the strong is also of course very prominent in Communist thought. The weak, the declining lower middle classes, are worthy only of contempt—only the powerful class enemy is worthy of being taken seriously. In Communist thought the weakness/strength dichotomy is almost as fundamental as the Party/non-Party dichotomy. The Communist fascination by power is manifest in a common tendency to exaggerate the strength of the powerful and the weakness of the weak.

Finally, with respect to the belief in conspiracies in modern society—the Leninist-Stalinist theory of politics is scarcely less conspiratorial than the Protocols of the Elders of Zion. In the latter instance it is the Jews who are the conspirators, in the former, the leaders of the bourgeoisie, once British and now American. It is the Communists who believe that wars are brought about by small cliques of munitions makers and bankers, that a small number of business men control the press in order to guarantee the power of their class and that economic life itself in Western society is controlled by a small number of monopolists whose actions and decisions are hidden from the public eye. It is through these conspiratorial actions that the bourgeoisie conducts the class struggle and it is through a sharply defined band of professional revolutionaries inspired by Leninist doctrine that the working class defends itself and contends for its own class interests.

III

In the preceding section we have argued that the questionnaires were designed to disclose not the authoritarian personality as such but rather the "Right"—the nativist-fundamentalist Authoritarian. This restriction of range of interest we believe rested on the proposition that political opinions are distributed on a unilinear scale and that the Left being at the other end of the scale from the Right was of necessity its opposite in every respect. Finally we have contended that as a result of this restriction of attention, the investigators have failed to observe that at the Left pole of their continuum, there is to be found an authoritarianism impressively like the Authoritarianism of the Right.

It is our view that the resemblance becomes vividly apparent once we move from the level of the questionnaire to that of the data provided by the interview. This is so because the contents of the questionnaire are composed of the concrete cliches of nativist thought and the negative cliches (with a few positive cliches) of "progressive" thought during the period when the Communists followed a peoples Front policy. As a product of the war-time collaboration, Communist tactics and a well intentioned lack of political and economic sophistication, the intellectual currency of American humanitarian liberalism for some years was much influenced by a Marxist outlook.

If we go below the surface of the concrete cliche to the deeper cognitive and emotional dispositions, such as Dr. Frenkel-Brunswik observed through her clinical interviews, the analogies and incongruities in Rightist and Leftist authoritarianism would become much more obvious. We shall now select some of the major categories which she employs to pursue our search for similarities a little further, and while doing so to formulate some of the major differences.

We have already asserted that both authoritarianisms were characterized by hostility towards parents. That of the Right is usually covered over by respect as a reaction-formation but like that of the Left it often breaks out into capricious rebellion.

Among Low Scorers we find a sizable minority (seven) who think that they were "victimized" by their siblings, a belief even more common among the High Scorers. Six Low Scorers reject their siblings[10] allegedly on grounds of principle, a symptom of left authoritarianism which tends to justify all its actions in terms of general principles in contrast with the more emotional justifications of the Rightist authoritarian when his defensive reaction-formation against his own rebelliousness breaks down. Both authoritarianisms reveal reaction-formations against their hostility towards siblings —the Rightists by idealizing their actual siblings, and the Leftists by rejecting their actual siblings but constructing the spurious sibling relationship of comradeliness with their fellow members of the Party, in which exploitation and manipulation of comrades, especially new recruits, is covered with protestations of solidarity. Leninist ideology which asserts the solidarity of the working classes across national boundaries, without a trace of benevolent sentiment such as could be found among more humanitarian socialists, certainly conforms with this interpretation.

---

[10] We do not know whether these six are included in the seven who feel victimized by their siblings.

A very substantial difference between the two authoritarianisms seems to exist regarding the sex. Those on the "Right" combine great preoccupation with sexual activity with a very tense demand for sexual purity and propriety. The Leftists, aided by the liberal tradition of weakening repressive sexual conventions in favor of a freer expression of affection between the sexes, do not insist on sexual purity and propriety in the same way. Much less emotion is aroused by sexual behavior which deviates from conventions, e. g. homosexuality. Both are below the surface antipathetic to "bourgeois" sexual morality but as in the case of hostility, alienation from or rebellion against the parents, the Leftists feel much less need to defend themselves from the painful emotions aroused by this antipathy. Nonetheless, even among the Low Scorers, there were as many as ten who followed the High Scorers' pattern of "rejection of the *id*" and seven who shared the Rightist authoritarian pattern of sharply distinguishing between sexuality and love.[11]

In their attitudes towards other persons, Left and Right authoritarianisms again reveal basic similarities. Both are distrustful and suspicious. As many as six of the Low Scorers show this authoritarian trait and the behavior of Communists gives repeated evidence of a deep lying suspicion even towards comrades, to say nothing of their contempt and distrust for persons outside the Party. The need in which every comrade stands to scrutinize his actions and those of his closest associates in the Party to discover and eradicate traces of "deviations" is a part of this generalized distrust, for which the assertions of comradeliness and fraternal solidarity are only reaction formations.

Rightist authoritarians prefer a hierarchical scale of human beings and in this they show their aggressiveness and contempt towards their inferiors and their submissiveness towards their superiors—both of whom they sharply distinguish from themselves. Liberalism has historically been more equalitarian but it is only at the revolutionary extreme that we find an intense claim for complete equality. Doctrines are often adopted only because they are part of a cultural tradition or because they conform with more general standards which are embedded in that tradition, but they can also be espoused because they function as a reaction-formation in the face of practices which diverge widely from the imperatives of the doctrine. So

---

[11] p. 392

it seems to be with the equalitarianism which Dr. Frenkel-Brunswik finds in such predominance among her Low Scorers. The rigid hierarchy of the Communist Party, the very strong feelings about the moral inferiority of various classes, the contempt for non-Communists—these are hardly the benign equalitarianism which the Berkeley group think is characteristic of the "left" sector of the political continuum.

Dr. Frenkel-Brunswik also finds the disposition to blame others (extra-punitiveness) to be characteristic of Rightist authoritarianism in contrast with the relative freedom from guilt feelings or excessive guilt feelings which she finds among the Low Scorers. Excessive guilt feelings and the denial of one's own guilt are however very intimately related to one another. The latter is often only the mechanism of defense brought into play by the strength of the former. Does not Communist doctrine and daily practice attribute the ills of the world to the actions of the non-Communists, and does not this usual self-exculpation from the responsibility for every error and defeat alternate in the history of Communism with extraordinary outbursts of confessions of guilt in persons who had previously exceeded all others in attributing guilt to the rest of the world? Are not the Communist "trials"—not just the famous purges, but those which take place regularly within even the smaller units of Communist parties—organized demands for self-accusation—and do they not often succeed in eliciting the now well-known catalogues of vices of which errant Communists accuse themselves? Hence although some of the manifestations may be different and although the jargon is certainly different, it does not seem reasonable to deny that there are fairly close affinities between the two authoritarianisms in this respect too.

One final instance of the affinity will be selected. The Rightist authoritarians are correctly asserted to be "intolerant of ambiguity." They demand definitiveness and freedom from vagueness in distinctions which they regard as crucial. Their beliefs must be unqualified; there must be no doubt and there must be no restrictions to the validity of their beliefs. Their actions too must be unequivocal and always on the right side of the clearly defined boundary which separates good and evil. Six of the Low Scorers possess this "intolerance of ambiguity" and although it is unjustified on the basis of the data available at present[12] to impute it to the five Leftists

---

[12] p. 462

included among the Low Scorers, it is certainly justifiable to regard this characteristic as a very important one in Leftist authoritarianism. It is of course a common property of alienated sects of many kinds, religious, political and literary, but it is especially noticeable in Leftist sectarianism and particularly in the Communist Party. There, no judgment can be left in suspension, there must always be a clear prescription which lays down the correct "line." Indeed the very conception of a *correct line* springs from the need never to confront an ambiguous situation. This is of course closely related to the need for clear boundaries to which we have already referred. The Bolshevik rule that when temporary tactical collaboration with other groups is necessary, the greatest pains must be taken to retain the complete identity of the Party and to avoid any trend of collaboration which at any point might approximate a genuine fusion provides evidence that the "intolerance of ambiguity" in the definition of situations is certainly not a monopoly of the authoritarianism of the Right.

The same process of assimilation of the extremes of Right and Left which we have performed on the preceding pages could be continued for many others of the deeper cognitive and emotional dispositions which are treated by Dr. Frenkel-Brunswik. We have dealt with most of the more important ones. Further examination would only repeat and refine what we have already set forth: great affinities in most of the underlying dispositions (except for sexual preoccupations) and superficial differences connected with the different concrete objects of love and hatred which the authoritarians select or which arise from differences in the strength and frequency of certain defensive mechanisms such as repression and reaction-formation.

The authors of *The Authoritarian Personality* have demonstrated in a more plausible manner than any previous investigators that there is a determinate relationship between particular attitudes towards public objects and symbols and "deeper" cognitive and emotional attitudes or dispositions.[13] There are many technical scientific questions concerning the adequacy of the canons of precise

---

[13] The evidence concerning the operation of the mechanisms of repression and reaction-formation is much less convincing than the evidences about the deeper dispositions but it is plausible. The operation of these mechanisms must be adduced in order to bring systematic coherence into the data gathered in the clinical interviews.

interpretation of the interview data, and earlier sections of this paper have criticized the conceptual scheme used in the analysis of political orientations. Nonetheless the consistency of the results as well as the statistical significance of many of the more important differences provide grounds for accepting their claim that general disposition and particular concrete political attitudes are intimately related.

The authors are not however content with this conclusion. Their interest is to estimate the probability of Fascism in the United States. By their analysis of personality structures, they seek to predict which types of persons will accept Fascist propaganda and become Fascists. They assume except for a few passages where the Marxist heritage reasserts itself that political behavior is a function of deeper personality characteristics. Social structure only plays the role of setting off the chain of personality-impelled actions. Once these are started, political activity and the political system take their form directly from the content of the impulses and beliefs of those participating in them.[14] The entire discussion is very remote from the actual working of institutions—the interviewers did not seek to obtain information about how the subjects actually behaved in their workshops or offices, in their churches and voluntary associations, in their trade union meetings, etc. The authors tell us nothing of the *actual* roles of their subjects and for this reason, they encounter no obstacles to their view that political conduct follows from personality traits.

Yet it is obvious that this is so only within very broad limits and under rather special circumstances. The expectations of our fellow men are certainly of very great weight in the determination of our conduct—to varying degrees, of course, depending on our responsive capacities or our social sensitivity. Persons of quite different dispositions, as long as they have some reasonable measure of responsiveness to the expectations of others will behave in a more or less uniform manner, when expectations are relatively uniform. Naturally not all of them will be equally zealous or enthusiastic about the action which they perform in accordance with the expectations of particular colleagues, superiors and inferiors who are present and in accordance with the expectations symbolized in abstract

---

[14] The ambiguity of the discussion of the role of personality in political institutions and movements, and of the Authoritarian political and social system is so great that an exegesis of their views would serve little purpose.

rules, traditions and material objects. To a large extent, large enough indeed to enable great organizations to operate in a quite predictable manner, they will conform despite the possibly conflicting urges of their personalities. The foreign policy of a country is not ordinarily a direct and primary resultant of the personality of the Foreign Minister even though aspects of his personality will enter into his policy. The traditions of his country, the realistic perception of the international situation and of the situation with which he is presented by his civil servants, the expectations of his colleagues in the Government, the demands of the leaders of his party who wish to be re-elected as well as his own conceptions of justice, of the national interest, of superior and inferior nations, etc.—all weigh in the balance in which policy is decided. The position of a civil servant or a business executive in the middle ranks of the hierarchy of this organization is even more restrictive of the range of freedom enjoyed by the personality qualities of the individual than is that of a leader or high official.

Now it is certainly true that these actions are not completely divorced from the personality of the actor. He must have sufficient sensitivity to the expectations of others, he must be capable of understanding the symbols in his situation. He must be oriented towards the approval of his colleagues and of his constituency and he must have some degree of reality-orientation which enables him to persist in a course once undertaken. Other qualities are necessary too for this capacity to act in a diversity of situations but they are all compatible with a fairly wide range of variation in such categories as tolerance of ambiguity, distrust and suspicion, preoccupation with sexual concerns, aggressiveness towards outgroups, and others of the sort dealt with by the Berkeley group. The Berkeley group has no realization of the extent and importance for the proper functioning of any kind of society of this kind of adaptiveness to institutional roles. For them conformity is only compulsive conformity, adherence to conventions is rigid conventionalism, both of which are obviously more closely related to the substantive content of the dispositional system of the ordinary run of conformity and respect for conventions which enables any society to run peacefully and with some satisfaction to its members.

Their belief that personality traits dominate public behavior has more truth when we turn to situations which have no prior organization, where there is, in other words, no framework of action set for the newcomer by the expectations of those already on the scene.

A new political party, a newly formed religious sect will thus be more amenable to the expressive behavior of the personalities of those who make them up than an ongoing government or private business office or university department with its traditions of scientific work. Personality will play a greater part in positions of leadership than in positions in the lower levels of an organization, because by the nature of the organization the higher positions have a greater freedom from elaborate expectations of fixed content. Personality structure will also be more determinant of political activities when the impulses and the defenses of the actors are extremly intense, e. g., when the compulsive elements are powerful and rigid or when the aggressiveness is very strong.

However, even when we have made these qualifications, the fact remains that it takes more than one set of personality characteristics to make a political movement,—even one which has the more favorable conditions we have just stated. The Middle West and Southern California are well strewn with small scale nativist-fundamentalist agitators of the type which might be called Fascist. Yet they have never had any success in the United States despite their numbers and despite the existence in the Middle and Far Western population of a vein of xenophobia, populist, anti-urban and anti-plutocratic sentiment, distrust of politicians and intellectuals—in fact very much of what the Berkeley group would regard as the ingredients of Fascism. Since an *Ethos* or general value system are not the same as differentiated behavior in a system of roles, these people have never been able to constitute a significant movement.

The failure of American nativism to organize its potential followers in the United States has been a consequence of a lack of organization skill in its aspirants to leadership, by the unstable and fluctuating relationships of the anti-authoritarian and the authoritarian components in the personalities of their followers and their consequent inability to sustain loyalty. They have had the necessary orientation or *Ethos* but they have lacked the minimum capacities to act in the roles necessary for a movement or an institution.

The internal organization of the various nativist groups in the United States has always been extremely loose, while the interconnections among the groups have despite repeated efforts to establish some degree of unity, been perhaps even more tenuous. The nativist leaders have almost without exception been characterized by their inability to organize an administrative apparatus for their movements, or to hire or attract others to do the work for them. The organization of an administrative apparatus involves a minimum of the capacity to trust other individuals and to evoke their trust and affection to an extent sufficient for them to pursue the goals set by the organization or its leaders. American nativistic-fundamentalistic agitators have lacked this minimum of trust even in those who share their views.

In the main, nativist leaders have been personalities who were driven into their "vocation" by strong paranoid tendencies or what is now called an authoritarian personality. Their paranoid tendencies have, however, been so diffuse in their objects, that even their own fellow nativists have been looked upon as potential agents of deprivation. Where the leader has been either so distrustful of others or, in order to overcome his fear of his own impotence, maintains in himself certain illusions of omnipotence, he seeks to do everything in the organization. It is usually too much for him. Especially since his aggressiveness keeps intruding into his efforts to do the routine work of his group. Demanding affection and loyalty, and fearing it when it is given, the aspirants to nativist leadership in the United States have had a hard row to hoe.

Their intense and self-inhibiting demands for affection and their interpretation of any failure as a deliberately inflicted deprivation are exacerbated because the normal modes of social ascent are closed to them. In the United States, the person with diffuse aggressiveness is likely to fail in his efforts to enter any of the occupations demanding persistent routine effort or offering high rewards of creativity in the exercise of authority. Hence, the paranoid tendencies of the nativist agitators which must have been generated quite early in their careers are accentuated by failures suffered during their adult years. Practically none of the nativist leaders could be called a reasonably successful individual in the conventional sense except perhaps for one who despite his external vocational success is alleged to have suffered for a long time from his social rejection at Harvard on account of his negroid appearance.

The impulsiveness which has driven these men into extremely aggressive behavior and speech has likewise prevented them from developing the flexible self-control required to build the administrative machinery in their organizations. They have been people who are driven by their immediately pressing impulses to take instantaneous action: their defenses, although strong on one side are completely open on the flank. They hate authority, for example,

Authoritarianism: "Right" and "Left" 47

sufficiently for them to build up by reaction-formation a belief that the best society is one in which there is a great concentration of authority—but they cannot control their anti-authoritarianism in actual situations. Hence the movements remain small because they cannot tolerate leaders and any effort to unify the fragments is attacked as the gesture of a menacing authority. Their poor reality-orientation led them to think that they were constantly on the verge of success and therefore to underemphasize those techniques necessary to consolidate their position for a long slow movement.

An examination of the physical state of their offices and files, even among the more successful ones, has revealed extreme disorder, and they themselves in their offices show impatience and irrationality in the use of their equipment. The manner in which they transacted business, as revealed both by observation and from their correspondence has indicated inability to conduct coherent, continuous discourse. The frequent quarrels among the leaders within a group have testified to their undisciplined, unchanneled aggressiveness. Their local followership and indeed even their more remote followership have been based largely on a direct unilateral personal relationship between the leader and the group. There is no hierarchical structure of the sort which is absolutely necessary if the actions of large numbers of people are to be coordinated. The leaders and their lieutenants who come and go seem to be incapable of the sustained continuous work of the "wardheeler" who also uses direct personal contact as a means of control.

Public meetings were often conducted in an informal unplanned manner—more like a religious revival in a storefront church—without any of the highly organized arrangements employed so successfully by the Nazis in calling forth the awe and devotion among their followers. At a meeting in Chicago organized by G. L. K. Smith, for example, the speakers strolled in individually, stopping to chat with the audience; during the speeches there was a constant movement to and from the platform. The speakers were too informal to inspire discipline among their followers, and the movement gave the appearance of being limited in size by the number of people with whom the leaders could personally be acquainted while the difficulties in personal relationships of these persons imbued with the authoritarian ethos meant there had to be a constant turnover in membership.

The hostilities of the nativists flow out against all groups who appear distinguishable from themselves. The symbol "national" and "Christian"[15] seem hardly adequate to bind such random aggressiveness which by its very diffuseness prevents unification and solidarity.

Despite the intensity of their animosities against those who diverge from the standards of nativist Americanism, the nativists have not on the whole appeared to be persons who have been capable of separating their love and hate components, and to attach them to objects in a persisting manner. The amount of attachment to objects, to say nothing of affection or congeniality of which they have been capable, has not offered the possibilities of sustaining a continuously ongoing organization. Furthermore, inasmuch as there has been no formal authority to articulate their actions, and to tie them to the organization, their spontaneous affection for their fellow members has had to carry a burden far too heavy for its meager supply. It is entirely possible that these same people with their prickly anti-authoritarianism and their universally diffused distrust, could not have sustained the structure of a more formal hierarchical body even as well as they do the present internal organizational disorder of the nativist sects.

This brief summary of certain features of American nativist organization and personality structure hardly support the Berkeley Group's views that a large number of authoritarian personalities as such could produce an effective authoritarian movement. Movements and institutions, even if they are authoritarian, require both more and less than authoritarian personality structures. On the other hand, a liberal democratic society itself could probably not function satisfactorily with only "democratic liberal personalities"[16] to fill all its roles.

---

[15] The fantasies of nativist fundamentalist Protestantism in the period between the wars were among the elements which prevented the unification of two of the main strands of nativism. The fundamentalists were about as anti-Catholic as they were antagonistic to any other institution or symbol. This antagonism prevented, for example, the unification of Father Coughlin and Huey Long's organizations, the two largest, even though they made overtures to one another. The war, and especially the pre-war isolationist agitation seemed temporarily to overcome this antagonism. The anti-British Catholic Irish were found to have numerous points of affinity with the anti-British Protestant nativists. Since the British were allied with international bankers, and the Protestant nativists saw this as well as anyone, they were for a time at least, able to sink their antipathies towards the Catholics out of their greater hatred for the British, the Jews, the war mongers, etc.

[16] From which the "leftist Authoritarians" have been separated.

Authoritarianism: "Right" and "Left"

The tasks of a liberal democratic society are many and many different kinds of personality structures are compatible with and necessary for its well being. Even authoritarian personalities are especially useful in some roles in democratic societies and in many other roles where they are not indispensable, they are at least harmless.

The fact that there is no point to point correspondence of personality and social role does not however mean that they have no approximate relationship to one another. The task of social research in this field is to clarify and make more determinate the scope of this relationship. *The Authoritarian Personality* both by its very solid achievement and its very significant deficiencies has contributed towards our progress in the solution of this task.

HERBERT H. HYMAN *and* PAUL B. SHEATSLEY

"THE AUTHORITARIAN PERSONALITY" — A METHODOLOGICAL CRITIQUE

I. INTRODUCTION

*I*N the recent annals of social science, *The Authoritarian Personality* is rivalled only by *The American Soldier* and perhaps by the *Kinsey Reports* in scope, prestige and influence. It has already, in the relatively brief time since its publication, achieved the status of a classic in its field. Like these other studies, it has obtained widespread circulation and prominence. It is authored by notable names in social research, and sponsored by a national social agency which provided generous financial support. Like Kinsey, the contents are sure-fire topics for discussion and assert a magnetic attraction for the applied social scientist. Problems of politics and prejudice are of interest to the ordinary citizen and are the concern of many groups and individuals; and the volume speaks to us persuasively on the causes and implications of such problems, and redirects much of our current thinking. And like the four volumes of *The American Soldier*, the work is generally recognized as a milestone in social research, and may well affect the methodological and substantive trends in the field for many years to come.

It is this atmosphere surrounding the volume which makes a minute and critical examination of its methodology a matter of some importance. For, like many classics, *The Authoritarian Personality* is less likely to be studied carefully and weighed critically than it is to be condensed, simplified and quoted. Its thousand pages, loaded with tables and statistics, and replete with technical terminology, are formidable—so formidable, indeed, that they may discourage all but the most stout-hearted from any careful scrutiny of the material. But even apart from the volume's prestige and formidableness, it offers a most appropriate vehicle for methodological analysis. Although one obvious way of increasing our research skills is through the empirical examination of past studies and the profit we may achieve from their example, most studies do not lend themselves well to such examination. They are either so limited in scope that the gain from a methodological analysis is small, or they are presented in so summary a form that we are unable to observe the total research process. In *The Authoritarian Personality*, however, we have a rich field to examine: the range of problems covered is wide and the description of the research design and execution is detailed.

But the importance of the work, its broad scope and the detail in which all the data are presented place upon the critic a heavy responsibility to be sober in his judgments. No work of social research is perfect. Human beings, scientists no less than critics, are fallible. Practical limitations impose themselves on every empirical investigation and force departures from the ideal. Unexpected contingencies destroy the most perfect of research plans. Especially is this true of studies like the present one, in which the inquiry was an attempt to break new ground, was protracted in time, ambitious in scope and supervised by many hands in many stages. It would be unfair to expect more than an approximation to the ideal that hindsight might suggest, or to carp at minor blemishes among the thousand pages of report. But while perfection cannot be expected, sound canons of criticism require in this instance the adoption of high standards. The protracted investigation also allowed time for reflection, experiments and improvements. The many hands also permitted the pooling of judgment and talents. The ample financial support was a cushion against contingencies and practical difficulties. The authors are of high repute, skilled, experienced and insightful researchers. If it is unfair to expect perfection, it is no less than fair to expect a great deal.

The Nature of Our Task. What guided *The Authoritarian Personality* was the general hypothesis that "the political, economic and social convictions of an individual often form a broad and coherent pattern . . . and that this pattern is an expression of deep-lying trends in his personality." (1)[1] More specifically, anti-Semitism was

---

[1] Numbers in parentheses refer to page numbers in *The Authoritarian Personality*.

seen as only a part of a larger constellation of anti-minority sentiments, which in turn were related to politico-economic attitudes of a "potentially fascist" nature. It is also hypothesized that the personality structure within which these sentiments are imbedded is derived from actual early family experiences, and that these sentiments "could not be derived solely from external factors, such as economic status, group membership, or religion" (603). A research design to test this theory was developed, and a massive array of data are presented in its support.

Our own basic task, in examining the methodology of the project, is to determine how well these data actually do support the theory. Methodology deals with the principles of effective research inquiry, so we are not here concerned with whether the theory itself, in the light of previous and subsequent research, is plausible or even correct. A theory may well be correct without having been proved in a particular instance, and many faulty pieces of research have nevertheless provoked new ideas and led to increases in knowledge. As methodologists, we are concerned only with the question: How effectively do the data collected in *this* research support the theory they were intended to test?

Our evaluation will, however, lead us occasionally to trespass on the territory of the theorists. For not only must we examine, for methodological soundness, the procedures which were used; we must also determine whether the data derived from these procedures are interpreted properly, reasonably and with due regard for research principles. And in weighing the reasonableness of the interpretations and the soundness of the inferences, we shall inevitably be guided by past literature and theory in the general area of social psychology. So, too, in evaluating the wisdom of a particular research procedure, we shall be guided by past theory, since the good plan methodologically is the one that takes full account of available knowledge.

A proper concern of methodology, no less than the soundness of the procedures and the interpretation, is the efficiency with which a research inquiry is conducted, for an effective study is one which obtains the maximum of relevant information for the minimum expenditure of time, money, personnel and resources. Such evaluation, while decidedly pertinent, is unfortunately seldom possible on the basis of published reports. From time to time in this critique we may notice instances in which more efficient procedures might have been utilized or devised, but in general, we must refrain from any broad judgments in this field.

Finally, the methodologist is concerned not only with the proper use of recognized research tools but also with the invention of new modes of inquiry, and we regard it as our further task to inquire into the larger methodological contributions of *The Authoritarian Personality*. On this score, the study is a most stimulating work in at least three respects. First, it represents a philosophy of research in stages, each stage representing a modification and improvement of an earlier design or procedure. Second, we have here a research project which stems from a well developed theory, a circumstance all too rare in social research. All of us would do well to ground our empirical procedures in a framework of theoretical principles. Third, and perhaps most important, the project represents the joining of two general, but heretofore separate research approaches and bodies of theory—the quantitative, statistical or survey methodology in the service of social psychology, and the intensive, clinical, case-study approach in the service of psychodynamics. From the first we presumably obtain precision, rigor and the ability to generalize our findings. From the second we presumably achieve depth, understanding, insight. The statistical treatment is to be enriched by the insights of the clinical method, and the clinical findings are to be controlled by the quantitative data. Insofar as these two approaches are effectively combined, *The Authoritarian Personality* represents an example worthy of emulation, for through the combination, we can achieve a superior methodology having the virtues of both methods. As the writers put it: "The attempt was made . . . to bring methods of traditional social psychology into the service of theories and concepts from the newer dynamic theory of personality and in so doing to make 'depth psychological' phenomena more amenable to mass-statistical treatment, and to make quantitative surveys of attitudes and opinions more meaningful psychologically" (12).

On the basis of our own study of the published volume, we believe that the verification of the author's theory must be questioned, that the procedures used were not the most efficient, and that in the attempt to combine the two general approaches, each was handled to some disadvantage. We shall demonstrate in this paper a great number of methodological weaknesses in the project, and we are concerned lest our remarks appear unduly critical. We would emphasize that many of the criticisms we are about to make could be levelled equally, and perhaps with even greater effect, at other research studies, and we find much to praise in the volume. But in subjecting *The Authoritarian Personality* to a rigorous *methodological* examination, we must perforce leave to others the deserved praise and concentrate our attention on the shortcomings of the techniques and procedures employed. A detailed criticism of the methodology is especially important, we feel, in view of the many derivative and follow-up studies which have used *The Authoritarian Personality* as their guide.

Here we shall take up in order the various stages of the total research process—the sampling, the measuring instruments, the data collection, processing and analysis—noting any striking or consistent weaknesses in each of these areas which would affect the conclusions drawn. Since in a work as large as the one under study, it is always possible to seize on isolated weaknesses or to pick remarks out of context, we shall document each of our criticisms with more than one reference, and we shall cite the page numbers so that the interested reader may check the contexts.

II. THE POPULATION STUDIED AND THE SAMPLING METHOD

The express methodological purpose of the study was to develop a series of measuring instruments which would provide data for a test of the organization of sentiments and the relation of such patterns to underlying personality trends. Such instruments were developed and administered to a considerable number of respondents, and the conclusions must of necessity be qualified in some manner in the light of the population studied. The actual sampling design on which the various conclusions rest is rather difficult to describe briefly. The extensive investigation of the patterning of sentiments was based on approximately 2,000 questionnaires, but since a variety of questionnaires were used, any given statistic from a particular questionnaire is based on only some portion of those 2,000. A number of intensive investigations using other types of instruments were conducted with small subsamples of this original total group.

A Methodological Critique

The general character of the larger group is clearly detailed by the authors, and its lack of representativeness freely admitted: "Save for a few key groups, the subjects were drawn almost exclusively from the middle socio-economic class" (22) "The working-class group shows a distinct sampling bias in a liberal direction: almost half the members of this group are from the United Electrical Workers (CIO), a militant union, or from the California Labor School, a strongly left-wing institution" (171). Minority group members were excluded. "The great majority of the subjects of the study lived within the San Francisco Bay area. . . . Unless a person had at least a grammar school education, it was very difficult, if not impossible, for him to fill out the questionnaire properly. . . . The average educational level of the subjects in the study is about the twelfth grade, there being roughly as many college graduates as there were subjects who had not completed high school. . . . It is important to note that the present samples are heavily weighted with younger people, the bulk of them falling between the ages of twenty and thirty-five" (23). It should be added that access to these individuals was generally obtained through groups and organizations such as a union, school, church, Rotary Club or the like. Thus, virtually all of the respondents were members of some formal organization, and in addition, they may be regarded as volunteers in the sense that they were agreeable to taking the questionnaire. "In some cases it was impossible to gain the cooperation of the leadership of a group; in other cases cooperative leaders were unable to put the idea across or to have it carried out. . . . There is some indication that resistance of the type mentioned above is correlated positively with ethnocentrism" (129).

As may be seen, the authors frankly describe the limitations of their sample and they expressly state in their Introduction that "The subjects of the study taken all together would provide a rather inadequate basis for generalizing about the total population of this country" (23) and "The (non-college) subjects are in no sense a random sample of the non-college population nor . . . can they be regarded as a representative sample" (20). They emphasize in advance that their concern is not with estimating the magnitude of a particular sentiment among the total U.S. population, but rather with demonstrating the inter-relationships between sentiments. And for demonstrating relationships, they regard the representativeness of their sample as of less critical importance.

Yet even if we grant this distinction (to which we shall return later), the authors do not adhere to it with any rigor. Throughout, there are broad generalizations which can easily mislead the uncritical reader. For example, after administering a scale on anti-Semitism to about 500 students, they remark, "The imagery described above seems to characterize the thinking of *most anti-Semites.*" (97—all italics in this series of quotes are ours, rather than the authors'). In interpreting the results from the questionnaire administered to 110 San Quentin prisoners, they state: "These gross findings point immediately to an important conclusion. *The general run of criminals* are not to be thought of as genuine rebels ... whose conflict with authority is accompanied by some consideration for the weak or oppressed. On the contrary, they would appear to be full of hate and fear toward underdogs" (823). Later they remark, "It would seem that *criminals tend in general* to be conservative in their politics" (836), and again, "This suggests that *nearly all forms of criminal behavior* tend to be incompatible with the kind of liberalism reflected in very low scores on the F-scale" (844). Apart from the fact that these conclusions are predicated on a total of 110 inmates of a single prison, the generalizations are in defiance of the fact that the sample deliberately excluded inmates over 55 years of age, those with less than eight years of schooling, Jews, Negroes and psychotics. Since criminologists have demonstrated that detected crime decreases with formal education, and that the rate of commitment is considerably higher among Negroes than among whites, the sampling requirements certainly appear to make the respondents to this questionnaire a far from representative group of prisoners.[2] Similarly, in discussing political sentiments as revealed by interviews with approximately 150 subjects[3], the writers say, "Our general impression concerning our subjects' attitude toward Russia may be summed up as follows. To *the vast majority of Amer-*

---

[2] For example, Taft notes that the rate of commitment of Negroes to prisons and reformatories was 3.2 times that for whites in 1936. He finds that from one-half to three-fourths of the prison population had not gone beyond the sixth grade in school, and that some 10% to 25% are unable to read or write. See Taft, Donald R., *Criminology,* New York, Macmillan, 1942, Chs. VI, XXIX.

[3] As nearly as can be determined. The major analysis is based on 80 interviews with extreme scorers, but there are also involved 63 interviews from a special labor study in Los Angeles (605-7). It is often difficult, throughout *The Authoritarian Personality,* to determine the exact number of respondents on which particular findings are based.

A Methodological Critique

icans, the very existence of the Soviet Union constitutes a source of continuous uneasiness" (722).

Now it is true that such broad generalizations are sometimes qualified (as above, where the authors speak of "our general impression"), and that it is easy for any writer to over-generalize his data on occasion in the course of a thousand pages. But at times even the qualifications represent such an understatement that the uncritical reader may feel the authors are only being modest. Thus, in discussing results on political ideology, they comment, "It is *perhaps safest* not to draw inferences about the total male and female population" (174—italics ours). Moreover, such instances as those cited above are so numerous that we feel the casual reader may easily be misled.

The Generalization of Attitudinal Relationships. Let us turn, however, to a more significant sampling consideration. The writers, as we have noted, distinguish the generalization of simple estimates beyond the confines of an unrepresentative sample from generalizations of a more dynamic sort. While they grant that the former is improper, the latter, they feel is quite warranted: "It is not likely that such sampling factors have distorted to any appreciable degree the relationships among the variables of ideology, personality and group membership under investigation. Since we are primarily concerned with the causes and correlates of anti-democratic trends, that is, with correlations and differences, rather than with the average amount of any single trend per se, the diverse groups comprising the total sample provide, it would seem, an adequate basis for study" (288). They present evidence which we shall accept for the moment that there is a high degree of organization and interrelationship between these respective levels of functioning. Can this be generalized to other populations? We are in agreement with the writers that one does not need a representative *number* of cases in each stratum or cell of a given population in order to demonstrate such conclusions and to generalize them to *that* population. One merely needs enough cases from all cells, and it is inefficient to take a large number of cases from a large cell, just to achieve over-all sampling representativeness, when the aim is only to establish some correlation or difference. But the question of whether such relationships or differences extend beyond one population to some or all *other* populations is a thoroughly different matter. Correlation coefficients, just like means or percentages, fluctuate from sample to sample and may well vary in different populations.

The authors use the split-half reliabilities of their questionnaire as proof of the organization of sentiments, and incidental to this argument they present evidence of considerable variation in these correlations from sub-group to sub-group within their total sample. For example, the reliability of a scale measuring ethnocentrism varied from .65 to .91 for five small groups studied (134). Conceivably such variations are within the bounds of sampling variance. Nevertheless, one would expect that if variations of this magnitude occur among these few groups, the sampling of a wider assortment of groups would yield even more marked variation. Similarly, the authors use the intercorrelations between scores on different attitude scales as proof of their theory that these sentiments are highly organized. Yet the relationship between ethnocentrism and political ideology, for example, varies among the groups studied from .14 to .86—certainly a striking demonstration that the degree of mental organization is a function of the population studied (179).

Actually, there is considerable empirical evidence from other studies that one cannot generalize the degree of attitude organization from one group to another—or even for the same group from one point in time to another. This whole problem of the specificity vs. generality of attitudes is a very old one in the psychological literature. In the Character Education Inquiry, the children became more consistent in their moral traits as they grew older.[4] Horowitz and Horowitz have demonstrated that the intercorrelations between different kinds of prejudice among children, and the reliabilities of the tests, increased with the age or school grade of the children studied. Murphy, Murphy and Newcomb, in summarizing such literature, report that correlations between related attitudes tend to increase with increased exposure to academic influences during college, that such correlations were found to be a function of religious affiliation, and again that intercorrelations between pairs of attitudes were much higher among a group in extreme financial straits than they were among the larger group of unemployed from which this extreme sub-group was selected.

A clear demonstration of the way in which interrelations between specific attitudes of *tolerance* can vary in different populations is

---

[4] Murphy, Murphy and Newcomb, *Experimental Social Psychology*, Harper's, New York, 1937. The other citations in this paragraph are also summarized in this volume.

available in the classic study by Hartley into the generality of prejudice.[5] In 1938-39, students at a variety of colleges were given a Social Distance Scale which measured prejudice with regard to a variety of groups. Intercorrelations revealed that generality of prejudice was the rule among the subjects. But for two of the categories —"Communists" and "Fascists"—the proportion of individuals which showed opposing attitudes toward these two groups varied from 8% to 33% among students at five different colleges. Hartley remarks, "Under appropriate influences the principle of generalized tolerance may be destroyed and individuals can respond with specialized differentiations."

That this finding is not unique to such political categories is shown in a more recent study by one of the authors of the work under discussion.[6] Levinson reports that slightly modified forms of the scales used in *The Authoritarian Personality* to measure ethnocentrism, authoritarianism and political ideology were administered to 32 participants in an Intergroup Relations Workshop. In the present study the intercorrelations between attitudes as measured by these scales were found to be fairly high, but Levinson reports that this group of 32 was unusually low on ethnocentrism, only slightly below college students in authoritarianism, and unusually high on political conservatism. The correlation coefficient for scores on ethnocentrism and political ideology approximated zero, whereas in the major study the r's ranged from .14 to .86 with a mean value of about .57. Levinson says that the workshop members were "most sensitive to anti-Negro prejudice, and that for many of them, this sensitivity does not carry over, even at an ideological level, to other aspects and more subtle forms of ethnocentrism." He states that "The workshoppers are unusually inconsistent and poorly integrated in their overall social outlook . . . their attitudes regarding minority problems are not completely acceptive, nor are they imbedded in a larger democratic pattern of political and religious thought, nor do they express a thoroughgoing equalitarianism of outlook. Indeed, for many of the workshop members, the opposition to prejudice is a lone attitudinal exception in an otherwise conventionalistic, authority-accepting outlook." The same phenomenon is demonstrated

---

[5] Hartley, E., *Problems in Prejudice*, King's Crown Press, New York, 1946.

[6] Levinson, Daniel J., and Schermerhorn, Richard A., "Emotional-Attitudinal Effects of an Intergroup Relations Workshop on its Members," *J. Psych.*, 1951, 31, 243-256.

in a study by Hatt conducted among three samples representing, respectively, upper class adults, middle class high school students and college students below the middle class level.[7] Intercorrelations between attitudes toward different groups were computed separately for each of the three samples, and it can be observed that the patterning of ethnic attitudes varies with the type of sample studied. Thus, as between the middle and lower class groups, the correlations between attitudes toward Jews and attitudes toward foreign-born were .35 and .61, respectively, and the intercorrelations between attitudes toward foreign-born and attitudes toward Negroes were .30 and .60.

Our purpose in citing such findings as these is not to deny that there is considerable generality in the organization of sentiments of prejudice. The point is too well documented by a variety of studies and methods, and we readily grant it. Our purpose is to raise a broader question of *methodological* concern; namely, whether inquiries into the *organization* of sentiments can afford to ignore sampling considerations in the course of the study design and analysis of results. We feel that the slighting of this matter by the authors is unsound methodology, and from a practical standpoint, it tends to perpetuate the implication that the level of organization of sentiments is a kind of universal, an intra-psychic process which bears little relation to environmental conditions. Actually, as we realize that the organization of sentiments is dependent in part on the organization of the social world and on the circumstances and experiences of the individual, we then naturally realize that the sampling of people in different circumstances will affect the degree and nature of organization found. The evidence we have cited is clear testimony to this theoretical principle and, we feel, to the necessity for qualifying such findings as those reported, in the light of sampling considerations.

As the nature and degree of attitude organization can be shown to vary from sample to sample, so also does the relationship between attitudes and other *personality* functions. On the basis of eighty interview cases, the authors report a highly significant relationship between ethnocentrism and "rigid set and outlook," that is, "preconceived categorizations, inaccessible to new experience" (461). Rokeach, in an independent investigation growing out of the pres-

---

[7] Hatt, P., "Class and Ethnic Attitudes," *Amer. Soc. Rev.*, 1948, 13, 36-43, quoted in Hartley, E., *Fundamentals of Social Psychology*.

ent study, confirms the general finding.[8] Yet Sullivan, in another study at California inspired by the same general theory, reports contradictory evidence.[9] Rigidity was revealed by a variety of behaviors involved in the categorizing of forty photographs of adult males. Sixty-one students and 28 prison inmates were the subjects, and their behavior on this task was correlated with their scores on ethnocentrism. Among the prisoners, there were no significant differences between ethnocentric and non-ethnocentric in the content of the concepts they used in categorizing the photos nor in any formal aspects of their categorizing. Among the students, however, the ethnocentric were *less* rigid in certain respects. Now the concept of rigidity is ambiguous, and perhaps some of the contradiction between Sullivan and *The Authoritarian Personality* can be ascribed to the difference in their methods and procedures. Sullivan remarks, however, that it is "reasonable . . . to assume that the importance of ethnic attitudes to the general personality make-up varies among sub-cultures with the amount of importance placed on ethnic attitudes." Again, one is led to question the position of the authors that generalizations about interrelationships of attitude do not need to be qualified in the light of sampling considerations.

The Effect of Sampling Biases. While organization of attitudes can result from many causes, there are at least two aspects of the sampling procedure used in *The Authoritarian Personality* which, in our belief, tend to *overstate* the normal degree of this organization and the relation of attitudes to personality structure. The authors, as we have seen, point to a number of respects in which their sample is not representative, but let us note one particular feature of the sampling procedure to which we alluded before and which is not commented upon by the authors. Apart from the college students studied, the respondents were obtained through their membership in some readily accessible formal group. About 500 of the subjects, for example, came from such groups as the Parent-Teachers' Association, Unitarian Church, Kiwanis and Rotary Club, United Electrical Workers, I.L.W.U., League of Women Voters,

---

[8] Rokeach, M., "Generalized Mental Rigidity as a Factor in Ethnocentrism," *J. of Abnormal & Soc. Psych.*, 1948, 43, 259-278.

[9] Sullivan, Patrick Lee, "An Investigation of the Conceptual Properties Governing the Categorization of People, with Special Reference to Certain Social Attitudes and Values." Unpublished doctoral dissertation, University of California, 1950.

etc. Furthermore, these subjects were not only members of the group; they were the more *active* members who were sufficiently motivated to attend the groups' meetings.

Now membership in such organizations is far from universal among the American public. Probability samples of urban populations have repeatedly shown that fewer than half of the adult public claim any formal group membership whatsoever. When national survey agencies have concluded interviews on social, political or economic issues with the question, "Do you happen to belong to any group or organization which discusses problems like these?," fewer than *one-fifth* of the adult citizenry report membership in such groups.[10] More important, this minority of "joiners" differs in many important respects from the remainder of their fellows. As the following data from an NORC national survey show, the group members are more likely to hold opinions about issues, they are more likely to discuss them with their neighbors, and they are more likely to take political action such as voting.

TABLE 1

Percent Who:	Group Members	Non-Members
Say they voted in last Presidential election	72%	63%
Discussed labor problems in last week	63	36
Discussed the atomic bomb in last week	43	24
Discussed relations with Russia in last week	53	31
Express opinions on atomic energy policy	78	59
Express opinions on China policy	91	85

Data from unpublished NORC survey, 1947.

One would naturally expect that voluntary membership in organized groups and active participation in those groups, to the point of attending meetings, reflect a greater concern with social and political matters, while non-participation in such activities reflects a greater apathy. Further, these organized groups generally have institutional power and a positive program to influence those who

---

[10] Almond Gabriel, A., *The American People and Foreign Policy*, Harcourt, Brace & Co., New York, 1950, p. 82. According to Ira Reid and Emily Ehle, "Leadership Selection in Urban Locality Areas," *Pub. Op. Quarterly*, 14, 1950, pp. 262-284, 85% of the Philadelphia area population belong to no civic or charitable organization and 74% report no affiliation with any professional, business or union group. Fifty-five per cent of the women belong to no organization of any kind.

belong. It is only to be expected that individuals selected from the ranks of organized groups would be more likely to show both some patterning of their sentiments and some greater relationship between sentiments and personality factors. The patterning would be a function of the influence of the group; the relationship to personality factors would reflect the individual's initiative in joining the group. A person who shows sufficient motivation to participate in a group is more likely to regard political and social questions as central concerns, and thus to imbue these aspects of life with energies derived from more central factors of personality. On the other hand, a person who is so politically inert as to avoid or refrain from group membership is likely to be an individual to whom social and political questions are peripheral and thus not penetrated by more fundamental values and energies. This speculation is supported by an interesting finding by Smith, who noted, in the course of an inquiry into political sentiments toward Russia, that individuals varied in the degree to which their views on Russia were related to more general value systems.[11] For some individuals, the political area did not, as he put it, "engage" their value system, and he observed that one of the conditions for such engagement is that the person's interests and activities be broad enough that they can extend to the object of the attitude. "Since foreign affairs are rather distant from the immediate concerns of daily life, some breadth of interests is required for a person to extend his values to so remote an area."

We would also speculate that the remainder of the sample—the college students—are more likely than others to show a higher degree of organization of attitudes, and to relate ideological questions to more fundamental levels of personality. There is abundant evidence from national polls, some of which we present in Table 2, that the college educated are more concerned with political and social questions—they vote more, join associations more, know more, have more opinions—and it is only likely that for them social processes are much closer to central levels of functioning. Is it not probable, therefore, that this part of the large sample, another 700 cases, considerably overstates the findings as compared with the vast majority of less educated citizens?

---

[11] Smith, M. Brewster, "Personal Values as Determinants of a Political Attitude," *J. Psych.*, 1949, 28, 477-486.

TABLE 2[12]

Representative Cross-section of U. S. Adults, by Amount of Formal Education

Percent Who:	Attended College	High School Only	Grammar School Only
Know what a tariff is	64%	50%	22%
Belong to groups, organizations	32	15	7
Have opinions on reciprocal trade policy	90	76	51
Dissatisfied with progress of United Nations to date	69	53	42
Voted in 1948 Presidential election	82	70	56

Srole, on the basis of his own analysis of *The Authoritarian Personality*, reasoned in a similar manner. He theorized that on different status levels there might well be different kinds of interrelationships between prejudice and authoritarian personality trends, and he put this to empirical test in the course of a study in Springfield, Mass., using a modified probability sample of 401 adults.[13] Separately for three educational groups, Srole cross-tabulated prejudice as measured by a social distance scale against authoritarian personality trends as measured by an abbreviated F-scale developed from the original one reported in *The Authoritarian Personality*.[14] Within the low education stratum the correlation is negligible and in the high school group it is only moderate; but within the college segment the correlation is sizeable. Srole remarks: "The limited theoretical framework of the California researchers could permit them to load their sample with college level students and adults, to discount the social, cultural and personality differences associated with social class differences, and to draw from their data broad conclusions about the generality of the personality-ethnocentrism nexus. Our data suggest that on the several status levels there may be rather different kinds of interrelationships among the anomie, authoritarianism and social distance attitude factors."

---

[12] Data from Almond, *op. cit.*, p. 129, except last statistic from Gallup Poll release, July 16, 1952.

[13] Srole, Leo, "Social Dysfunction, Personality and Social Distance Attitudes," paper read before the American Sociological Society, 1951 (now in press).

[14] It should be noted that in this cross-tabulation a third factor, tendency toward personal anomie (self-to-group alienation), was measured, and the above relationships were established while controlling on this factor. We shall refer again to this aspect of Srole's analysis, for its relevance to another part of the methodology of *The Authoritarian Personality*.

A Methodological Critique

Biases Arising from the Study of Extremes. As previously indicated, the design of *The Authoritarian Personality* involved a two-stage procedure. Some of the evidence in support of the general theory is based on the answers to questionnaires which were administered to the total group. But in addition, a more intensive investigation was made of eighty individuals who showed extreme scores on the ethnocentrism questionnaire. These eighty were drawn in approximately equal numbers from both extremes, and were used as contrasted groups to isolate the personality correlates of social attitudes. We shall discuss later the methodology of the intensive investigation, but here we wish to consider certain aspects of the procedure as they relate to sampling problems. Obviously, since these extreme groups were a sub-sample of the large group, the same qualifications which we have attached to the conclusions drawn from the total group apply equally here. The sub-groups which were subjected to the intensive interviews are still, for example, drawn largely from urban, middle class, relatively well educated, participating members of American society. Their one important difference from the larger group is the fact that they represent individuals who hold extreme positions with respect to ethnocentrism.

Insofar as any generalizations drawn from the intensive study are limited to such extreme individuals, there is no problem. But insofar as inferences are drawn from these extreme cases about the dynamic processes underlying attitude formation *in general,* the question must be raised as to whether the sampling of extremes permits any inference as to the processes of similar but less extreme individuals. This question involves some assumption as to the linearity of the regression between any attitude measure and some specific other variable such as a personality trait. The writers raise this question explicitly, but do not resolve it. In one place they appear to accept the assumption of linearity: "The impression gained from a few interviews with middle scorers, and from the examination of many of their questionnaires, is that they are not indifferent or ignorant with respect to the issues of the scales, or lacking in the kinds of motivation or personality traits found in the extremes. In short, they are in no sense categorically different; they are, as it were, made of the same stuff but in different combinations" (27). But again it is remarked: "How far the relations would hold for those with middle scores on prejudice has to be left open, since such individuals were not included in the present intensive investigation by means of interviews" (473). The volume has little to say about these middle scorers, and it must be emphasized that the major conclusions of the study are based on findings obtained from the extreme groups. This is important not only as it affects the validity of the present research, but also as it may guide the efforts of future investigators in this field.

While the authors do take passing notice of this point, it is unfortunate that they did not definitely ascertain whether and how the extreme scorers might differ from the middle groups. The matter could have been established at relatively small cost, and in view of the scope of the study and the attention devoted to less major aspects of the methodology, the omission is surprising. Research studies have frequently revealed a curvilinear relation between social attitudes and various determinants of those attitudes, and a number of investigations have indicated that extreme individuals differ from others in the degree of organization of their sentiments and in the relation of such sentiments to personality factors. For example, Vetter, in a very early study of the personality correlates of social attitudes, compared groups arrayed along the reactionary-radical continuum on the basis of their questionnaire answers. The design is rather similar to the current study, except that Vetter also examined the intermediate groups, and he noted curvilinear functions on a number of variables. Thus, while radicals had an average income of $7,100 and reactionaries of $7,700, the "conservative" group, contrary to what one would expect on the assumption of linearity, had a mean income of $10,500. Similarly, the mean score on the Allport Ascendance-Submission scale for reactionary men was .2, for radicals 1.2—but for conservatives it was 9.3. On the Laird Personal Inventory, an index of introversion, reactionary men scored 16.1 and radicals 18.5, but conservatives scored only 14.8. In this instance a mere study of the extremes would have provided no adequate estimate of the middle group.[15] In a wartime study of industrial morale, it was noted that when workers were contrasted by length of employment, new employees and old employees had approximately the same level of morale. However, any assumption that there was no relationship between length of employment and morale, on the basis of analysis of these two extremes,

---

[15] Vetter, G. B., "The Measurement of Social and Political Attitudes and the Related Personality Factors," *J. Ab. and Soc. Psych.*, 1930, 25, 149-189.

would have been misleading. Individuals with short terms of employment showed lower morale than either new or old workers.[16]

The Value of National Norms. Our remarks thus far have dealt mainly with the qualifications which must be placed on research findings, in the light of the particular population being studied and the sampling design which is used. We have noted that although the authors of *The Authoritarian Personality* recognize the unrepresentativeness of their sample, they often generalize the results to the total population, and that they unwisely assume that lack of sample representativeness is no bar to the generalization of their findings, so far as relationships and determinants of attitudes are concerned. We have not criticized them because their samples were unrepresentative. That is permissible, and often wise—provided that the limitations of the sample are not ignored in drawing sweeping conclusions. Rigid orthodoxy in selecting national samples or precisely representative samples of any kind is often inefficient or unnecessary, and we hold no brief for the researcher who applies the same sampling considerations to all problems, regardless of his resources or of the nature of the problem under investigation.

Particularly in exploratory research, where the primary aim is to develop hypotheses and investigate ideas, the use of rigorous sampling methods is usually unjustified. More limited studies of less representative samples permit a greater concentration of research funds and effort on the questionnaire design, interviewing and analysis. But such studies, while quite proper for the purpose mentioned—the development of hypotheses—do not permit of generalization, nor do they provide a *test* of the hypotheses. For a definitive test of the findings obtained from an unrepresentative sample, a similar study of a representative sample is required. There is no inherent virtue in sampling the heterogeneous national population, but such a population has one often overlooked virtue which would have improved the quality of the analysis and cast doubt on certain conclusions in *The Authoritarian Personality*. For such a sample reveals the extent and social location of attitudes. Without this knowledge, interpretation is difficult and often dangerous.

Thus, one might well find in a national sample that a particular attitude is almost universal. Yet this same attitude, studied in a small ho-

---

[16] Unpublished report of the Surveys Division, OWI. A summary of these studies is reported by Katz and Hyman, "Worker Morale in War Industry," in Newcomb & Hartley, *Readings in Social Psychology*, Holt, New York, 1947.

mogeneous group, may appear to be deviant. Lacking national norms, one would attempt to explain the latter finding in terms of some *idiosyncratic* personality process, when in reality it is highly correlated with a major social fact. Or in a heterogeneous national sample one might often find a particular attitude, but largely concentrated within a particular segment of the population, whereas in the sampling of a more homogeneous group it might turn up rarely. In the former case, the researcher would have a good clue to its origins and would not, as perhaps in the second case, misinterpret the phenomenon and institute a devious search for some hidden determinant. For example, the same attitude of radicalism may have completely different functional meanings for a rich man as compared with a poor man. In the former, it is deviant, irrational; in the latter, it is normative and easily understood. But if the researcher, because of his sampling design, cannot tell whether the given attitude is normative for the general population, he may seek the explanation in the wrong place. We are suggesting that a sample of the heterogeneous total population illuminates the direction for analysis and makes less likely the drawing of broad conclusions which may be unwarranted. We shall return to this topic in discussing the analytical methods employed in *The Authoritarian Personality*, and will merely illustrate it here with one example.

In discussing the political ideology of ethnocentric individuals, the authors note that such persons are distinguished by an emphasis on the "inevitability of war." The interpretation is then given in individualistic psychodynamic terms: the high scorer has much "psychological passivity," "an underlying sympathy for war-making," "cynicism and contempt for man" and "underlying destructiveness" (719). When this same question is put to representative samples of the population, one notes that the expectation of future war is characteristic of a great many people and not a deviant few; that it fluctuates in a rather orderly fashion according to the objective facts, and that it shows a high negative correlation with formal education.[17] Illustrative figures are presented in Table 3. If one had at his disposal the data from such samples, one might have interpreted the meaning of this sentiment quite differently. For example, belief

---

[17] Five items on an abbreviated F-scale administered to a representative cross-section of U.S. adults reveal an identical pattern. The "authoritarian" response is in most cases selected by a clear majority of the population, and has a high negative correlation with education. See Table 4, P. 94.

A Methodological Critique

in war's inevitability may be a function of formal education, and the high scorers who hold this sentiment may simply represent the small number of less educated in the particular sample used. One could then control for this factor in the analysis.[18] Or it may be that the association of the belief in war's inevitability with certain irrational personality trends and prejudice is true only for relatively sophisticated, educated people. For such persons to deviate from their fellows in respect to this belief may well mean some kind of irrationality; for the ignorant soul to believe, along with his fellows, that war is inevitable may be a reasonable consequence of external factors.

TABLE 3

	Percent
"Wars are inevitable" (sample of Cincinnati, 1947, NORC)	73%
"There will always be wars" (sample of Baltimore, 1947, American Jewish Committee – NORC)	79%
Percent of national sample who expect war in 25 years at various times (Almond, op. cit. p. 90)	
August 1945	40%
March 1946 (Iran crisis)	64
February 1948 (Czechoslovakia crisis)	76
Percent of national sample who think U. S. can do something to prevent war, by education (Almond, ibid)	
College	71%
High school	54
Grammar School	47

We have stated our major criticisms of the sampling methodology. The sample on which the conclusions are based is far from a representative one, but improper generalizations are frequently made. These generalizations are of three types: (1) In spite of initial disclaimers, the incidence of sentiments in the sample population is often projected to other populations or (as with the prisoners) to an entire subgroup of the total population; (2) The nature and degree of organization of sentiments and the relationship to personality traits found in this sample are often generalized to other populations; and (3) The findings obtained from interviews with opposing extreme groups are generalized to the non-extreme middle groups.

---

[18] We discuss later in some detail the failure of the authors to control the education correlate.

III. MEASURING INSTRUMENTS

In order to test the theory, a series of questionnaires were developed to describe anti-Semitism, ethnocentrism and political ideology. The questionnaire responses permitted the measurement of social attitudes, the study of the organization among these attitudes, and the study of some correlates of attitude, notably group membership, by means of personal background items attached to the questionnaire. The *personality* correlates of the attitudes and patternings were studied in the main by such specialized instruments as depth interviews, projective questions and TAT's administered to sub-groups, although a special questionnaire was developed to measure some of these.

An inherent feature of any standardized measuring instrument is the element of artificiality. The nature of the phenomenon under investigation is inevitably affected by the design and technical features of the measuring instrument. The decision as to the content of the questionnaire, the number and types of answer-categories and the formulation of the items — all these technical, and often minor, features of the instrument influence and may even determine the results achieved. This act is recognized as a virtual truism in all empirical research, and allowances are made for it in the course of analysis. But one would expect an increased sensitivity to the problem in a study like *The Authoritarian Personality* which seeks to combine the usual survey techniques with the more clinical method. Such a joining of methodologies loses much of its possible value if the rich clinical data are merely juxtaposed against questionnaire responses which are quantified and interpreted in a positivistic way. The directors of the study applied penetrating insight in their conceptualization of the variables and in the formulation of the questionnaire items, and one would have wished that the statistical findings had been treated with equal discernment. But once the procedure had been settled, one notes that in the treatment of the data the limitations of the responses are periodically ignored, the answers are accepted at face value and the statistics manipulated in an unimaginative way. In the marriage of the two methodologies, the quantitative statistical method is all too often cast in the role of the stodgy husband who just answers "Yes, dear" to all the bright suggestions made by the wife.

The authors note (fn. 60) the lack of "rigorously obtained data" in the many public opinion polls dealing with anti-Semitism, and it is true that such polls are often superficial and badly designed. Nevertheless, the pollsters, through long experience, are acutely aware of such sampling problems as those we noted in our earlier section and most of them, again through long experience, are acutely sensitive to the nuances of question wording and the likelihood of non-statistical errors in their data. We would not expect them, as do the present authors, to ask the bald question, "What is your present income?" of groups of housewives and students, and stolidly assume that all respondents had given valid answers in comparable terms.[19] Nor would we expect them to be impervious to the ambiguity in a question like "What might drive a person nuts?"[20] But it would be profitless to discuss minor flaws of question wording, scale construction and other petty weaknesses in a study of this size and scope, and we shall turn to more general instances of a lack of feeling for the limitations of the quantitative data.

Development of the Scales. The first scales constructed were designed to measure anti-Semitism and ethnocentrism, and comprised a series of statements to which the respondent indicated his degree of agreement or disagreement. No provision was made for the expression of a qualified opinion or an ambivalent opinion; though he could indicate the extremeness of his agreement or disagreement, the respondent had to be for or against the proposition. Now this represents a perfectly legitimate and in this case wise decision on the part of the study directors, but one cannot then treat the absence of qualifications in the responses as one of the findings of the

---

[19] It is interesting that 11 out of 47 university student women in one group left this question blank, and none of the others reported more than $3,000 (198). Among the middle-class women (mostly housewives, presumably), over half reported no income, while others reported amounts up to and exceeding $10,000. More than 10% of this group, too, left the question blank. Had the question specified "your own earnings during the past year" or "total family income last year," more complete, meaningful and comparable data could easily have been obtained.

[20] This was deliberately framed as an unstructured "projective" question, but the inherent ambiguity of the "nuts" creates difficulty in the analysis. Should the respondent give the causes of insanity, as he sees them, or do the researchers merely want to know the sorts of things he considers highly irritating?

study. Such a finding was predetermined when the decision was made to construct the scale in that manner. Yet in discussing the scale results for their relevance to the structure of anti-Semitic ideology, the authors treat the lack of qualifications as a characteristic of anti-Semitic respondents. They write: "One striking characteristic of the imagery in anti-Semitic ideology is *stereotypy*, which takes several forms. There is, first, a tendency to overgeneralize single traits, to subscribe to statements beginning 'Jews are . . .' or 'The Jews do not. . . .' Second, there is a stereotyped negative image of the group as a whole as if 'to know one is to know all,' since they are all alike. Third, examination of the specific characteristics comprising the imagery reveals a basic contradiction in that no single individual or group as a whole could have all these characterstics" (94). Now this may be perfectly true, but it can hardly be inferred from the questionnaire data. It was a property of the scale, which no respondent could escape. An anti-Semite, by the rules of the questionnaire, could not reply to a question on Jewish business practices, for example, that it was true for some Jews and not for others. He could express seemingly contradictory opinions by subscribing to two such statements as "Jews seem to prefer the most luxurious . . . way of living" and "Districts containing many Jews always seem to be smelly, dirty . . . ," but he had no way of explaining that he had different segments of the Jewish population in mind. He could indicate his general prejudice and dislike, but he had no way of expressing the refinements of his prejudice. By the same token, the low scorers—the non-prejudiced—were also forced to "overgeneralize single traits," to reveal "a stereotyped image" of the group and to demonstrate a "basic contradiction" in their thinking, since they had to take the stand that "No Jews are . . ." or "None of the Jews do. . . ." This was an inherent feature of the scales as constructed, for the cognitive refinements of anti-Semitism could have been elicited only through free-answer questions or by means of answer-categories which permitted of qualification.

A similar instance of unimaginative manipulation of the quantitative data, while neglecting the more fundamental properties of the questionnaire, occurs in the demonstration of significant intercorrelations between the scale on politico-economic conservatism (PEC) and those on ethnocentrism (E) and authoritarianism (F). Here the actual content of the scales is given little regard, while many pages of text and tables are devoted to statistical means, rank order correlations, standard deviations, reliability coefficients, etc. After all, one can invent a hundred different questionnaires to measure any complex attitudinal area, each of which will be internally consistent, and one can give the same name to all these scales or questionnaires; but an inspection of the contents is really the only way to know just what it is that one is measuring. One can also study the intercorrelation between attitudes by reference to the intercorrelations between scale scores, but again the statistics take on real meaning only when one studies the content of the scales. The means and r's and S.D.'s have importance only by reason of the content on which they are based. Let us illustrate. The authors demonstrate a certain correlation between scores on their PEC scale and scores on the E and F scales. When we think of politico-economic conservatism, we normally think of an individual's position with respect to such issues as government ownership, labor-management conflict, taxation, social welfare measures, etc. While the investigators in the present study naturally included such items, they were even more concerned "to get behind the specific issues, to move . . . from a purely political to a more psychological level." So in formulating their items they were guided by the hypotheses that conservatives tend "to idealize existing authority," esteem such personal values as "practicality" and "ambition," etc. (153-154). A research director obviously has the right to select any items he chooses in constructing a scale, but equally obviously, his interpretation of the scale results is limited by the nature of the items he selects. In this case, it would seem that a major finding of *The Authoritarian Personality* — the demonstration of a syndrome of attitudes of political conservatism and authoritarianism, as revealed by the formal statistics of a correlation between the numerical scores—could instead reflect the mere fact that the PEC scale and the F scale both contain questions which are basically similar in content. The point can only be determined through an inspection of the contents of the two scales.

When we do look at the items included in the initial PEC scale, we see at a glance that in considerable degree they relate not to the usual view of the politico-economic conservatism dimension, but instead to the very kind of thing dealt with in the F or authoritarianism scale. For example, the item, "Young people sometimes get rebellious ideas, but as they grow up they ought to get over them and settle down," seems to us more closely related to authoritarianism than to politico-economic ideology. So, too, does the item,

"Whether one likes them or not, one has to admire men like Henry Ford or J. P. Morgan, who overcame all competition on the road to success." Indeed, no less than eight of the sixteen items in the initial PEC scale suggest to us a closer relation to the dimension of fundamental values tapped in the F scale than to what is normally conceived of as the politico-economic dimension. The fact that both the split-half reliability of this scale and its item-analysis indicate less internal consistency than that shown for the scale on ethnocentrism also suggests that there is a diversity of dimensions incorporated in the instrument; and it is noteworthy, too, that when intercorrelations between single items were computed in the final form of the scale, the average value was only .14 (175), again supporting the view that several different dimensions are tapped by the same scale. The authors take early note of this difficulty and even move some of the items from one scale to another because of their contents, but when they later demonstrate a positive correlation between authoritarian personality trends and politico-economic conservatism, there is no hint of the possibility that the relationship may be a spurious one owing to the overlapping content of the scales. A brief examination of the items included in the F-scale adds considerable weight to the suspicion. One notes that the "rebellious youth" item in the PEC-scale has its parallel here in "Obedience and respect for authority are the most important virtues children should learn." The item on "admiration for Ford and Morgan in overcoming competition" has a close counterpart in "Although leisure is a fine thing, it is good hard work that makes life interesting and worthwhile." Whereas on the PEC-scale, we have "America may not be perfect, but the American Way has brought us about as close as human beings can get to a perfect society," on the F-scale we find, "America is getting so far from the true American way of life that force may be necessary to restore it." Many of the items seem almost interchangeable on the two scales, and it is therefore not surprising that a correlation is found.

We cite one further example of what seems to us a signal lack of perception with regard to the inherent limitations posed by the content and format of the scale items. In this case, certain methodological problems with respect to the construction of the F-scale strongly affect the conclusions drawn about the origin of prejudice. Much of the evidence for the relation between personality trends and prejudice comes from the intensive interviewing, which we discuss later, but other evidence is based on the correlation between scores on the E and F scales. Now the F scale had a double purpose, of which the empirical test of the relation of authoritarianism to prejudice was only one. The other purpose was the construction of a disguised instrument for the measurement of prejudice, which would be useful to "survey opinion in groups where 'racial questions' were too 'ticklish' a matter to permit the introduction of an A-S or E scale" (222). The authors suggest that the two goals are quite compatible: "This second purpose—the quantification of anti-democratic trends at the level of personality—did not supersede the first, that of measuring anti-Semitism and ethnocentrism without mentioning minority groups or current politico-economic issues. Rather, it seemed that the two might be realized together. The notion was that A-S and E would correlate with the new scale because the A-S and E responses were strongly influenced by the underlying trends which the new scale sought to get at by a different approach. Indeed, if such a correlation could be obtained it could be taken as evidence that anti-Semitism and ethnocentrism were not isolated or specific or entirely superficial attitudes but expressions of persistent tendencies in the person" (223). We submit that the two goals are compatible only in the *initial* construction of the instrument—for the development of a hidden test or predictor always involves the empirical procedure of adding and deleting items until one settles on those which are found to correlate best with the criterion one is trying to predict. Insofar as one goes through stages of this type, the *final* instrument can be used as a predictor; but insofar as one goes through these stages, it also becomes less and less meaningful as a test of the *relationship* to the criterion.

That the purpose of producing a prediction instrument, a hidden test of prejudice in the F scale, was well served is demonstrated by the fact that the successive forms of this scale show increased positive correlations with scores on ethnocentrism. In the initial form the r was .65; in the second form, it was .69; in the third, it was .73, and in the fourth and final form, the r was .77. It is permissible for the authors or anyone else to use the final form for practical research purposes, as a disguised predictor of prejudice, but it is not permissible to use the correlations obtained by means of the later forms as a test of the theory, since one has stacked the cards in favor of the highest possible correlations. In the present case, an item-analysis was conducted on the original scale of 38 items, to see which ones were most worthy of being kept in the later, improved scale. "The 19 items from the F scale that ranked highest in order of goodness were retained . . . in the new scale. Thus, statistical differentiating power of the item was the main basis of selection. As stated above, however, the items which came out best statistically were, in general, those which seemed best from the point of view of theory, so that retaining them required no compromise with the original purpose of the scale" (250). But it is clear, after a study of the items retained and the items dropped, that the two purposes are not compatible and that the successive refinements in the prediction instrument *did* compromise the scale's original purpose to provide a test of the theory. We note, for example, that three of the items which were omitted on the final scale were among the best in discriminating total scores on authoritarianism, but they had very low correlations with scores on anti-Semitism.[21] In other words, here were three items which by the logic of internal consistency were very good measures of personality on the F scale, but because they empirically did not correlate with anti-Semitism, they were discarded. These items appear to provide *negative* evidence on the theory, but they are thrown away in the process of developing a good prediction instrument. Four other items which were found to correlate highly with anti-Semitism were retained in the scale, even though they were *poor* measures of the larger personality dimension which was being tapped.[22] In other words, these items are employed to provide evidence on the theory in spite of the fact that they are among the least appropriate as measures of authoritarianism. Here then are no less than seven decisions, in a 19-item scale, each of which enhances the predictive value of the scale but simultaneously renders it misleading as a test of the theory.

Another example of a curious lack of insight in the questionnaire construction lies in the authors' handling of the classic problems of reliability and validity. The emphasis on validity is most commendable, since all too often the current attitude research in the public

---

[21] As well as can be determined (Table, 245), Items 9, 66 and 67 were dropped from Form 78 because they correlated poorly with A-S, although they were good measures of F.

[22] Items 17, 32, 47 and 70 were kept in the scale because they correlated well with A-S, although they were poor measures of F.

A Methodological Critique

opinion field simply assumes the questions to be valid on the basis of the general context and an inspection of the items. Here the concept of validity is treated for each of the four scales by the measure of agreement between the scale scores and the later responses to the intensive interview by selected subjects. An orthodox definition of validity is advanced: "One meaning of the concept of validity as applied to a psychological test is that the test, which involves only a small sample of the individual's responses, tells us something that is generally true of that individual as judged by an intensive study of him. The A-S scale may be said to have validity of this kind to the degree that the subjects, in their responses to the scale, reveal the same tendencies which come out in their interviews" (89). One can hardly quarrel with this definition, provided one obvious condition is met. Any such approach to the validation of an instrument by means of some outside criterion presupposes that the two sets of results have been *independently* derived. If the scores obtained by the instrument and those obtained by the criterion are not independently achieved, such an approach to the problem of validity is not only pointless, it is both naive and grossly misleading.

Yet for each of the four scales, a serious discussion of the validity of the questionnaire is presented, despite the fact that the criterion data, from the intensive interviews, were not independently obtained. Scattered through the text, although never noted in the context of the discussions on validity, are many references to the fact that the interviewers were armed with a thorough study of the respondent's scale scores when they initiated the interview. "In each case the interview was preceded by the study, on the part of the interviewer, of the information gathered previously, especially a detailed study of the questionnaire responses" (302). Instructions to the interviewers urged: "It must be emphasized that *careful study of the questionnaire beforehand* is essential for an adequate interview. The questionnaire by itself reveals many important points under each topic; it also suggests hypotheses which can be verified in the interview. Pre-interview study of the questionnaire, then, gives the interviewer a more structured approach to the interview and should be done in all possible cases" (304).

This is another example of a legitimate research decision on the part of the study directors, but the consequences of the decision are then ignored and the logic of the analysis consequently perverted. It cannot be gainsaid that the interview achieves greater focus and penetration when it follows the leads of the questionnaire; the procedure cannot be condemned and needs no defense. But one cannot achieve these advantages and simultaneously point to the resultant responses for purposes of validation. There is abundant evidence, even from surveys in which the freedom of the interviewer is deliberately and maximally restricted, that large areas still remain for the operation of interviewer bias, and that interviewers are inevitably guided in their probing, their resolution of ambiguous responses and their recording of verbatim material, by whatever clues they may have as to the natural or expected response.[23] Especially in this case, in which the interviewers were deliberately urged to use the prior scale scores as leads in the interview situation and were given maximum freedom to improvise their lines of inquiry, one would naturally expect a high motivation on their part to make the interview data conform to what they already knew about the respondent on the basis of his questionnaires. In such circumstances, it is difficult to treat the interviews as an objective test of the validity of the scale scores.

We are not contending that the scales are not valid, but rather that the data presented in evidence are not appropriate for validation purposes.[24] In one paragraph of the text, there is a passing reference to other validation procedures: "Unpublished data from the present study indicate that both conservatism and ethnocentrism are significantly correlated with support of the un-American Activities Committee, Hearst, the American Legion, and militarization . . ." (152). It is of course impossible to evaluate this statement in the absence of the data, but the remark is interesting. No further information is provided on this possible method of validation, while the text is four times interrupted with a detailed "validation by case studies" which lacks any significance. The lack of independence

---

[23] See, for example, Smith, H. L., and Hyman, H., "The Biasing Effect of Interviewer Expectations on Survey Results," *Public Opinion Quarterly*, 14 No. 3, 491-506. See also the forthcoming monograph on "Interviewer Effects," to be sponsored by the Social Science Research Council, covering three years of research on this subject by the National Opinion Research Center.

[24] In a study using a modified form of the F scale, Eager and Smith showed that scores on authoritarianism achieved by counselors in a summer camp agreed with campers' perceptions of the degree to which their counselors engaged in behavior that represented authoritarian leadership. This is a legitimate test of validity. Eager, J. and Smith, M. Brewster, "A Note on the Validity of Sanford's Authoritarian-Equalitarian Scale," *J. Abnorm. Soc. Psych.*, 1952, 47, 265-267.

between the questionnaire and the interview procedures had much more serious consequences for the study to which we shall return in our discussion of the analysis. We cite the point here only as a further example of the rather mechanical handling of the questionnaire problem.

Let us note one additional point in this general area. With all questionnaire instruments, one can order individuals with respect to a particular attitude dimension. One can say that a certain respondent or group of respondents is "high" or "low", for example, relative to a scale on ethnocentrism, or higher or lower than someone else on the scale. But the scale scores have no *absolute* meaning in relation to the total quantum of ethnocentrism. Other equally good scales could be devised which would establish the same relationship but produce different means. Moreover, since there is no way to equate two different scales for their completeness of measurement of different attitude dimensions, it is meaningless to compare the absolute levels of two different scales. Yet one finds periodic statements in *The Authoritarian Personality* which ignore this obvious consideration. For example, in discussing political conservatism and ethnocentrism, it is remarked: "Thus, while the rank order of conservatism (the position of sub-groups along the dimension) is similar to that of ethnocentrism, the general level of conservatism is considerably higher. People are, so to speak, more conservative than ethnocentric, at least as measured by these scales" (159). An almost parallel statement appears later on (173). Statements of this kind, based on scores achieved on two separate incommensurable scales, are meaningless.

Collection and Processing of Interview Data. As indicated earlier, the relationship between attitudes and deeper personality factors was established in the main by intensive interviews with a subsample of eighty respondents selected from the high and low extremes on ethnocentrism. Approximately ninety variables within six major areas were to be covered in the course of a long interview. A list of the variables and a suggested schedule of questions were provided for the interviewer, but he was free to modify the procedure to suit the particular circumstances of any given interview. The authors note that the nine interviewers varied in their backgrounds, and in consequence of their differing orientation, "some difference of emphasis in the collection of data had to be anticipated" (301). But judging from the description, the interviewers appear to have been well trained, and they were allocated to particular respondents in such a way as to minimize any biasing effects due to disparities in group membership between interviewer and respondent. Thus, prejudiced respondents were interviewed by American-born Gentiles, men by male interviewers, etc.

Evaluations of the quality of interviewers' work are always difficult to make, even when the field staff is under one's own close supervision, and at this distance we can make few comments on the skill with which these nine interviewers handled their task. In many cases in which the volume cites excerpts from the actual interviews, the verbatim accounts have been summarized and paraphrased in the third person; e. g., "Her parents definitely approve of the engagement. Subject wouldn't even go out with anyone if they didn't like him" (351) and "with regard to the Jews she feels that assimilation and education will eventually solve the problem" (755). It is stated that "the interviewer wrote as rapidly as he could, in a 'shorthand' of his own, throughout the interview and then immediately used a dictaphone to record all that he had written" (33). The verbatim material may easily be distorted by such summaries —an important point, in view of the subtleties of the coding which we discuss later—but the difficulty of accurate and complete reporting of the respondents' language is well-nigh universal in survey research. Periodically, too, one notes the use of probes which tend to lead the respondent or to put words in his mouth. Thus, when a respondent spoke of pre-marital sex relations, the interviewer asked, "All momentary relationships?" (393), and when another spoke of Jews as "all alike," the protocol states: "When asked if she did not feel that there were variations in the Jewish temperament as in any other . . ." (614). In another instance we find "When it is pointed out to her that people of her own extraction probably also fall into good and bad groups, she admits this . . ." (626). But probing and recording errors occur in any interview study, and if anything, these interviewers appear to be far above average—well educated, highly motivated, thoroughly trained and closely supervised.

The interview data were coded by two individuals under the approximately ninety variables defined in the interview schedule, and the relationship between personality factors and social attitudes was then determined by comparing the size of the categories for the two contrasted groups of respondents. Considerable attention was given to the danger that the coding might have been biased if the coders

A Methodological Critique

knew in advance the ideology of the respondents whose interviews they processed. Because of this danger, all the coding was done blindly, with the coder in ignorance of the respondent's scale scores. Such a procedure represents a rigorous control of one source of error, but the attention devoted to this type of precaution is largely wasted when one recalls that the interviewers, whose material the coders processed, were given all available information on every aspect of the respondent's ideology. If, as the authors admit, there was danger of bias if the coders were familiar with the respondent's scale scores, the same consideration applies with even stronger force to the interviewers. If, as may be argued, the interviewers could operate with greater effectiveness when armed with this information in advance, one could advance the same point in regard to the coders. The inconsistency strikes us as a flaw in the research procedure. In this case, any systematic bias caused by the interviewer's awareness of the level of the respondent's ethnocentrism was fully incorporated into the data at the time the coder did his work blindly. There is no evidence whatever in the text of the volume to support the authors' implicit assumption that the interviewers' awareness did not systematically enhance the correlations in the direction of proving the original hypothesis. If it were deemed advisable for the interviewers to orient their procedure in the light of a full knowledge of the respondent's ideology, it would seem almost elementary to test this procedure by means of a small experimental study to determine whether there was any difference in results for high vs. low respondents under the two conditions of blind vs. informed interviewing. In this context, the elaborate attention to the problem of bias in coding seems misplaced.

But let us turn to other problems in the coding process. Admittedly, the judgment of the two coders could not have been influenced by the full knowledge of the respondent's questionnaire scores which were in the possession of the interviewers. But there are other sources of error to be considered. The ninety code categories were quite complex, and there is the problem of the reliability of the coder's judgment; a variety of transient factors might affect his decision in any instance. The usual procedure was employed to check on this point: each of the two coders processed the same interviews in a small sub-sample, and since they showed a high level of agreement in their judgment on these cases, we can assume that any of the later findings are not due to the idiosyncrasies of the particular coder who rated the case. It is a fair assumption, too, that the coders handled their work consistently over time. But this demonstration of *reliability* does not insure us against all forms of error in the coding process. Let us look at some of the coders' problems, remembering that there were approximately ninety complex and subtle categories to be rated, and that given the free interview procedure there may often have been no response to correspond exactly to the variable to be rated.

It is hypothesized, and supported by the data of the text, that ethnocentric individuals will show a "conventionalized idealization of parents: overestimation of qualities and status, expressed in . . . conventionalized generalities," whereas the non-ethnocentric will show an "objective appraisal of parents." Another hypothesis with respect to the family constellation is that the ethnocentric will report "victimization: neglect . . . unjust discipline . . ." by parents, while the non-ethnocentric will show "genuine positive affect" toward the mother and father (339). One can immediately see coding difficulties here. The distinctions are subtle, and a coder might easily confuse idealization of parents (high) with positive affect (low), or victimization (high) with objective appraisal (low). And the distinctions have to be made on the basis of the interviewer's transcript or summary of the respondent's language. But the coders appear to have mastered the difficulties. "Very, very fine man — intelligent, understanding, excellent father, in every way" (343) is classed as conventionalized idealization rather than positive affect (the respondent is a high scorer) and "Can't say I don't like him . . . but he wouldn't let me date at 16. I had to stay home . . ." (348) is coded as victimization rather than objective appraisal. A parallel set of codes is established for attitudes toward siblings. The same problems arise, but the coders, much more often than not, find the hypothesized "high" variants in the ethnocentric respondents and the "low" variants in the non-ethnocentric. Thus, the following remark of a high-scoring respondent who states of his brother, "He's a wonderful kid. Has been wonderful to my parents. Always lived at home. Gives most of his earnings to my parents" (378), is coded as "conventionalized glorification" rather than "positive affect," while "She was lucky if she heard from her sister once in three months" (381) goes under "victimization" and not "objective appraisal." Similar difficulties occur among the variables surrounding the "self-image." Ethnocentric persons were hypothesized to engage

A Methodological Critique

in self-glorification in contrast to the critical self-appraisal of the non-ethnocentric. But the ethnocentric were also hypothesized to show "ego-alien self-contempt." Again these relationships are demonstrated in the data, and the coders somehow manage to make the elusive distinctions. The remark of a low-scoring subject, "I work best by myself—have difficulty working with other people . . . it's a strain on me. I'm rather shy, don't like competition" (426) is judged as critical self-appraisal, while in a high scorer, "I'm inclined to be nervous, haven't the confidence in myself . . . I'm the clinging vine type . . ." (427) is rated as "ego-alien self-contempt." In addition to the intricacies of these distinctions, the coders had another problem in the apparent logical contradictions of the codes. We have noted that toward parents and siblings the high-scorers on the ethnocentrism scale were hypothesized to show conventionalized idealization as well as victimization; toward themselves, both self-glorification and ego-alien self-contempt were expected. Under "childhood environment," references to the father as "distant, stern, bad temper," illustrated by the remark, ". . . He's as stubborn as an ox . . . And he can fly off the handle" (360), is scored as a "high" variant, though it seems incompatible with the hypothesized "conventional glorification." Under "conception of childhood self," high scorers are presumed to report themselves more often as "difficult children: unmanageable, stubborn, aggressive, spoiled, sensitive, etc." This seems contradictory to the hypothesized "self-glorification" and also to their significantly greater tendency to report a "bland childhood: happy, active, no worries, etc." (435). The authors take note of this latter difficulty: "We were aware of the fact that this assumption (of a happy childhood) is in apparent contradiction to the trend just referred to, namely that high scorers lean toward describing themselves as having been difficult children. However, it is quite common to find denial of difficulties in such subjects side by side with revelation of difficulties" (438). This is no doubt true, and we would grant also that the other apparent illogicalities of the coding system have some psychological validity. But this merely emphasizes the problem of the coder. How does he decide, when he confronts a remark that could with equal logic be scored as a "high" variant such as conventionalized idealization or as a "low" variant such as genuine positive affect? How does he decide, when a respondent speaks of childhood difficulties, whether this confirms the "high" trait of "a difficult child" or denies the "high" trait of "a bland childhood?" How does he decide whether criticism of parents reflects victimization or objective appraisal?

The criteria for such decisions, though they are often not too hard to understand, are at other times completely baffling to the reader. We give one final example. High scorers, in speaking of their parents and siblings, are expected to show conventionalized idealization or victimization, but never open rejection. A quotation from a high scorer, which we noted earlier, runs as follows: "With much bitterness, subject replied that she was lucky if she heard from her sister once in three months. She feels that this sister has the family characteristic of being self-sufficient and independent, and that she has never really shown any gratitude for all that subject has done for her." The authors then say, "This record shows clearly that the subject resents both mother and sister, *without daring to criticize them*" (381—italics ours). Yet, as we have noted, the coders proved able to make these subtle distinctions, their reliability was checked, and most of the hypotheses are borne out by the data in the text. How can we explain the apparent success of this coding system which is so elaborate, artful and abstruse?

It should be noted first of all that the reliability check is based on only nine cases and the agreement was not complete, of course, on those nine. A second consideration is that while attention is given to reliability (i.e., errors due to inconsistency between the two coders), no notice at all is taken of the possibility of *bias*—the likelihood that both coders may introduce the same systematic type of error. Agreement between the two, as indicated by the high reliability, could well reflect only a common bias. Both coders, for example, were "well-trained psychologists and were thoroughly familiar with the nature of the categories and the underlying implications as to personality theory. These raters had participated actively in numerous conferences at which the scoring procedure was thoroughly discussed, prior to making the ratings" (328). Two such coders, high-level research people who were thoroughly indoctrinated with the particular point of view of the study directors and who had participated in other phases of the study, might well have a common bias. Such coders were presumably able to perceive the subtle distinctions required by the theory, whereas two others, trained in another school or with no particular attachment to the study, might have found themselves thoroughly confused by the overlapping and mutual contradictions of the coding system. It is somewhat as if two lawyers for the prosecution independently report the same opinion on the basis of their careful study of a large mass of evidence. They agree on almost every point. But one must continue to have reservations about their opinion until independent judges can follow their logic and arrive at the same conclusions.

But even a common background, training and approach to the task are not sufficient to explain the coders' regularity in finding the presumed "high" traits in the high scorers and the "low" traits in the low, in spite of the puzzling verbal similarities. It should be noted in this connection that although the coders coded "blind," without knowledge of the respondent's scale score, they still coded in an over-all fashion. That is, they read the entire interview before deciding the proper category of doubtful items. Since the coders knew what the expected relationship among the personality variables was to be (even though they did not know which respondent had which constellation), they could perhaps order themselves according to the distinctions of the theory and know that the appearance of a particular remark in one part of the interview would automatically exclude the likelihood of a particular code in another part of the interview. We must remember, too, that the respondents whose interviews were coded represented *extreme* cases at both ends of the scale; the middle, less determinate groups were excluded from this phase of the procedure. Although all references to topics of political ideology and prejudice were deleted from the protocols before the coders received the material, it is not unlikely that the remainder was still sufficiently indicative to give the coders a strong impression that the respondent represented a "high" or a "low." And such strong impressions as to the respondent's over-all ideology would inevitably have guided them when they had to decide whether an ambiguous remark reflected a presumed "high" variant or a presumed "low" variant. The authors of the study were aware of this likelihood, which they call the "halo-effect," but left its control to "special analytical attitudes the raters were asked to maintain" (334). They point out also that a certain amount of correlation may reflect valid relationships and be fully justified by the facts, and that the variability of "high" and "low" ratings ascribed to various subjects indicate that the "halo effects" were kept within reasonable bounds. In the absence of contrary proof, however, one can only assume that the system of over-all coding and the coders' intuitive awareness of the ideology of many of the respondents helped them to reconcile the difficulties of the coding scheme, and is likely to have produced spurious relationships between the factor of ethnocentrism and certain of the personality traits.*

Other Techniques Employed. In addition to the four questionnaires (on anti-Semitism, ethnocentrism, politico-economic conservatism and authoritarianism) and the personal interviews with selected members of the groups which scaled very high and very low on ethnocentrism, two other procedures were employed in testing the theory concerning the relation between personality and prejudice. The first of these involved a series of projective questions which were attached to the regular questionnaires. These were free-answer questions which yielded data that were then coded into certain categories indicative of personality functioning. Results were then compared for contrasted groups on ethnocentrism, and differences were demonstrated. The second procedure involved the administration of a thematic apperception test to two contrasted extreme groups, and again differences were demonstrated. The results derived from these two procedures seem among the most substantial from the point of view of methodology, in that they are free from the likely bias incorporated into the interviews through the interviewer's complete awareness of the scale responses of each of his respondents. Replies to the projective questions and to the TAT were elicited in each case through standard stimuli, uninfluenced by the impromptu questioning and probing of interviewers. Therefore, whatever differences are noted in the responses of the contrasted groups cannot possibly be attributed to bias, influence or variation of the stimulus. But there are other possible pitfalls in the coding, analysis and interpretation of the responses. We discuss the latter points in our next section, and comment only briefly here on the coding procedures.

As with the coding of the interview data, the research directors were aware that the coding of the projective material might be unfairly influenced if the coders knew whether the respondent was a "high" or a "low," so on four of the six groups studied they adopted a procedure of "blind" scoring. "The high and low quartiles from a given group were combined and their responses to each item typed in a single, randomly ordered series. Each response was identified

---
*Editors' note. A more detailed examination of the raters' halo effect may be found in Chapter IV.

by a code number, so that the scorer did not know whether it was given by an individual scoring high or by an individual scoring low on ethnocentrism. . . . The scorer was, therefore, entirely on her own in deciding whether each response fell into a high, low, or neutral category" (581). It is noted that in the case of the first two groups studied, "the scoring was not done blindly. This was recognized as a methodological error and corrected on all subsequent groups." That the methodological error affected the results is admitted: "It appears that the scorers, try as they did to be unbiased, were systematically influenced by the fact that they knew the E-quartile standing of the (two groups which were not coded blindly)" (590). Discounting this fact, however, we believe that the blind coding procedure used on the projective questions, just like the blind coding procedure used on the interview data, was an ineffectual precaution against bias—because the bias had already been incorporated into the material before the coding stage was reached. In the case of the interview data, the bias entered through the interviewers' knowledge of the person's questionnaire responses; in the case of the projective question data, the bias was built into the coding system.

The authors describe the way the codes were built: "The procedure in determining the specific categories for each item was as follows. The responses of the low scorers to that item were transposed by typing onto one or a few sheets, thus permitting easy inspection of group material; and similarly for the high scorers. Closer examination of the responses of each quartile as a whole revealed a few major trends characteristic of each group and differentiating it from the other group. These trends were formalized into categories which seemed both empirically differentiating and theoretically meaningful. The final step involved the preparation of a Scoring Manual in which each category is defined, discussed briefly, and illustrated with examples from the groups on which the Manual is based" (549). It will be noted that the categories decided on were those which had already proved "empirically differentiating" between the two groups, and that the presumed "high" and "low" categories were illustrated by example in the Scoring Manual. In such a procedure, the coder's ignorance of the subject's scale score is unimportant in most cases; by reference to the Scoring Manual, he merely translates the response back to the "high" or "low" score already determined by the person who constructed the Manual, and who constructed it in full knowledge of each subject's scale score. If we understand this procedure correctly, it worked something like this: In response to the projective question, "What great people do you admire most?," it was empirically found that people engaged in "the arts and philosophy" were more often mentioned by low scorers, and in the Scoring Manual such names were therefore listed as a low category. The coder when he came to such names, then coded the response as low. The empirical demonstration of differences in the responses of the high and low groups to these questions is entirely legitimate, but the further procedure of "blind scoring" of these differences and the use of the results of such coding to provide a test of the theory strike us as meaningless.

Any scoring, coding or classification scheme of this type presupposes an examination of some or all of the responses in order to set up the necessary categories in a workable manner, and such an examination was apparently conducted here. But to test the theory, it seems to us that one of two alternative procedures should have been employed from that point on. Under the first procedure, in building the code the answers would merely have been classified according to content areas; i.e., the "most admired men" could have been coded as political figures, military, arts and philosophy, etc. The coders would then merely indicate the content category within which each response fell. Then, and only then, would the high and low groups be compared. If significant differences appeared, confirming the hypotheses suggested by the theory, the point would be established. As noted earlier, the authors state that such differences were indeed evident when the material was examined during the code-building process and the Scoring Manual was actually constructed on the basis of these differences. But the differences were merely observed by the analyst; they were not objectively demonstrated. Alternatively, the analyst could examine the sample of responses, and *without reference to the respondents' scale scores*, decide, in terms of his theory, which types of replies were to be coded as "high" and which as "low." The coders would then classify each answer in these terms, again without knowing the respondents' scale scores, and only after the coding was completed would the responses be validated against the scale scores. Again, if the correlations between scale scores and results from this code were significant, the evidence would be convincing. Under the procedure actually followed, however, the "blind scoring" contributes nothing, since the coding system itself was constructed in full knowledge of the respondents' scale scores and the categories decided upon were those which had already been found to be differentiating.

Two separate techniques were used in the analysis of the TAT material. The first, using the Murray-Sanford scoring scheme, demonstrated differences in the content of the stories told by prejudiced and unprejudiced subjects. The findings appear to be substantial. The second technique, a "thematic analysis," is subject to the considerations mentioned above in regard to the coding of the projective question data. The Murray-Sanford results were carefully studied, in terms of the differences between highs and lows, and hypothetical "high" and "low" thema categories were constructed on this basis. The coders then coded the TAT material into these categories, again on a "blind" basis, without knowledge of the subjects' scale scores.[25] The expected differences are demonstrated, but in view of the procedure through which the categories were built, they cannot be accepted as a test of the theory.

IV. ANALYSIS

Our consideration of the coding process leads directly to a discussion of the analytic procedures, which yield the findings in support of the theory. As indicated, the theory's major support is found in the different personality syndromes which are characteristic of the contrasted extreme ethnocentric and nonethnocentric groups which were interviewed. We have tried to show that the conclusion must be highly qualified in the light of sampling considerations, and that in view of the interviewing and coding procedure, some of the differences may simply be artifactual. But with regard to the analytic methods themselves, we have a number of points to make.

The analytic scheme assumes that differences in the level of ethnocentrism of the two contrasted groups can be attributed to

---

[25] It is clearly stated that this scoring was blind (507), although later it is noted that "the analyses of the stories . . . were 'blind' in the sense that the analyst was not familiar with any of the other material on these two subjects. All that was known was that Mack scored high, and Larry low, on the E scale" (530). The reference is puzzling, since this is all one would need to know in order to introduce a spurious relationship into the findings.

the types of factors which are found to differentiate their personalities. It might well be, however, that the differences are due not to the demonstrated personality variables but to other factors not controlled in the analysis; or it might be that the personality differences which are demonstrated are really pseudo-differences arising from certain inadequacies of the analysis. The classic procedure in field research studies is to approximate laboratory conditions by matching the contrasted groups in other respects in advance of the comparisons, or by higher order cross-tabulations to compare the responses of equivalent sub-groups. Obviously such controls must be applied in the light of certain principles. Some factors are intrinsic to the variable under study, and to control for them is not only unnecessary; it may prove misleading. But other factors are merely associated accidentally with the variable under study, and the influence of these factors must be held constant if the demonstrated differences are to be accepted as valid proof of the hypothesis. The authors were of course aware of this problem, and they indicate in the initial discussion of the interview material that the ethnocentric and nonethnocentric cases were balanced as well as possible "in terms of age, sex, political and religious affiliation, as well as national and regional background" (294). So presumably these factors cannot have contributed to the findings.

However, the controls exercised do not by any means exhaust the possibilities. There is still the potentiality that some uncontrolled factor which is correlated with the personality factors observed is what really accounts for the ethnocentrism of the subjects. In such an instance, the relationship demonstrated would be spurious. Srole, in the paper previously cited, demonstrates this very type of spurious relationship between ethnocentrism, as measured by a social distance scale, and authoritarian personality trends. Srole constructed a scale for the measurement of "anomic tendencies," which was administered to a representative sample along with two other scales which measured authoritarian personality trends and social distance in regard to minority groups. He finds that the relationship between authoritarianism and social distance is dissipated in *the entire sample* when anomic tendencies are controlled. In the presence of such control, the relationship persists only for the sub-group of college-educated. He remarks: "Our data suggest the possibility that the California Study's finding of a correlation between authoritarian personality tendencies and ethnocentrism may in some measure be spurious, i.e., may be accounted for by the high correlation between authoritarianism and the anomic factor, which factor in turn is significantly and independently correlated with our social distance scores."

Now obviously we cannot expect the analyst to control every possible factor which could remotely account for the correlations. No matter how many factors are controlled, there will always remain others which could conceivably be responsible for whatever differences are found. All we can ask is that the analyst take account of the more obvious variables, the ones which would normally occur to any reasonable reader of his findings, and either control for those in his analysis or qualify his conclusions in the light of the omission. We submit that, despite the authors' concern in matching their groups on such demographic characteristics as sex and age, they completely overlook a quite obvious factor which could easily account for the correlations they report. That factor is formal education, or years of schooling completed. Neither in the original choice of the groups nor through higher order cross-tabulation in the subsequent analysis was there any control of possible education differences among the ethnocentric and non-ethnocentric respondents. Although there is never any detailed description of the educational level of the two groups, it is clear from a number of sources in the text that the non-ethnocentric have had considerably more formal schooling. The twelve San Quentin inmates who were included in the study, for example, comprised four non-ethnocentric and eight ethnocentric individuals. No one of the former had less than eleven years of schooling and the median number of years completed was twelve; among the ethnocentrics, on the other hand, the median was 9.5 years and two of them had completed less than four years (820). Elsewhere in the discussion of the correlates of various scale scores, it is reported that ethnocentrism shows a "slight negative correlation with amount of education" (287), and detailed distributions of the relationship between these two variables for a number of subgroups generally support this statement.

We do not feel that we are being academic in raising the issue that the findings reported may reflect uncontrolled differences in education. As one examines the interview excerpts in the text, one is continually and vividly struck by the fact that some of the differences obtained, which are treated as determinants of ethnocentrism, seem actually mere reflections of formal education. For example, one of the factors found to differentiate the ethnocentric most significantly is a conventionality with respect to sex. As a manifestation of this, it is shown that high scorers emphasize conventional virtues in a mate, and the authors state: "In contrast with the stereotyped and conventional description of their desired or real mates given by the high-scoring subjects, the typical low-scoring subject takes a much more individualized attitude, as shown in the following quotations" (403). One of the quotations then goes as follows (italics ours): "She has to be intelligent, mature, emotionally stable, have *adequate physiological characteristics*, as well as have *culture and personality* that goes with this. . . . She should have a maximum of *femininity*, since we're all *bisexual*. You can think of it in terms of a polyfactorial setup (subject then quotes *Rosanoff's theory* of four factors in sex)." As one reads this case, the thought occurs that this is not at all an individualized attitude. This is the language of a pseudo-intellectual student. It seems strange for the authors to follow this quotation with the remark: "The preceding descriptions by low-scoring subjects of their real or ideal mates reveal a conception of *real people*." The high scorers, on the other hand, say "It was love at first sight. He has brown hair, brown eyes, white teeth, not handsome, but good clean-cut looking" and "A very good wife, good mother, and darned good cook."[26]

It is later noted that high scorers are more likely to explain phenomena in terms of heredity, physical or accidental factors, whereas low scorers tend in general toward socio-psychological explanations. Again, one thinks immediately that this is a common correlate of formal education, and our suspicions are not reduced when we find that the first four quotes used to illustrate the manner in which low scorers think of prejudice in psychological terms come from "a student-minister . . . who has strong intellectual leanings," "a thoroughly liberal teacher, head of the English department in a junior college," "a 33-year-old Stanford graduate who served for four years in the navy, finally becoming a Lieutenant Commander" and "an executive secretary in the movie industry" (644-46). Again,

---

[26] Perhaps we should repeat that we are not criticizing the authors' *theory*. The quotations cited may not be representative, and it may be that if education were controlled, the same differences would be found. But our point is that the examples fail to provide any demonstration of the theory, and indeed strengthen the suspicion that educational differences could account for a large part of the findings.

A Methodological Critique

one notes that the ethnocentric have an exaggerated regard for property, while the low scorers see it as a means toward an end and refer more to enjoyment of books and music. This is illustrated by the low scorer who, when asked what he missed most on his present income, replied, "A good radio with a record player on it;" the one who, when asked what he would do with $7500, referred to the fact that his wife "always likes to go to plays and concerts," and the third who described the good life in terms of "a good record player with lots of records" (434). In contrast, the high scorers are quoted as desiring "security," "more cattle, more land." Such matters of taste are well known to be a function of education.[27] The frequent emphasis by low scorers on the "record player and lots of records" impresses us not as a real personality difference but simply as the conventional ordering of tastes among the intellectuals and better educated.

These are far from isolated examples; they occur throughout the analysis. The low scorers, for instance, are distinguished as having a childhood which involved "orientation toward the adult and the espousal of internalized standards, as manifested in reading a lot, an interest in school and teachers . . ." (439). An illustration of this is the low scorer who describes his childhood as "Oh, very serious. Read Rippant's 'History of the World' at nine. My grandfather, when I was nine or ten, gave me Washington Irving's 'Conquest of Granada,' which meant a great deal to me. . . ." The low scorers are distinguished by a "scientific-naturalistic attitude" as compared with the high scorers who accept "stereotyped, pseudoscientific answers" and who "escape into ready-made hereditarian explanations" or show a "tendency toward superstition" (464-5). In discussing the contrasted ethnocentrics and non-ethnocentrics among the criminals studied, it is noted that the low scorers, "when they do attribute certain character traits to Negroes, tend to offer sociopsychological explanations for such traits in terms of environmental pressures" (830).

All of the differences referred to could well be artifacts of an uncontrolled educational difference. That these "personality traits" do vary with education has been demonstrated in many representative samples of the adult population, of which we cite a few in Table

---

[27] For detailed discussion of just such differences in taste among differing strata of the population, see Lazarsfeld, P. F., *Radio and the Printed Page*, Duell, Sloan and Pearce, New York, 15-48.

4.[28] It is surprising indeed that in the kind of detailed inspection and analysis which the interviews received, there was never any concern expressed regarding this factor of education, nor was it reported as being taken into consideration when the contrasting groups were matched. We are certainly not implying that ethnocentrism is caused by lack of education or that formal education determines basic personality structure, but we contend that the significance of these personality variables to the problem of ethnocentrism seems dubious in the light of the known correlation with education of many of the indices employed, and the failure to take account of this factor in the analysis of the two groups.

TABLE 4

EDUCATIONAL DIFFERENCES AS FOUND IN NORC NATIONAL SURVEYS

	College	High School	Grammar School
n=	217	545	504
Agree that:			
The most important thing to teach children is absolute obedience to their parents	35%	60%	80%
Any good leader should be strict with people under him in order to gain their respect	36	51	66
Prison is too good for sex criminals. They should be publicly whipped or worse	18	31	45
There are two kinds of people in the world: the weak and the strong	30	53	71
No decent man can respect a woman who has had sex relations before marriage	14	26	39
Believe cancer is contagious	9	12	27
Know what a nuclear physicist does	50	16	5
Think the world is better off as a result of man's ability to exploit atomic energy	58	40	25
Believe that most people can be trusted	77	70	52
Mention reading as a favorite activity	62	43	33
Think it's more important for government to guarantee jobs than to assure opportunities	24	39	51
Rate interest in work as most important thing in choosing a job	44	34	21
Rate financial return as most important thing in choosing a job	9	12	21

---

[28] The first five items cited form an abbreviated F scale which was administered to a representative national sample sponsored jointly by the American Jewish Committee and the Anti-Defamation League of B'nai Brith in the Fall of 1950.

A similar disregard for the influence of formal education occurs in a parallel analysis of the correlates of ethnocentrism, as revealed by a series of projective questions, rather than by interview data. It is noted, for example, that low scorers emphasize such values as "intellectual, aesthetic, and scientific achievement, social contribution and democratic social change" as manifested in their replies to the question, "What great people do you admire most?" (559).[29] Examples cited include the following: Whitman, Pushkin, Beethoven, Voltaire, Bertrand Russell, Comte, Maimonides, Confucius, Sir William Osler, Freud, Pestalozzi, etc. The high scorers, on the other hand, emphasize values of "power and control, conservative Americana, etc." as illustrated by such names as: Marshall, MacArthur, Lindbergh, the Pope, Henry Ford, Washington, Teddy Roosevelt, Kate Smith, Bing Crosby, etc. What strikingly distinguishes the two lists of names, apart from their content, is the fact that the first are largely unknown to non-intellectuals while the second spring readily to the popular mind—certainly a likely correlate of formal education.[30] On the basis of another projective question, "What might drive a person nuts?," the lows are found to emphasize "psychological conflict and frustration. They have an intraceptive orientation and they emphasize the role of the individual himself in the neurosis," whereas the highs emphasize extern-

---

[29] The use of this type of question for projective purposes has a long history in psychological research. In a 1929 study conducted among more than 8,000 school children, Hill found that the mention of characters from a "remote environment" increased steadily with the children's age, i. e., education. He notes that the question he used, "Of all persons whom you have heard, or read about, or seen, whom would you most care to be like or to resemble? Why?" is "practically identical with the one used in . . . pioneer American studies," one of which dates back to 1898. Hill, David Spence, "Personification of Ideals by Urban Children," *Journal of Soc. Psych.*, 1:3:379-392.

[30] When this question has been put to representative cross-sections of the public (of which only 10-15% have attended college), by far the most frequently mentioned names are those of political and military leaders. In general, fewer than 1% name persons who represent such values as "intellectual, aesthetic and scientific achievement." Thus, in a 1947 Gallup Poll on the ten most admired persons "living today in any part of the world" General MacArthur ranked first, with Eisenhower, Churchill, Truman and General Marshall following. (Gallup release March 9, 1947.) In a Philadelphia study, also based on a representative sample of the total public, F. Sanford reports that only F. D. Roosevelt, Lincoln and Washington were named by as many as 5% of the public when asked to "tell me the name of a great person, living or dead, whom you admire the most." Sanford, Fillmore H., "Public Orientation to Roosevelt," *Public Opinion Quarterly*, 15:2:191.

als like heredity or excessive drinking (561ff). This difference too could be a function of specialized knowledge and education.³¹ Again, we do not deny that personality factors are involved. We are simply dubious of the interpretation when the very *manifestation* of these factors could easily be a function of education. We suspect that what is often being scored here are not personality differences but simply the variations in the language of different social classes.³²

The Derivation of Causal Inferences. Let us turn to another feature of the methodology of the interview study. Apart from the validity of the coding and the meaning of the personality traits which are evidenced, there is the larger question of the method by which conclusions are drawn from the data. Let us assume that the contrasted groups were found to differ significantly with respect to ninety variables of personality. Such would be the findings, but a meaning must still be read into them. How, for instance, does one relate a variable of early childhood to an ideology in adult life? How can we understand the significance of the formal cognitive dimension of "intolerance of ambiguity," for example, as it relates to prejudice? All such correlations must be interpreted through some logic by which the two entities are bound together. It is not always readily apparent how certain variables, separated by many years in time and experience, ultimately become converted into prejudice, and in any analysis of such relationships, one wishes to safeguard the interpretations of these processes and, if possible, to illumine them directly. So, in the clinically oriented method, one observes the growth in time, following the process longitudinally and noting directly the logic of the relationship. In more experimental work, one attempts to measure directly some of the factors which intervene between the two variables, and so highlight the process.³³

---

³¹ It might also be a function of differential understanding of the question. "Harry James' orchestra," for instance, is scored as a "high" answer, though the respondent may have interpreted the question popularly as "What sort of things irritate you?" Had he interpreted it to ask, "What are the causes of insanity?," he might have expressed a "low" reply such as "Continual worry about family problems, continual striving to earn a living."

³² It should be noted that in Srole's sample in Springfield, both authoritarian personality tendencies and anomic tendencies were more prominent in the lower educational groups. Consequently, the failure to control education may also mean that some of the differences between ethnocentric and non-ethnocentric simply reflect these differences in anomic tendencies. Srole, *op. cit.*

³³ An illustration of this method is provided by a project which grew out of *The Authoritarian Personality*. Rokeach, by *experimental* procedures, demon-

A Methodological Critique

Or taking a cue from phenomenological work in social psychology, we might seek to understand such relationships as the authors demonstrate through detailed cognitive material which would help us understand, for example, how a respondent sees a Negro in the image of some more prototypical problem of his own.[34] Such analyses provide a safeguard against the highlighting of some statistical demonstration which could occur by chance when many variables are correlated seriatim. They also put a constraint upon the analyst of the data and caution him against imputing his own dynamic theory to the bare statistical finding.

We would anticipate in an intensive-type interview a considerable emphasis upon questions which solicit the *reasons* for particular ideologies, upon inquiries into the way in which Negroes, Jews and other minority groups are *perceived*, etc. Admittedly, such verbalizations must be sifted and weighed, but they nevertheless have a value for the study of the dynamics which underlie statistical relationships—if only the negative value of constraining the analyst. But in the interview procedures here used, while the content of the variables is the quintessence of dynamic psychology, the formal mode of analysis is as statistical as can be. All the dynamics are simply imputed by the analyst, without benefit of any of the direct types of data that we have referred to above. For example: "The assumption behind this question, later proved correct, was that the pattern developed in the relationship to the father tends to be transferred to other authorities and thus becomes crucial in forming social and political beliefs in men" (315). But the transference is never demonstrated, the process never explained. Prejudice and childhood relationship to father merely correlate. Again: "Where

---

strated that ethnocentric individuals show more rigidity in tasks involving problem solving. By means of this procedure, he demonstrates precisely that cognitive factors of a general sort are present in the ethnocentric. Such a rigidity factor can then be used as a link between personality factors and ethnocentrism. See M. Rokeach, *op. cit.*

[34] In Part IV, "Qualitative Studies of Ideology," and particularly in Chapter 16, "Prejudice in the Interview Material," the authors suggest that the subject's ideology should be explored directly by examination of the nonclinical parts of the interview material, and reference is made to an auxiliary study in which a detailed questionnaire on the more qualitative aspects of the subject's anti-Semitism was administered. Examination of this material might have enabled one to perceive the link between personality and ideological trends through what we have labeled a phenomenological approach. But these materials are not used in the manner we suggest, and the analysis accordingly suffers the limitations which we discuss.

there is no readiness to admit that one's parents have any weakness in them it is not surprising to find later an indication of repressed hostility and revengeful fantasies behind the mask of compliance" (343). It occurs to us to wonder *why* this is not surprising, or why this repressed hostility necessarily relates to the person's attitude toward Jews. "Since typical low scorers do not really see their parents as any too overpowering or frightening, they can afford to express their feelings of resentment more readily" (346). Does the one necessarily follow from the other? "Submission to parental authority may be closely related to submission to authority in general. And submission to authority, in its turn, has the broadest implications for social and personal behavior both toward those with power and those without it" (350). Here is a clear instance of the way in which the dynamic explanation is simply attached to the statistical finding. The authors continue: "It is therefore interesting to note that this category (submission to parents) shows marked differences between prejudiced and unprejudiced interviewees."

We present a number of similar quotations: "It is in the area of social and political attitudes that the suppressed yet unmodified impulses find one of their distorted outlets and emerge with particular intensity. In particular, moral indignation first experienced in the attitude of one's parents toward oneself is being redirected against weaker outgroups" (385). "The resentment, rendered ego-alien, is the more active through the operation of mechanisms of displacement" (386). Indignation about people considered as inferior "seems to serve the double purpose of externalizing what is unacceptable in oneself, and of displacing one's hostility which otherwise might turn against powerful 'ingroups,' e.g., the parents" (407). The low scorer, as a child, "seems to have enjoyed the benefit of the help of adults in working out his problems of sex and aggression. He thus can more easily withstand propaganda which defames minorities or glorifies war" (483). To this latter "conclusion," as well as to the others, it is fair to ask, "How come?" We have presented, we hope, enough quotations of this type to show that the dynamic processes are simply imputed to the statistical findings or juxtaposed against them. Armed variously with such concepts as "projection," "displacement," "generalization," "repression" and the like, the analyst "explains" the data. But nowhere are the processes illuminated directly nor is it clearly demonstrated how they actually work out in the particular forms of attitude described.

A Methodological Critique

The Use of Retrospective Reports and Other Analytic Weaknesses. A third analytic procedure which merits discussion is the use of the respondents' retrospective reports on their early family life. We noted in our statement of the theory that the work aimed at providing a test of the relation of ideology to personality, and that implicitly the personality structure was regarded as a product of *actual familial experience.* In the interview data, which provided the measures of personality, were subjective reports by each respondent of his childhood attitudes, behavior and relations with the family group. The authors, throughout, oscillate between the view that these reports have only a *psychological* reality in conveying the subject's personality, and the view that they have *objective* reality as an accurate description of the subject's actual family life. In discussing the question, they remark: "As stated in Chapter IX, it is difficult to say how much the image of a parent corresponds to reality and how much it is a subjective conception. However, this distinction may be of less importance when, as is the case here, personality structure rather than its genesis is the major concern. The notions our subjects have of their parents are psychologically relevant in the discussion of the parent-child relationship whether they are true or not. In a separate project, parents of prejudiced and unprejudiced children were actually studied, substantiating in kind many of the statements our present interviewees make about their own childhood" (358). Parenthetically, we would remark that the distinction is of considerable significance from the standpoint of action or implementation of the study's findings. If the differential accounts of childhood experiences by ethnocentric and non-ethnocentric persons are factually true, one course of action suggests itself; if they are merely psychological distortions, we must look elsewhere.

Actually, in spite of the above disclaimer, the authors frequently accept the respondents' retrospective reports as objectively accurate. For example, when the low scorers report a friendly father, they conclude (italics ours), "It is quite *convincingly evident* from the last three records that the fathers of these men *possessed, as well as displayed,* a good deal of affection for their sons" (361). Later they state that "For the establishment of the psychology of the unprejudiced man a non-threatening father figure may indeed be of great importance. . . . The unprejudiced man *did not as a rule have to submit* to stern authority in his childhood" (364). And again: "The difference in the *type of discipline found* in the families of our high-scoring as compared with those of our low-scoring subjects, in conjunction with the difference in the family structure and the *personality of the parents* (stern vs. relaxed) may be considered part of the foundation for an authoritarian vs. democratic approach to interpersonal relationships" (375). In another place we find: "These preoccupations (with moralistic typologizing) may be considered as an outcome of *a certain type of child training;* thus, sociopsychological factors are brought into the picture" (448).

In view of the elaborate evidence which the authors bring to bear showing that the prejudiced are characterized by irrationality and distortions of objective reality, and that they tend either to glorify their parents or to report victimization by them (339ff), it appears inconsistent to accept their retrospective reports of distant events as factual accounts. In the absence of any validating data, one is compelled to qualify very seriously any conclusions which relate to the influence of *actual* childhood upon prejudice. It may well be that the individual who is characterized by the prejudiced, authoritarian outlook in adult life is simply generalizing his *Anschauung* back upon his childhood, and that the non-prejudiced, non-authoritarian similarly distorts his experiences. While the authors, as we have shown, are obviously aware of the danger, their later neglect of it can easily mislead an uncritical reader.

We have already touched upon a further consideration which affects the analysis when we noted that, for the interview study, two contrasting extreme groups were selected on the basis of their scores on the scale of prejudice. While some effort was made to include "atypical" subjects who obtained a prejudice score which was opposed to their score on political ideology or authoritarianism, inspection of the eighty cases reveals only about ten respondents who showed contradictory patterns of sentiments. Moreover, these cases are never treated separately in the analysis. In the light of the value of deviant case analysis[35] for the construction of theory, and in view of the express interest of the project in the problem of mental organization, it seems to us that there would have been considerable wisdom in a deliberate study of contrasted groups varying in the *profiles* of their sentiments. This might have provided illuminating

---

[35] For a discussion of deviant case analysis, see Kendall, Patricia, and Wolf, Katherine, "The Analysis of Deviant Cases in Communications Research," in Lazarsfeld and Stanton, *Communications Research*, Harper's, New York, 1948-49.

data on the manner in which differentiations in prejudice develop out of a particular matrix of experience.

Let us speculate for a moment about the implications of this matter. In addition to the fact that the ethnocentric respondents who were interviewed are *extreme* in their prejudice, with the consequences for generalization which we referred to in our discussion of the sampling, all but a handful of them are also individuals with *highly organized* patterns of prejudice. They are like the man in the Peter Arno cartoon who stands at the bar and proclaims, "I hate *everybody*, regardless of race, creed, or place of national origin!" If one had taken individuals who showed inconsistent profiles of sentiment, one might have uncovered a rather different relation between prejudice and personality structure. It may be that the individuals chosen show such an internal relation between sentiment and personality just because their psychic systems show more interpenetration generally. That could explain why for them personality factors are so highly related.³⁶ Or consider another possibility. A person who hates everybody is perhaps irrational, and maybe he can only be understood in terms of personality. But a man who is generally unprejudiced and politically liberal except for a focus of resentment upon one particular group might be understood in terms of other factors, such as competition or unhappy personal contacts.

Qualitative Handling of the Interview Material. The primary analysis of the materials, though subject to such weaknesses as we have just noticed, nevertheless proceeded according to accepted conventions of methodology. In Part I of the book, dealing with the scale scores based on the questionnaires, there was concern for problems of statistical reliability, the significance of differences, and the like; and in Parts II and III, which contain the analysis of the coded results of the interview material and of the projective tests, attention is properly given to problems of quantification, coder reliability, interviewer bias, etc. We have pointed to a number of major defects in this part of the analysis, but the broad outlines are in

---

³⁶ In a study by French one notes that if individuals are contrasted purely by the formal fact of the degree of *organization* of their religious sentiments, apart from the *content* of these sentiments, personality differences are found between the organized and non-organized. Perhaps the findings of the interview analysis here implicitly refer to those with highly organized sentiments. See French, V. V., "Structure of Sentiments III, A Study of Philosophico-Religious Sentiments," *J. Personality*, 16, 209-244.

accordance with good procedure. There is one aspect of the total analysis, however, which departs from the usual methodological safeguards.

In Part IV of the book, the ideology of the individuals who were interviewed is subjected to a qualitative analysis, in an effort to understand some of the types and patterning of sentiments and to discern directly the way in which ideology and personality mesh. As we suggested in our earlier remarks, such a qualitative analysis is most desirable in an attempt to understand the dynamic processes which underlie the statistical findings—but it should proceed according to certain conventions of scientific method. Admittedly, it is in this very area that we have the least codification of research principles. There is a huge literature available to the research worker on such matters as sampling, statistics, coding, interviewing and the like, but on qualitative analysis there is very little.[37] Consequently one cannot expect the same degree of scientific rigor in the handling of the materials. Moreover, as the writers indicate: "A subjective or what might be called speculative element has a place in this method, just as it does in psychoanalysis, from which many of our categories have been drawn. If, in places, the analysis seems to jump to conclusions, the interpretations should be regarded as hypotheses for further research, and the continuous interaction of the various methods of the study should be recalled: some of the measured variables discussed in earlier chapters were based on speculations put forward in this part" (604).

The implications for future research make it important to examine critically this portion of the text, and granted the lack of detailed principles for such analysis and the tentative use of the findings, we nevertheless feel that here the analysts often exercise license far beyond what is permitted the scientific investigator. There is no reference whatever to any other qualitative analysts working on the same materials, and in many instances the judgments are subject to no scientific restraint. In the very first part of this treatment of the materials, in connection with a discussion of prejudice as revealed in the interviews, we find psychiatric diagnoses rampant. The sentiments of a vehemently anti-Semitic woman who sees Jews conspiring everywhere are reported to reveal their "proximity to delusion"

---

[37] At the present time, a research project under the direction of Paul F. Lazarsfeld is under way on the problems of codifying certain principles of qualitative analysis. Publication of these materials should help us considerably.

(615). In the case of another woman we are told that there is a "merging of semipsychotic idiosyncrasies and wild anti-Jewish imagery" (615). When she remarks "I am not particularly sorry because of what the Germans did to the Jews. I feel Jews would do the same type of thing to me," the author notes that "The persecution fantasy . . . is used, in authentic paranoid style . . ." (615). Another respondent is described as engaging in "paranoid storytelling" (616), and elsewhere it is parenthetically remarked that "the whole complex of the Jew is a kind of recognized red-light district of legitimized psychotic distortions" (617). In a later comment about stereotypes it is noted that the stereotype is "an expression of a psychological trait which probably could be fully understood only in connection with the theory of paranoia and the paranoid 'system' . . ." (632). This last view flies in the face of most accepted social psychological thinking about the near universality of stereotypes and their recognized "economical" function for the human being. One cannot quarrel with the use of figures of speech in a scientific text. They liven up reader interest and none would accept them literally. But this discussion in the present volume appears deadly serious, at the same time that no other data in its support are presented in the text. Worse, it suggests to the casual reader that anti-Semitism is an aberrant pathological phenomenon which has no relation to reality.[38]

Even departing from this psychoanalytic usage, we still find arbitrary applications of judgment. In examining the sentiment of one respondent who says, "Well, the Jews are a ticklish problem," the analyst notes that "The term 'problem' is taken over from the sphere of science and is used to give the impression of searching, responsible deliberation. By referring to a problem, one implicitly claims personal aloofness . . . a kind of detachment and higher objectivity. This, of course, is an excellent rationalization for prejudice" (620). Such dynamics may well operate among anti-Semites, but to peg it all on the author's inspection of the connotations of the word "problems" seems to us completely arbitrary. While we have no direct evidence on the point, it appears probable that the very phrase,

---

[38] In Chapter XXII, a direct study of these same attitudes in psychiatric clinic patients provides substantial evidence bearing on the author's ascription of psychopathology to high scorers. And in this less simplified, more rigorously controlled study, there were found at best only very modest relationships between psycho-pathology as such and prejudice.

"the Jewish problem" or "Negro problem," is in such common usage that it has none of the properties imputed to it here. It is merely synonymous with "trouble" or "difficulty," as in "What's your problem?" Thus, national polls routinely ask people, "What is the biggest problem facing you and your family?," and the answers invariably come in terms of an assortment of personal troubles. Later, in discussing anti-Semites who allege that Jews bring anti-Semitism upon themselves, it is remarked that this idea "is used as a rationalization for destructive wishes which otherwise would not be allowed to pass the censorship of the ego" (631). With respect to one respondent who utters such a remark, it is said that "the interrelation between death-wish and moralistic rationalization becomes truly terrifying" (632). We pondered the particular remark cited, but the analyst's reasoning continues to elude us. In summarizing some of the extreme anti-Semites, allusion is made to the case who "suffers from color-blindness and from psychogenic sexual impotence, determined, according to the interviewer, by a severe Oedipus complex." The interpretation is given that "His radical wishes for the extermination of the Jews are probably conditioned by severe, early childhood traumata: projections of his own castration fear" (636). But in the material presented one notes nothing permitting this particular explanation of his anti-Semitism. Such interpretations, as the authors point out and as we earlier agreed, have a place in their suggestion of variables for study and of hypotheses for future research, but we see no reason for publishing them as part of the *findings* of an elaborate research undertaking.

In the realm of the political and ideological materials the qualitative interpretations remain questionable. In the introduction to this chapter (XVII), it is noted that the gap between high- and low-scorers is least clear in the political area, and that many of the broader ideological trends must therefore have their roots in widespread cultural or environmental factors. But as we enter upon the analysis of the detailed cases, this fact becomes more and more neglected and the interpretations take on a narrowly psychologistic hue. Here, as noted in our earlier discussion of sampling considerations, what was needed was data from a representative national cross-section which would have provided automatically the very perspective required to determine whether a particular sentiment was widely dispersed in the culture. In the absence of such data, the good intentions and proper orientation of the introduction cannot be implemented, and the analyst consequently mistakes the universal for the particular, a typical sentiment widely held among the population for an idiosyncratic psychological phenomenon which calls for a dynamic explanation. We shall illustrate this point in a number of ways.

Thus the authors note the emphasis among high scorers upon the personal traits of "honesty and sincerity" in evaluating Dewey as a Presidential candidate, and upon such personal qualities as strength, youth and courage in making their political choices, and from this is drawn the interpretation that the emphasis on honesty involves "a rationalization for vindictiveness" (since Dewey was honest in that he punished wrongdoers as district attorney). "Speaking psychologically, the image of Dewey is a projection of the punitive superego . . ." (670). Actually, emphasis upon the attributes of honesty, sincerity, strength, youth and courage is very widespread in American political preferences, and such traits are not attributed only to candidates like Dewey, where the honesty *was* pointed up in relation to the punishment of wrongdoers.[39] In discussing the case of the high-scorer who says, "Naturally, I get my Republican sentiments from my parents," it is remarked that "The overt link between the father-fixation . . . and authoritarian persuasions in politics should be stressed" (680). We do not contest the theory; we are concerned with the interpretation of the datum. In this case, the view that such parent-child relationships are specific to authoritarians is mistaken. There is much evidence to show a consistent positive correlation between attitudes of intra-family members in the ideological and value realm.[40] Elsewhere, the tend-

---

[39] In a May 1948 study conducted by NORC among a representative cross-section of voters in New York, Illinois and California, respondents were asked to name "the one person now in public life who you think has the best qualities for President," and then to explain "what are the qualities that you think would make him the best man." "Honesty, good character, fairness, sincerity" were mentioned by about one-fourth the sample in all three states, and "aggressive, young, forceful, decisive, firm" were mentioned by almost as many. The qualities named were attributed almost equally to Dewey, Eisenhower, Truman, Stassen and MacArthur — the five most popular choices.

[40] A large-scale study of college alumni, reported last year, found that 58% of the graduates belonged to the same political party as their fathers, and only 10% had shifted to the opposite party. "If we disregard the independents, we find that 85% follow the politics of their fathers and that only 15% have switched." Havemann and West, *They Went to College*, Harcourt, Brace & Co., N. Y., 1952, p. 117.

ency to be "realistic," i.e., pessimistic about improvements in the social order, is commented upon: "Psychologically, the anti-utopian pattern of political thinking is related to sadomasochistic traits" (697).[41] The tendency of high scorers to have "no pity for the poor," as evidenced by such statements as "I think we ought to let them starve, especially them Japs" or "Only reason they are unemployed, they are lazy like me," is analyzed.[42] Variously, the interpretations are given that "the ideas involved have a tinge of punitiveness and authoritarian aggressiveness which makes them ideal receptacles of some typical psychological urges of the prejudiced character. . . . The mechanism of projectivity is also involved: the potentially fascist character blames the poor who need assistance for the very same passivity and greediness which he has learnt not to admit to his own consciousness." In the case of the high scorer who did admit his passivity in the remark quoted above ("They are lazy like me"), it is remarked: "This may be regarded as one of the most authentic examples of sadomasochistic thinking in our interviews" (699). In discussing the high scorers' emphasis in their antilabor ideology upon racketeering, the authors comment: "Viewed from a purely psychological angle the idea of 'labor racketeering' seems to be of a nature similar to the stereotype of Jewish clannishness. It dates back to the lack of an adequately internalized identification with paternal authority during the Oedipus situation. It is our general assumption that the typical high scorers, above all, fear the father and try to side with him in order to participate in his power. The 'racketeers' are those who by demanding too much . . . run the risk of rousing the father's anger—and hence the subject's castration anxiety" (709).

Now practically all of these sentiments and others which we have not space to quote, interpreted here as traits mainly of the high scorer, derived from psychodynamic processes, can be shown to have a wide distribution in American society and, quite regularly, to show a clear correlation with such objective factors as formal education. We have cited some of this evidence in footnotes on the

---

[41] "Realism" in regard to "political utopias" is characteristic of the majority of the American people. Thus, in an NORC national survey conducted in October 1950, only 33% approved of the world government concept.

[42] In March 1946, an NORC survey found one person in every five answering "Send them no food at all" if the Japanese people are starving. Such attitudes were significantly related to educational level.

A Methodological Critique

preceding page. In this perspective, several observations seem justified. First, such sentiments are not unique to high scorers generally (though they may characterize the high scorers within the authors' unrepresentative sample or within particular sub-groups of that sample). Secondly, it may well be that whatever such differences are found may be caused simply by uncontrolled differences in education. Thirdly, it seems a little extravagant to seek such depth explanations when there are much more obvious environmental determinants involved. And finally, if these dynamics are involved, they should at least be given some social location. They may define the *process* of such attitude formation, but the location of this process within some part of the social order would seem to require that adequate reference be made to the fact. Methodologically, what appears responsible for the arbitrary and perhaps mistaken interpretations of these data are the narrow type of sampling used and the study directors' bias toward psychodynamic explanations.

Other analytic procedures employed by the authors similarly involve the inspection of certain data (either qualitative or quantitative), the noting of particular features of the attitudes, and the drawing of inferences that such features occur because depth psychological factors are at work. In other words, we have a method which comprises (a) inspection of the findings, (b) a subsequent judgment put upon the results, and (c) an inferential process which then leads to the conclusion: namely, that personality factors are responsible. The method has considerable plausibility in the text, though we have noted earlier that it cannot be regarded as scientific, in that no causal factors are demonstrated by the data. As an illustration of the lack of scientific rigor in this method, let us examine some of the judgments and inferences, and see how a researcher with another orientation could, with perhaps even more plausibility, interpret the data otherwise.

One such theme which pervades the treatment of the questionnaire and interview findings is that of "irrationality." It is perhaps typical of the authors' use of psychopathological terms to explain the sentiments of certain ethnocentric respondents. Thus, the sentiments of such respondents are frequently inspected, and when they do not conform to the demonstrated truths revealed to us by science or to the superior knowledge of the researcher, the judgment is made that the sentiment is irrational. The inference is then drawn that a person who holds an irrational sentiment cannot be judged to hold it on simple intellectual grounds, but rather because it is somehow functional for him or represents some distorted expression of deeper, unconscious tendencies. As a result, the findings are said to support the theory that personality trends underlie ideology. Let us illustrate this methodology by a few examples from the text.

"When it comes to the ways in which people appraise the social world, irrational trends stand out glaringly . . . prejudice against, or totally uncritical acceptance of, a particular group often exists in the absence of any experience with members of that group. The objective situation of the individual seems an unlikely source of such irrationality; rather we should seek where psychology has already found the sources of dreams, fantasies, and misinterpretations of the world—that is, in the deep-lying needs of the personality" (8-9). "The irrational quality in anti-Semitism stands out even in casual everyday discussions. The fact that people make general statements about 'the Jew,' when the Jews are actually so heterogeneous . . . is vivid evidence of this irrationality . . . when the belief that Jews possess financial power out of all proportion to their numbers persists in the face of overwhelming evidence to the contrary, one is led to suspect not only that the individual holding this belief has an unusual preoccupation with power but also that he might himself wish to assume the kind of power which he supposes Jews to have. It is clear that research into the emotional sources of ideology is required for the understanding of such phenomena as these" (57). "It would appear that the more a person's thinking is dominated by such general tendencies as those found in Mack, the less will his attitude toward a particular group depend upon any objective characteristics of that group, or upon any real experience in which members of that group were involved. It is this observation that draws attention to the importance of personality as a determinant of ideology" (51). A host of similar quotations could be provided, as illustrations of the way the argument is bolstered.

That prejudice is irrational when judged against the standard of logic or of the best available knowledge may well be true. But it by no means follows that the judgments of particular respondents are arrived at *in irrational ways* and therefore reflect the operation of underlying non-intellectual processes. To assert this is to ignore the fact that there are social conditions which define knowledge, which define what is rational, which define the information available to any individual when he makes a judgment. What the authors do here is to substitute their own knowledge, that of the scientific observer, for the less accurate knowledge possessed by the ordinary subject they interview. To put it another way: They take the irrationality out of the social order and impute it to the respondent, and by means of this substitution, it is decided that prejudiced respondents derive their judgments in an irrational way. A moment's thought or a simple analogy is sufficient to expose the flaw in this reasoning. Most Americans, for example, would probably affirm that the earth revolves around the sun, and not vice versa; but we suspect that an interviewer would be hard put to get a "rational" explanation of this belief from most people. It is just something we have been taught and which we accept without question. Is the belief therefore irrational? A savage might well believe that the sun circles the earth each day, but we would look on him simply as ignorant and untutored, not as irrational. So, too, when people absorb prejudice on the basis of incorrect but widely current belief, their process of thinking cannot be regarded as irrational. One of the very examples cited by the authors—that prejudice often exists in the absence of any direct experience with members of a minority group—and from which is drawn the conclusion that such prejudice is irrational and must represent deeplying personality needs, was studied long ago by Horowitz.[43] His conclusion was that prejudice against Negroes is determined not by contact and experience with Negroes, but by contact with the *prevalent attitudes* toward Negroes. Knowledge does not come to us solely through direct experience, nor is it always obtained through access to the best scientific knowledge; much of our information comes from others who may indoctrinate us in irrational ways. That most of us do have prejudiced, irrational beliefs is well supported by a variety of data which demonstrate both the pervasiveness and the persistence in time of prejudice in America.[44]

Of course, it may still be asked how the irrationality originated in the first place, but this is quite a different question from that of the origin of the person's current prejudice. It may be true, too, that for the educated segment which comprised the basic popula-

---

[43] Horowitz, E. L., "The Development of Attitudes toward Negroes," *Arch. Psych.*, 1936, No. 194.

[44] For a summary discussion of prejudice as a social norm, the reader is referred to Hartley, E. L. and R. E., *Fundamentals of Social Psychology*, Knopf, New York, 1952.

tion of the present study, better sources of knowledge are readily available and their prejudices are indeed derived irrationally; but the generalized inference which the authors consistently draw is quite unwarranted on the basis of the data. The process which produced this inference—the inspection of the data for their accuracy or logical basis, and then the drawing of questionable inferences— was incidentally aggravated by a particular omission in the research design, to which we have already alluded: namely, the neglect in the interview study of questions of cognition. It might well be that if the subject's views of minorities had been directly explored, rather than placing a preponderant reliance on indirect measures, many of the *social* determinants of these views could have been revealed, and some constraints would thus have been placed upon the inferences drawn.

The same procedure is applied by the authors in the analysis of *contradictory* sentiments. When a pattern of attitudes toward a given object of prejudice is found to include contradictory sentiments, it is argued that since such prejudice is self-contradictory it must be irrational—and therefore caused by deeper personality factors. Thus, in the statistical analysis of the scale scores, it is noted that respondents regard Jews as both "seclusive" and "intrusive," and the authors state: "This categorical, self-contradictory rejection of an entire group is, however, more than a matter of faulty logic. Viewed psychologically, these results suggest a deep-lying irrational hostility directed against a stereotyped image to which individual Jews correspond only partially if at all" (75). The discussion is then expanded upon, and various single questionnaire items are juxtaposed and shown to be contradictory in content. This finding is somewhat more convincing than the "irrationality" of single prejudiced comments, as an indication that prejudice is not logical or reasonable and that its roots lie within the personality, but the evidence from the data is hardly as satisfactory as we would wish. For one thing, the authors do not cite the intercorrelations between single items on these scales. Thus, while the r between total prejudice scores on the "seclusive" and "intrusive" sub-scales approximates .7, the *inter-item r,* as nearly as we can determine, approximates the value of .4—a rather weak demonstration of the occurrence of such contradictory sentiments. Moreover, an inspection of the content of the items involved indicates that the referent of the questions is not always the same. Thus, the respondent may

A Methodological Critique

hold two different kinds of sentiments about Jews, but he does not necessarily hold contradictory sentiments toward the *same* Jew or Jews. For example, in some questions the referent is Jewish businessmen or "Jewish millionaires," while in other items on the scale there is no reference at all to these particular subgroups of Jews. And as we mentioned earlier in our discussion of the formulation of the questionnaire items, the lack of provision for qualified or ambivalent answers undoubtedly lent a false encouragement to the expression of contradictory sentiments. These are perhaps minor considerations, but they are intended to show that the data do not provide any conclusive proof in support of the conclusions.

We shall cite one last example of the means by which the authors note a finding and then draw unwarranted conclusions on the basis of their own inferences—the theme of the generality or structure of prejudice. It is often noted that a person who holds one certain prejudice also holds another, and from this finding it is argued that, since such generality of sentiment cannot be explained in terms of specific factors relating to the particular objects of prejudice, the explanation must consequently lie in some personality factor. Let us look again at the quotation we cited earlier in this section: "It would appear that the more a person's thinking is dominated by such general tendencies as those found in Mack, the less will his attitude toward a particular group depend upon any objective characteristics of that group, or upon any real experience in which members of that group were involved" (51). In other words, a generalized attitude can be explained only in terms of some general factor. Then the inference is immediately drawn: "It is this observation that draws attention to the importance of personality as a determinant of ideology." An even clearer example occurs a little later: ". . . the conception of personality would be forced upon us by observation of the *consistency* with which the same ideas and the same modes of thought recur as the discussion turns from one ideological area to another. Since no such consistency could conceivably exist as a matter of sociological fact, we are bound to conceive of central tendencies *in the person* which express themselves in various areas. The concept of a dynamic factor of personality is made to order for explaining the common trend in diverse surface manifestations" (56). Again: ". . . we have seen that anti-Semitism or anti-Negroism, for example, are not isolated attitudes but parts of a relatively unified ethnocentric ideology. The present chapter suggests that ethnocentrism itself is but one aspect of a broader pattern of social thinking and group functioning. Trends similar to those underlying ethnocentric ideology are found in the same individual's politico-economic ideology. In short, ideology regarding each social area must be regarded as a facet of the total person and an expression of more central ('subideological') psychological dispositions" (207). And finally: "This does not mean, however, that those high scorers whose prejudiced statements show a certain rationality *per se* are exempt from the psychological mechanisms of the fascist character. Thus the example we offer is high not only on the F scale but on all scales. She has the *generality* of prejudiced outlook which we have taken as evidence that underlying personality trends were the ultimate determinants" (753).

One may accept without question, of course, the existence of generality, not only in the field of prejudice but over a wider domain as well. Obviously, there is some organizing principle in social attitudes, and such patterns suggest that the source is not to be found in the specific features of any particular object of prejudice. But whence does it necessarily follow that the organizing principle is a deeper psychological disposition, and that "no such consistency could conceivably exist as a matter of sociological fact"? Societies and groups do not necessarily indoctrinate the individual piecemeal. We find the extreme of this in the *Weltanschauung* sought by the totalitarian society, and we find patterns of sentiments expressed in the programs of almost every organized group. That the degree of patterning itself, and not just the content of specific attitudes, varies with different groups was noted earlier in our discussion of the sampling methodology, and such variation supports the fact that social factors affect generality. Certainly, consistency must be explained, not in terms of the specific objects of prejudice, but as a generalized disposition within the person—but the organizing factor behind this generalized disposition may very well be societal. We are far from being inevitably thrown back on deep personality factors.

The Argument from Group Membership. There is one aspect of the analysis that is subjected to far more rigorous methodological controls than the authors more usually employ, and in which they use the evidence of only moderate relationships as further inferential support for the theory. We refer here to the testing of that very fundamental part of the theory which argues that these patterns of prejudice are not explainable in terms of group membership. Since the conclusions are so fundamental and since the analytic procedures are complex and interesting to examine, we devote some attention to the matter.

The scale scores which were used as measures of social attitudes were examined separately for individuals who varied in certain group membership characteristics: political party affiliation, organizations drawing upon different social classes, current income, father's occupation, religion, and the like. Each of these was successively used as the independent variable. In addition, a number of exceedingly insightful cross-tabulations were made, using more subtle manifestations of group processes. For example, ethnocentrism was contrasted for individuals who expressed political affiliations different from their parents and individuals who claimed the same party choice as their parents. Aspiration level for income, as well as actual income, was used as an independent variable. A very nice "cross-pressure" treatment is presented in the form of ethnocentrism scores for individuals whose parents had the same religion, as compared with those whose parents differed in their religious affiliation. Something approximating reference group analysis is involved in a contrast of two groups differing in the degree to which they regard the church as an important institution. But though the approach is a discerning one, and though the data are handled carefully and moderately, there is again the tendency to use the evidence of moderate relationships as inferential support for the argument that since such social determinants are not proved significant, personality determinants must be the effective ones.

It should be noted first that the authors did not exhaust the universe of group memberships available to the individual. Out of the richness of possible affiliations, only a few were chosen and examined and these not necessarily the central ones. (It may be superfluous to suggest that a test based on education might have turned out differently.) The analysis hardly permits, therefore, after the examination of one rudimentary relationship—political party affiliation—the immoderate statement that "These intra- and intergroup variations suggest that group membership is not in itself the major determinant of ideology in the individual" (189). Secondly, it should be noted that some of these group membership characteristics take on an especially ambiguous meaning in the light of the population studied. Thus, the use of current income is a rather superficial measure for students, since they are not often regularly employed and their current income does not have the significance for them that it has for a more established adult group. Moreover, the analysis was not only limited to a small number of group membership characteristics, but it studied these individually, each in isolation from the others, whereas virtually all current work emphasizes the influence of *multiple* overlapping or contradictory group memberships. Thus, it is noted in the analysis that "No broad grouping in this study showed anything approaching ideological homogeneity" (204), and from the variations in attitude within each group, the inference is drawn that individual personality factors account for the attitude. But is it not equally possible that intra-group variability in attitude is due to the fact that individuals sharing one group membership in common often differ with respect to other group memberships? Lazarsfeld, in his classic study of political behavior in Erie County in 1940, showed that among Catholics, a predominantly Democratic group, almost one-fourth expressed Republican preferences. Under the principles of the present study, this intra-group variability would be accepted as evidence to deny the effect of group membership and to emphasize the importance of personality factors. But if we look only at those Catholics in the lowest economic level we find only one in seven expressing a Republican preference, and among Catholics who are laborers, the incidence of Republican preference is but one in ten.[45] Thus, the intra-group variability is progressively lessened as other memberships of the individual are taken into account, and in the absence of any higher order cross-tabulations to observe the effect of *multiple* group memberships on prejudice, the inference drawn from the variability within single groups is unwarranted.

Apart from these technical inadequacies in the handling of this section, there appears to us a logical fallacy involved. In general, the argument is advanced that insofar as objective group membership correlates are not significant, it then follows that emotional or personality factors are the determinants. But does this necessarily follow? Are there not other possibilities besides personality factors which could account for the attitude? Consider the argument advanced in the treatment of class differences in political ideology: "In view of the intergroup as well as the intra-group variability, it

---

[45] Lazarsfeld, Berelson, Gaudet, *The People's Choice*, Columbia Univ. Press, New York, 1948 (2nd edition). Ch. III.

seems safe to conclude that over-all class differences in political ideology are not extremely large, and that individual and group differences within each class are so great that they become the primary problem requiring explanation. . . . Why does one middle-class individual join a service club while another becomes a supporter of Henry Wallace? . . . These may be not so much questions of actual class or group *membership* as questions of class or group *identification* — and 'identification' is a psychological variable. . . . We shall have occasion to consider further, in the chapters that follow, the deeper emotional trends that help to determine the individual's group memberships and identifications" (172). The authors are correct in pointing to the phenomenon of group identification as a factor attenuating the relation between objective membership and ideology, but to interpret this, in turn, as indicative of deeper emotional trends is quite a jump. One need only examine Merton and Kitt's discussion of reference group theory to note a whole host of factors that may account for the selection of a reference group.[46] The fact that a person's social class does not determine whether he joins a service club or supports Henry Wallace does not prove that the choice is determined by deeper emotional trends. He may join for social or financial reasons, mere proximity to the group may lead him to identify with it, any one of a hundred accidental factors may be responsible. And even apart from questions of group identification and reference groups, there are a host of what we might call "situational factors" which operate in the individual's contemporary environment and which influence his ideology: he falls in love, loses his job, suffers a sickness, reads a particular magazine article, etc., etc. It is a vast oversimplification to argue that everything that is not determined by formal group membership must by default be due to deeper emotional trends. This is to make personality theory identical with all of psychology, which it is not, and to reduce all of the complexity of social structure to a few group memberships.

Details of the Statistical Treatment. We have already suggested that the quantitative handling of the questionnaire material is rather mechanical, and that the insights one would expect from the incorporation of clinical thinking into the project are missing in this dis-

---

[46] Merton, R. K. and Kitt, A. S., "Contributions to the Theory of Reference Group Behavior," in Merton R. K. and Lazarsfeld, P. F., *Continuities in Social Research*, The Free Press, Glencoe, Ill., 1950.

cussion. Parallel with this is a general lack of precision and sophistication in the application of statistical concepts throughout the volume. It is almost impossible, for example, in spite of the detailed and elaborate account of the methodology, to discover just what statistical treatment was applied in many cases. Nowhere, for instance, is it ever indicated what test of significance was used in evaluating the interview data. Scattered through the text one frequently finds allusions to statistical matters in which the usage employed is much too casual. Thus, in one chapter the word "random" appears in a rather strange way; elsewhere there is reference to conversion to a tetrachoric correlation coefficient, without regard for the assumptions underlying the application of that technique. Some of the comments regarding the outcome of significance tests are quite strange. In discussing the fact that the interview results are more clear-cut for men than for women, one of the possible reasons offered is "the unequal size of the two samples of women interviewees" (470). As we mentioned, it is not stated what tests of significance were applied but all of the standard tests would take full account of the size and distribution of the n's. Elsewhere, it is noted that a non-significant difference "may well reach significance in a somewhat larger sample" (453). So it might, but again it might not. Slightly more important in its effect on the interpretation is the statement that for men only four of the eighty-six personality variables studied in the interview fail to confirm the hypothesis, and for women there are only six exceptions (468). Such a box score is quite misleading when it is realized that the number of *independent* tests of the general theory is much smaller, and that because many of the eighty-six categories are overlapping in content and were coded on the basis of overall inspection of the interview, the scores on these variables were not determined independently.

But even more central from the point of view of the major findings is the application of a double standard of statistical treatment for the personality variables as determined by the interviews and for the study of group membership factors on the basis of the scale scores. In the interview study, two extreme groups are compared on a series of personality factors. Intermediate groups are not examined and the fact that all the individuals in one extreme are not homogeneous is ignored. Further, if there is *some group trend*, it is accepted as evidence. In the case of the group membership data, on the other hand, a whole series of small groups are compared and any minor inversions of the findings are noted. In addition, the procedure is carried out separately for each of the small groups: e.g., the relation of income to ethnocentrism is studied on the basis of six income groups, and this is done separately for college students, working class men, middle class women, etc. It is then noted that prejudice does not vary consistently by income over the entire range of values, and that the relation between prejudice and income is not the same among the different groups studied (199). It is also pointed out generally in this discussion that no grouping shows homogeneity. This procedure is admirable in its detail, and we have already commented on the superiority of studying the entire range of values of a variable, rather than merely studying the two extremes. We object not to the thoroughness and precision of this analysis, but to the use to which its findings are put, in contrast to the statistical analysis of the interview data. Had a single standard been applied, and the latter materials subjected to the same microscopic scrutiny, it is possible that similar irregularities would have turned up in the functional relations between prejudice and personality.

Documentation and Bibliography. One final observation about the analysis might be in order. The support for a theory comes not alone from the specific research of any single investigator, but from the larger totality of scientific research. Research, and the testing of theory are, after all, a collective endeavor. When the work of other researchers supports a theory, it is given additional strength. When the work of other researchers is in conflict with a particular set of findings, either doubt is cast upon the evidence or opportunity is provided for clarification of the conditions which produced the disparate findings. In either case, improved theory and knowledge should result. The problem of documentation is therefore a legitimate area for the methodologist. In the course of this critique, we have cited a number of studies in the research literature which cast additional light on the authors' findings and which help us interpret their results. Although some of our citations refer to evidence accumulated after the preparation and publication of *The Authoritarian Personality,* many others have been in the literature for years, but they are not alluded to by the authors. The lack of such references seems hardly in keeping with a thousand-page study to which is attached a 121-item bibliography, and in our view a great deal is lost thereby.

There are occasions, for example, when the authors do not do justice to their findings through their failure to cite earlier writings which provide substantial support for their argument. Thus, early in the work, in introducing the larger question of the measurement of ethnocentrism, as contrasted with simple anti-Semitism, there is a discussion of prejudice as a generalized attitude and allusion is made to past thinkers who have foreshadowed this point of view. But no reference whatever is made to Hartley's or Murphy and Likert's classic demonstrations of just this phenomenon.[47] More often, however, confirmatory evidence, where it exists, is regularly cited. What is generally missing in the volume is evidence in the literature which contradicts the current findings, and the reader is thus given an unbalanced perspective on the problem. Thus, the authors note that class differences in ideology are found to be small in their results, the finding is accepted as fact, and they consequently infer that deeper emotional trends are responsible. We need only think of Centers' work, or Kornhauser's early studies, or the evidence of practically any public opinion poll to feel that their hasty dismissal of this factor on the basis of their own inconclusive evidence is quite unwarranted.[48] The lack of attention to past findings not only does the reader a disservice, it misleads the authors as well. In another context, that of the relation between childhood experience within the family and ideology, it is remarked that there must well be sub-cultural determinants of family patterns within America, though they were unable to find such in the present study. Allusion is made to an unpublished study by one of the authors in which the families of prejudiced individuals were found to come from a particular sub-group. But is it not likely that if the classic work of Allison Davis or M. Erickson on differences in child rearing in different classes had been cited, the findings of the present study on the significance of early childhood would have been placed in proper social perspective?[49] Actually, the neglect of certain bodies

---

[47] Hartley, E., "Problems in Prejudice," *op. cit.* Murphy, G. and Likert, R., *Public Opinion and the Individual,* Harpers, N. Y., 1938.

[48] Centers, Richard, *The Psychology of Social Classes,* Princeton University Press, Princeton, 1949. Kornhauser, A. W., "Analysis of Class Structure in Contemporary American Society," in Hartmann and Newcomb, *Industrial Conflict, a Psychological Interpretation,* Cordon, New York, 1939.

[49] Davis, Allison, *Social-Class Influences upon Learning,* Harvard University Press, Cambridge, 1951. Erickson, M. C., "Social Status and Child-Rearing Practices," in Newcomb and Hartley, *Readings in Social Psychology,* Holt, New York, 1947.

of literature seems to run parallel to the neglect which we have noted of certain dimensions in the analysis. Our earlier discussion of the questionable assumption that the generality of attitudes is independent of sampling may be seen in this context also. The very literature we cited, neglected by the authors, would have immediately rendered their assumption doubtful and might have encouraged more attention to sampling factors, with a resultant increase in the substantiality of the findings.

V. CONCLUSION

After analyzing the research methodology of *The Authoritarian Personality*, we have set forth a variety of criticisms. At times we have cited even minor weaknesses in the procedures, but we have done so in the interest of thoroughness, and with the hope that future researchers, working along similar paths, may perhaps profit by the weaknesses we have observed. Our major criticisms lead us inevitably to conclude that the authors' theory has not been proved by the data they cite, and that in their commendable attempt to combine the statistical and clinical approaches, neither was employed to fullest advantage.

To recapitulate our main points: The findings rest on an admittedly unrepresentative sample, from which large generalizations are incautiously drawn. What is true of highly educated people, or of extreme ethnocentric or non-ethnocentric individuals, or of active participants in civic affairs, is not necessarily true of the majority of the population. Weaknesses in the authors' handling of the quantitative data invariably work in favor of the assumptions, and the procedures are often inadmissible. Thus, the hypothesized "stereotypy" of ethnocentric individuals is deemed supported by the questionnaire answers, although both high and low scorers were forced, by the nature of the scales, to subscribe or not to subscribe to arbitrary, generalized statements. A positive correlation between authoritarianism and political conservatism is claimed, although the contents of the two scales which produce the correlation are clearly overlapping and therefore inflate the value. A positive correlation between authoritarianism and anti-Semitism is claimed, although in the process of building the authoritarianism scale, several items which failed to correlate with anti-Semitism were omitted although they were good measures of potential Fascism. Again the magnitude of the correlation is thereby exaggerated.

The questionnaire data are not validated save by their correspondence with the results of personal interviews with extreme groups; and since the interviewers were in full possession of the respondents' questionnaire answers and were deliberately urged to use these responses as leads in the interview situation, the criterion for validation was not independently derived. That the subsequent coding of the interviews was performed without reference to the respondents' scale scores does not atone for this error. Any bias introduced by the interviewers remained in the data; the persons who constructed the elaborate coding system did so in full knowledge of, and with reference to, the respondents' scale scores; and the coders, working only with the interviews of extreme individuals and coding in an over-all fashion, had little opportunity to exercise any independent judgment. In such a situation, a significant correlation between the scale scores and the coded interviews is not at all surprising, and cannot be said to provide objective support for the hypothesis.

In analyzing the data, no control at all was exercised over the important variable of formal education, although national survey evidence demonstrates clearly that many of the differences cited as determinants of ethnocentrism may instead merely reflect differences in the respondents' educational levels. Nowhere do the authors clearly illumine the correlations they do find between ethnocentrism and personality traits. Statistical tables are presented, the relationships are noted, and they are then "explained" in terms of the authors' theory. But there is no safeguard on the interpretations, and they become mere statements of opinion. The analysis is further handicapped by the fact that all subjects were selected from extreme groups which had highly generalized sentiments of prejudice, and that retrospective reports of childhood incidents are frequently assumed to represent valid and complete information regarding the respondent's early years.

Much of the qualitative analysis of respondents' ideology is almost completely unrestrained by any attachment to scientific method. The authors' propensity for psychodynamic explanations leads them to ignore the widespread distribution of certain sentiments in the American population, their frequent correlation with formal education, and their obvious social determinants, and to attribute them instead to psychodynamic processes unique in the ethnocentric individual. Thus, the fact that prejudice is "irrational" or "contradictory" or "highly generalized" is assumed to prove that personality factors are responsible, though no objective evidence is provided in support of this contention and other explanations deserve at least equal weight. In contrast, the quantitative data on the influence of group membership are given elaborate statistical treatment to show that this factor cannot account for ethnocentrism, and when significant correlations are not achieved, the influence of personality factors is regarded as confirmed.

As we said in our introductory remarks, one does not expect any research project—and especially one of this scope and originality —to be beyond criticism. Mistakes and limitations of one kind or another are inevitable. But in this case, the mistakes and limitations —no one of them perhaps crucial—uniformly operate *in favor* of the authors' assumptions, and cumulatively they build up a confirmation of the theory which, upon examination, proves to be spurious. Even in their choice of past research for reference purposes, they have largely ignored contrary findings or hypotheses. Their theory itself may yet be correct and provable, but the methodological weaknesses of the present study prevent its demonstration on the basis of these data. This is unfortunate not only because the insight which went into the formulation of the study deserved a better methodology, but also because the size and detail of the volume, the abundant statistical tables, and the prestige and publicity attached to the project will deter many readers from a careful study and lead them to believe that all of the arguments find full support in the data.

It is perhaps unfair that in preparing a criticism of the methodology of the study, clearly its weakest point, we are allowed no opportunity to pay tribute to its more positive contributions. That we must leave to others, and perhaps in most cases we shall be in agreement with them. Here we would refer only to the authors' own conclusions which occupy six of the one thousand pages at the end of the book. In these six pages, the imperfections of the study which are so often neglected in the body of the text are again referred to, and in the most moderate of language, with all due attention to the various qualifications imposed upon them by their techniques, the authors sum up the impact and significance of their work. Their conclusion goes far to remedy the earlier inadequacies, and has an eloquence rarely found in psychological writings. One feels intuitively that they have wisdom in their views and soundness in their conclusions, and it is sad that the acumen which inspired the project, the energy in executing a research task unparalleled in scope, and the intuitive power devoted to the appraisal of the results, were not matched by equal methodological skill.

RICHARD CHRISTIE

AUTHORITARIANISM RE-EXAMINED

THE present chapter is designed to afford an overview of the burgeoning body of social psychological research which has been reported in or inspired by *The Authoritarian Personality*. Relatively few studies have provided *direct* tests of the theory underlying the work of the California investigators. There is no dearth, however, of studies which have utilized scales taken in whole or part from those developed in *The Authoritarian Personality*. These have been related to other scales and to various measures of behavior among varying samples. In brief, a great amount of effort has been spent upon research which has a bearing upon various problems raised in *The Authoritarian Personality* but the direct theoretical links between these studies and the original investigations have not always been explicit.

In part, the responsibility for this "discontinuity of continuity" may be traced to *The Authoritarian Personality* itself. The volume is devoted to an essentially descriptive account of a progressive refinement of attitude scales and corroborative clinical data which indicate that individuals high in ethnic prejudice differ in personality from those low in prejudice. Abundant evidence from such diverse sources as intensive interviews, case studies, TATs, projective sentences, questionnaires, and psychiatric case records is presented to buttress this conclusion. However, these varied and impressive results are not integrated so as to make the underlying theory explicit enough to permit the testing of unequivocally specific hypotheses in further research. As Brewster Smith has noted, "In no single place in the volume, in fact, is there to be found a concise statement of the hypotheses underlying the entire undertaking or of the integrated conclusions of the project as a whole."[1]

---
[1] Smith, M. B., "Review of *The Authoritarian Personality*," *The Journal of Abnormal and Social Psychology*, 1950, 45, 775-779.

It is therefore necessary in evaluating subsequent research to return again and again to *The Authoritarian Personality* in order to clarify the theoretical points under discussion. Since this rescrutiny is affected by knowledge of the results of more recent studies and theoretical perspectives which have changed in the eight years since the original research was started, the present interpretation of some of the original data differs from that made by the authors. Also, since theoretical viewpoints partially determine the methodology employed and the methodology leads to the type of data uncovered which in turn has implications for theory, certain methodological considerations must be raised. Whereas Hyman and Sheatsley[2] evaluated *The Authoritarian Personality* against generally accepted methodological standards, the present concern is only with those methodological points which, in the light of recent research, have important theoretical implications. Fortunately Hyman and Sheatsley's intensive scrutiny permits reference to their contribution in most cases and the present chapter elaborates only those methodological points which are germane to the present discussion.

One difficulty in evaluating recent research is that much of it has not as yet been published. In many instances it has been necessary to accept summaries and brief statements at face value without having the opportunity to examine the basic data critically. On the other hand, where access to original data was possible, the present writer's interpretations are frequently focused upon specific aspects which were of less salience to the researcher's basic interest. The necessity of compressing the present discussion within the confiines of a single chapter has inevitably led to a cursory treatment if not omission of a number of original and valuable theoretical points of view. Since the concept of the authoritarian personality has engaged the attention of many able young social scientists the interested reader will find it rewarding to examine for himself the references from which the present summary has, perhaps capriciously, plucked data relevant to the evaluation of research related to *The Authoritarian Personality*.

The primary focus throughout this chapter is upon authoritarianism and less attention is paid to ethnocentrism and very little to political-economic conservatism (as measured by the PEC scale developed by the California investigators). Initially, the concept of

---

[2] See the preceding chapter.

authoritarianism developed in *The Authoritarian Personality* is examined in an effort to determine what is meant by the term and what the F scale (nee fascism but more recently authoritarianism) actually measures. The second task is to summarize the evidence relevant to the validity of measures of authoritarian tendencies in social interaction. After this scrutiny of the concept of authoritarianism, the relationship between authoritarianism and related personality measures is examined in relation to various measures of ethnocentrism. A fourth area of interest is in the social correlates of authoritarianism, where and under what conditions does it flourish? The final set of queries relates to the genesis of authoritarianism, and the tenability of the theoretical position of the California investigators is re-examined.

The selection of the aforementioned five areas has not been arbitrary. The original outline of the present chapter was based upon the assumption that it would be primarily a summary of research following *The Authoritarian Personality*. In the scrutiny and re-scrutinies of the relevant material constant referral to *The Authoritarian Personality* was necessary and the importance of making a sober and considered evaluation of certain aspects of the original work in the light of more recent findings gradually became paramount. The present chapter therefore represents an attempt to answer certain questions about *The Authoritarian Personality* which a protracted consideration of it and more recent research have raised.

I

An initial consideration in any analysis of research dealing with authoritarianism is a definition of precisely what is meant by the usage of the term. The research to be described in this chapter has been based upon what appears (implicitly, at least) to be a highly operational definition. Individuals scoring relatively high on the California F scale have been designated as authoritarian, those scoring lower have been viewed as non-authoritarian. However, the particular version of the F scale used in these investigations has varied. In some cases the final version designated by the authors of *The Authoritarian Personality* has been used, in other cases abbreviated versions have been adopted without explanation, some reports indicate that most of the items were used verbatim but changes were initiated in a few, and in some instances the abbreviated and simplified Authoritarian-Equalitarian scale developed by Sanford and Older has been used.³

What is especially interesting about this practice is that the F scale is nowhere (as far as the writer can determine) explicitly referred to as an authoritarianism scale in *The Authoritarian Personality*. Its construction is described in a chapter entitled, "The Measurement of Implicit Antidemocratic Trends" and it was dubbed the "F" scale because it was designed to tap "implicit prefascistic tendencies" (p. 224).⁴ There are occasional references to "authoritarian" and "authoritarianism" in the text of *The Authoritarian Personality* but these appear to be used in a descriptive sense and not as implying that all authoritarianism is fascism— explicitly or implicitly.⁵

Before an examination of studies utilizing the F scale or its variations are analyzed it is of obvious importance to specify: (1) the ideological nature of the content of the scale, (2) the ability of the F scale to discriminate fascistic and non-fascistic authoritarians and (3) the structural relationships between various items on the F scale. These problems shall be separately examined.

Explicit in the construction of the F scale was the intention that its content should not refer directly to ethnic groups but that it should discriminate between individuals high and low in minority group prejudice. These items were taken from remarks made by prejudiced interviewees, from newspapers and magazines, from previous research, etc. However, the initial rationale for using certain items came from a gradually developing system of hypothesized

---

³ Sanford, F. H. and Older, H. J., *A Brief Authoritarian-Equalitarian Scale*, Institute for Research in Human Relations, Report No. 6.

⁴ Page citations not otherwise identified in the following discussion refer to pagination in *The Authoritarian Personality*.

⁵ The title, *The Authoritarian Personality*, appears to have followed rather than preceded the research reported. The first page of the text contains the word "fascist" nine times, "anti-fascist" once, and "authoritarian" is *not mentioned a single time*. The title would appear to be a misnomer if the authors did not refer in a footnote (p. 971) in the final chapter to the "syndrome which we have labeled the authoritarian personality." The precise point where the labeling occurred is unclear (although Chapter XX carries the phrase "Authoritarian Personality" as part of the title). What is clear, however, is that in recent investigations high scorers on the F scale have been identified as "authoritarians." The term "potential fascist" is more consistent with the text and with the content of the items in the F scale. However, to avoid confusion, the discussion in the present chapter follows general usage in equating high scorers on the F scale with "authoritarians."

variables which were believed to be of importance. The subsequent refinements were made with the following considerations in mind: (1) the individual items had to discriminate between high and low scorers on the F scale as a whole, (2) they also had to discriminate between high and low scorers on the AS and E scales,[6] and (3) the items were selected with attention to *"meaningfulness, contribution to the structural unity of the scale,* and proper degree of *rational justification"* (p. 251). In addition certain items became outmoded by the changing course of world events.

It is therefore clear that formal ideological considerations were not of paramount importance in the construction of the F scale. The usage of the term "fascist" in reference to the content of the scale was not explicitly based upon a study of the content of fascistic ideologies. The starting point was the identification of anti-Semitic individuals as "anti-democratic." At the time of the study (1944-45), the United States and its allies were viewed as democratic, the enemy as fascistic. Through a series of transmutations, the identification of subjects scoring high on the E and F scales gradually changed from "anti-democratic" through stages of "potential" or "implicit fascism" to "fascism," and finally to "authoritarianism."

What is of pertinence here is the degree to which the foregoing labels accurately describe the content of the F scale. To the writer's knowledge, no copies of the F scale have been administered to any known Fascists. There are several indirect lines of evidence, however, that indicate that the content of the F scale is related to political fascism.

Stagner's pioneer work in scaling fascistic attitudes was based upon an analysis of German and Italian fascistic writings in a search for general themes which seemed to characterize these political movements.[7] He isolated seven content areas: (1) nationalism, (2) imperialism, (3) militarism, (4) racial antagonism, (5) anti-radicalism, (6) middle-class consciousness, and (7) a benevolent despot or strong-man philosophy of government. The first five of these areas relate to the California E scale; the last two are more directly related to the F scale which also contains tinges of some of the other areas. In Table I some of Stagner's items are paired with F scale items which appear to tap somewhat similar sentiments.

---

[6] See the preceding chapter.
[7] Stagner, R. "Fascistic attitudes: an exploratory study," *The Journal of Social Psychology,* 1936, 7, 309-19.

TABLE I
SIMILAR FORMAL AND INFORMAL "FASCISTIC" STATEMENTS

Stagner[a]	The Authoritarian Personality[b]
24.[c] CCC camps where the boys learned military discipline and self control would be a good idea.	13. What the youth needs most is strict discipline, rugged determination, and the will to work and fight for family and country.
26. We will always have depressions.	6. Human nature being what it is, there will always be wars and conflicts.
44. America has plenty of plans— what it needs is strong men who are willing to work for recovery.	23. What this country needs most, more than laws and political programs, is a few courageous, tireless, devoted leaders in whom the people can put their faith.
48. People should not be allowed to vote unless they are intelligent and educated.	34. Most of our social problems would be solved if we would somehow get rid of the immoral, crooked, and feebleminded people.

a. Stagner, R. *op. cit.*
b. From Table 7, (VII), pp. 255-57.
c. Item numbers follow those in the original citations.

The four F scale items in Table I come from five of the nine "hypothetical clusters" mentioned in *The Authoritarian Personality* (a given item could belong to more than one cluster): conventionalism, authoritarian submission, authoritarian aggression, power and "toughness," and destructiveness and cynicism. Although the F scale items are less specific than Stagner's, and more personally oriented questions were added designed to elicit feelings of antiintraception and overconcern with sex, there is sufficient overlap to assume that the F scale gets at an individual ideology which is generally congruent with Stagner's analysis of Fascist ideology.[8]

Quite different support of the relationship between the type of items in the F scale and political fascism is evidenced in a report by Dicks.[9] Intensive psychiatric interviews were conducted with 138 Nazi prisoners of war including former members of the German army, navy, and air force. The interviewees had previously been screened for political proclivities. The sample consisted of 65 men considered high in fascism, including both fanatic, whole-hearted

---

[8] A useful review of the earlier material on various scales of fascist attitudes has been made by Edwards. Edwards, A. L., "The signs of incipient fascism," *The Journal of Abnormal and Social Psychology*, 1944, 39, 301-316.

[9] Dicks, H. V., "Personality traits and national socialist ideology," *Human Relations*, 1950, 3, 111-54.

Nazis and those who believed in Nazism with reservations. The remaining 73 were considered low in fascism and included those who were classified as unpolitical, passive anti-Nazis, and active, convinced anti-Nazis.

A number of comparisons between ratings of those high and low in attachment to the Nazi Party were made. Significant differences were found: the "highs" were characterized by a tenderness taboo, sadism, homosexual trends, projection, anxiety, low identification with the mother and lack of rebellion against the father. These have much in common with the power and "toughness," authoritarian aggression, concern with sex (possibly), projectivity, and authoritarian submission described by the California investigators. The impression of a strong similarity between the convinced Nazi described by Dicks and the middle-class person high in prejudice delineated in *The Authoritarian Personality* is heightened by a comparison of the interview material in both studies.

One further bit of evidence might be adduced—not because it is directly relevant to the content of the F scale but as a sidelight. Himmelhoch[10] empirically derived a special Rorschach scoring scheme based upon an analysis of differences in protocols among individuals scoring high on the F scale in contrast to lower scorers (the subjects were primarily Jewish college students). A second sample was utilized as a validating group, the Rorschach protocols being scored blindly before F scale scores were computed. It was possible to relate significantly the Rorschach "authoritarianism" index to high scores on the F scale. The index was then applied to the Rorschach protocols obtained from seven defendants at the Nuremberg trials (Goering, Von Ribbentrop, Rosenberg, Streicher, Ley, Frank, and Doenitz). Although the scores obtained are not presented, it is stated that all seven Nazi leaders scored high on the Rorschach authoritarianism scale. This ingenious demonstration is in accordance with the material in *The Authoritarian Personality*; however, the sample is so small and the approach so indirect that it cannot be safely maintained that *all* Nazis would score at the high extreme of the F scale.

In general, it would appear that the content of the F scale is such that it conforms to the formal content of Fascist ideology; the personality dimensions presumably being tapped are similar to other related measures which characterized Nazi prisoners of war

---

[10] Himmelhoch, J. *The Dynamics of Tolerance.* Unpublished Ph.D. thesis, Columbia University, 1952.

and a small sample of Nazi leaders. Although the material utilized in constructing the F scale was based upon items differentiating young adults in California who were high and low in ethnic prejudice, it appears justifiable to view it as tapping a dimension of fascistic receptivity.

Evidence as to the ability of the F scale to screen non-fascistic authoritarians is extremely meager. Relatively few Royalists, Junkers, members of the samurai, or other right wing authoritarian groups are available for investigation, and to the writer's knowledge none have been tested by means of the F scale. Similarly, affiliation with authoritarianism of the left has recently become so suspect that such individuals are not readily accessible for purposes of psychological investigation.

One possible indirect source of evidence regarding leftist authoritarians is available. Among the groups tested by the authors of *The Authoritarian Personality* a sprinkling of Communists and party liners may be found. Nine individuals who identified themselves on the questionnaire face sheet as Communists are included (Table 12, (V), p. 188-89). Fifty-four individuals were tested who attended the California Labor School (Table 1 (I), p. 21-22), this being an organization designated by the Attorney General as under control of the Communist Party. There is little reason to doubt that the students attending it were voluntarily exposed to, if not identified with, the ideology of the Communist Party.

It might be argued that when the scales were administered in 1945 many individuals who were not authoritarian in either terms of ideology or personality may have been members of the Communist Party or attending the California Labor School because of political naïveté rather than out of genuine ideological identification. This is a plausible argument although one on which there is little reliable data. However, a recent article by Krugman[11] indicates that the actual techniques of the Communist Party even in the 1930s in the United States were such that genuine liberals would find them alien. Krugman interviewed ex-members of the Communist Party in obtaining his material on the appeal of party membership and reasons for joining. What makes Krugman's material especially interesting is that it was not obtained from professional ex-Communists. The consistent and mutually independent descrip-

---

[11] Krugman, H., "The appeal of Communism to American middle class intellectuals and trade unionists." *The Public Opinion Quarterly*, 1952, *16*, 331-355.

tions by these individuals of the deliberate anti-intellectualism of Communist indoctrination, the inculcated cynicism, and the abject submission to party discipline (as expressed in formalized confessions of deviations from party standards) indicate authoritarianism in the sense of a formal definition and a striking similarity to fascistic practices.[12]

If the Communists and party liners included in the samples tested by the authors of *The Authoritarian Personality* are in truth authoritarians, do their F scale scores reflect it? A direct answer is impossible since the actual F scale scores made by these individuals are not reported. However, it is possible to utilize other data to obtain an approximate answer to the question. Data is presented on the E and F scales in groupings of "Middle-Class Men," "Middle-Class Women," and "Working-Class Men." Unfortunately, data on 19 California Labor School "Working-Class Women" tested (Table 1, [I], p. 19) are not presented in these comparisons. However, E scale scores are available on the remaining 35 California Labor School members, the nine self-identified Communists, and the F scale means of the larger groupings in which they are subsumed are given as well as the correlation between the E and F scales for the larger categories. Table II (see p. 132) represents a recombination of data from four tables in *The Authoritarian Personality*.

The Labor School students who are combined in the various class membership groupings (the criteria for which are not defined) vary from seven to 25 per cent of the socio-economic groupings under which they are subsumed and range from 1.90 to 2.84 mean points below the average E scale score of the other members of their socio-economic grouping.

Although the F scale scores of Labor School members and Communists are not given it is obvious that under the conditions summarized in Table I they could not be other than low on the F scale as well as on the E scale. The obtained correlations between the E and F scales could not have been obtained if the left wingers scoring low on E had scored high on F. Or as is stated in more rigorous fashion, "A correlation of .775 (between the E and F scales) means that about two-thirds of the subjects who score in the high quartile on the one scale, score in the high quartile on the

---

[12] Shils' chapter deals at length with the authoritarianism of the left. This has happily necessitated deletion of a less cogent discussion previously prepared for the present chapter.

TABLE II[a]
LEFT-WING ETHNOCENTRISM AND AUTHORITARIANISM

	E scale		F scale	E & F
	M	n	M	r
"Middle-Class Men"	3.89	69	3.69	.81
(Labor School)[b]	1.27	9		
(MCM - LS)	4.11	60		
"Middle-Class Women"	3.64	154	3.62	.83
(Labor School)	1.20	11		
(MCW - LS)	3.83	143		
"Working-Class Men"	3.83	59[c]	4.19	.76
(Labor School)	2.41	15		
(WCM - LS)	4.31	44		
All Labor School	1.73	35		
All Communists[d]	1.25	9		

a. All data for the E scale (except for Communists) was taken from Table 15 (V), p. 194. Communist E scale scores were obtained from Table 12 (V), p. 188. F scale scores were obtained from Table 12 (VII), p. 266, and the correlations between E and F scales were obtained from Table 10 (VII), p. 263.

b. The mean for the "purified" Middle-Class Men (as well as for the other groupings in which Labor School members were excluded) was calculated from the original tables.

c. In the tables in Chapter V summarizing the results of the E scale the n for "Working-Class Men" is given as 59. In Chapter VII, the n for "Working-Class Men" is given as 61 in both the summary table for F scale scores and also in the table reporting the correlation between the E and F scales.

d. Five of the Communists *may* have been in the Labor School sample. Three can be excluded because they took a different questionnaire form than that administered to the Labor School sample. At least one Communist was included in the interview sample (Table 6 (IX), p. 300) and none of the interviewees was drawn from the Labor School (Tables 1 [IX] and 2 [IX], pp. 296-97.)

other, and that there are practically no reversals, i.e., cases in which a subject is high on one scale but low on the other." (p. 264)

It follows that not only the nine self-admitted Communists but also the individuals attending the California Labor School were relatively low on the F scale. A number of possible explanations are available. The logical possibilities are: (1) the F scale does not measure authoritarianism in general but more specifically fascistic ideology, (2) the F scale does measure authoritarianism but Communism is not an authoritarian ideology, and (3) the Communists and party liners taking the questionnaires were more sophisticated than other members of the questionnaire sample and therefore simulated low scores. There is no evidence in support of either of the latter two possibilities. It therefore appears that the most probable reason that Communists rejected the items in the F scale was not an absence of authoritarianism on their part, but rather a well ingrained tendency to reject ideological cliches representative of the authoritarian right.[13]

This tentative conclusion raises questions as to what the F scale actually measures. The items themselves may be defined in terms of their content, i.e., they are phrased so that agreement implies a *Weltanschauung* which is characterized by dichotomization of complex issues, acceptance of authoritarian figures (traditional ones, at least) and a view of the world as hostile and threatening. In constructing the F scale, items were chosen in terms of hypothesized personality variables (p. 224-241). These were: conventionalism, authoritarian submission, authoritarian aggression, anti-intraception, superstition and stereotypy, power and "toughness," destructiveness and cynicism, projectivity, and sex. From four to eleven items were initially selected to tap each of these hypothesized variables, some items being assumed to tap two or three dimensions.

The third and final form of the F scale (Forms 40 and 45) reported in *The Authoritarian Personality* contained 30 items (Table 7 (VII), p. 255-257). The only analysis of the relationship between F scale items by the California investigators is briefly reported (p. 261-262). Five hundred and seventeen women students in an elementary psychology class constituted the sample. The average of the correlations of each item with every other item was .13, the range varying from -.05 to .44. The correlation of each item with the remainder of the F scale averaged .33, the range running from .15 to .52.

These results clearly indicate that the F scale is not measuring an unidimensional attribute. But since the items intercorrelate it is apparent that they are tapping something in common (or things in common). Do the empirical results indicate that the hypothetical clusters which were a factor in item selection exist in reality? The answer appears to be in the negative. "Proof that the variables or groups of items used in thinking about the F scale are not clusters in the statistical sense, is contained in the data from the present group of 517 women. Although the items within each of the Form

---

[13] This reluctance of Communists to accept disguised fascistic statements has been demonstrated previously. Raskin and Cook found that 35 communist students were significantly lower on Stagner's scale than those students who identified themselves as members of or sympathetic to major political parties. Raskin, E. and Cook, S. W., "A further investigation of the measurement of an attitude toward fascism." *The Journal of Social Psychology*, 1938, 9, 201-206.

Stagner also found that individuals favoring the 1932 presidential candidate on the Communist Party ticket (Foster) had lower fascism scores than supporters of Roosevelt and Hoover, Stagner, *op. cit.*

45 F-clusters tend to intercorrelate (.11 to .24), the items in any one cluster correlate with one another no better than they do with numerous items from other clusters." (p. 262).

Apparently no attempt was made to test the matrix of intercorrelation to find out if empirical clusterings of items existed which did not conform to those hypothesized. However, a subsequent study by Christie and Garcia[14] directly attacked this problem. A statistical analysis of the intercorrelations of F scale items for two samples matched for socio-economic factors was made. One sample was composed of individuals attending an introductory psychology course at the University of California; the other sample was composed of students in an introductory psychology course at a private university in the southwest ("Southwest City"). The range of inter-item correlations was markedly greater in both samples than that reported in *The Authoritarian Personality*. In the California sample the range was from -.50 to .77; in the Southwest City sample the range was from -.46 to .89. The greater range is probably related to the fact that the samples were composed of members of both sexes and that many of the males were veterans. With more heterogeneous populations it is to be expected that greater variability might exist than held true for the all college women sample reported in the pages of *The Authoritarian Personality*.[15]

Independent cluster analyses were made of the inter-item correlations in both the California and Southwest City samples. In cluster analysis, items are statistically isolated which correlate highly with one another but which do not correlate so highly with other items. Through successive refinements it is possible to isolate clusters or groupings of items which empirically hang together, i.e., a person who accepts one item in a cluster tends to accept the others whereas rejection of one item tends to be related to rejection of the other items in the cluster. Since the items in a cluster are responded to in a consistent fashion, the assumption may be made that they have some common psychological relationship.

---

[14] Christie, R. and Garcia, J., "Subcultural variation in authoritarian personality," *Journal of Abnormal and Social Psychology*, 1951, 46, 457-469.

[15] It is also possible that the use of tetrachoric correlations by Christie and Garcia and the smaller size of their samples (57 each) affected the range of correlations as compared with the unspecified correlational method used in *The Authoritarian Personality*.

the underlying reasoning leading to its acceptance. Thus Christie and Garcia report that an individual who had accepted wholeheartedly the majority of the F scale items completely rejected one stating, "Wars and social troubles may some day be ended by an earthquake or flood that will someday destroy the whole world." This behavior is at face value contradictory since the individual happily accepted the content of the majority of F scale items; however, it is genotypically consistent since the individual in question wrote in after the item the following explanation, "My church says it will be by fire," indicating agreement with the general philosophy of the item in conjunction with rejection of the specific statement.

A perusal of the items in the F scale indicates that in many cases the referent is unclear. In contrast to unidimensional scales such as Guttman's the meaning of the acceptance of an item is not generalizable with a high degree of certainty from one individual to another. However, the reliability of the scales is high enough to indicate that an individual who accepts one item *tends* to accept the rest, the more individual items he accepts the greater the probability that he will accept the remainder.

There is no question that the F scale does not tap a unidimensional component of "fascism," "authoritarianism" or whatever. Indeed, the authors never intended that it should. It may be that it includes a number of discrete attributes, each of which is capable of isolation and measurement upon unidimensional scales. If this possibility is correct, a great deal of testing upon a variety of samples with progressively more refined subscales will be necessary before such clarification ensues. Alternatively, it may be true that no rational scales to measure irrationality can be statistically purified to the desired extent. Any such attempt at isolation of "pure" dimensions faces serious problems. If the referents of the items are unequivocally specified (as would presumably be necessary to obtain unidimensionality) it may be that the items would lose much of their present ability to capture agreement from those who accept the looser formulations. It seems unlikely that items which have the general vagueness of referents which makes the F scale so uniquely able to capture indigenous authoritarian sentiments could ever be incorporated into an unidimensional scale. Since the items *mean* different things to different people it appears a difficult task to devise items which mean the same things to different individuals for the *same* basic reason. The study by Christie and Garcia indicated that similar clusters were found (in the sense that the underlying common denominator of meaning appeared similar) in two samples which apparently interpreted individual items quite differently.

This brief examination of the F scale leaves us with two conclusions: (1) it captures something common to fascistic philosophy but it is impossible to specify with any precision exactly what it captures, and (2) although there is evidence that the hypothesized dimensions have some validity the individual items are not related to these in a clearcut way.

The situation recalls Augustine's intellectual agony in trying to clarify the concept of time: "For so it is, oh Lord my God, I measure it, but what it is that I measure I do not know."

II

The preceding discussion indicates that the F scale is related to some dimension (or dimensions) of personality which are related to ideological proclivities toward fascism. The precise nature of the relationship is as yet unclear. However, the ultimate question to be asked of any scale is essentially an empirical one; how well does it work in measuring what it is assumed to measure? In the present section we shall be concerned with empirical correlates of the F scale. Although there are few relevant studies the consistency of results is encouraging.

For our present purposes the presence of authoritarianism will be considered demonstrated in social situations in which individuals high in authoritarianism in contrast to those low in authoritarianism are: punitive and condescending toward inferiors, unreceptive to scientific investigation, less sensitive to interpersonal relationships, and prone to attribute their own ideology to others. These criteria appear to be in accord with both the definition of authoritarianism specified in *The Authoritarian Personality* and a garden-variety interpretation of authoritarianism as manifested in interpersonal relations.

Eager and Smith have reported a study conducted in a summer camp.[17] Evaluations of counselors were made by six to eleven year

---

[17] Eager, Joan, and Smith, M. B., "A note on the validity of Sanford's authoritarian-equalitarian scale," *Journal of Abnormal and Social Psychology*, 1952, 47, 265-267.

old underprivileged children. These evaluations were made on a "Guess Who" basis; seventeen boys and seventeen girls were asked to guess which of 31 statements applied to which counselors. The counselors were eleven college girls who had been given the seven most discriminating items from the Sanford-Older A-E scale (modified from the California F scale and scored along a six response continuum) prior to the commencement of camp. The counselors were divided upon the basis of their test scores into five relatively equalitarian and six relatively authoritarian counselors. The item mean scores[18] of both groups was below the theoretical mean of 3.5,[19] being 1.79 and 3.03 respectively; hence it might be more accurate to speak of the two groups as "more equalitarian" and "less equalitarian." The pertinent point, however, is that even within this relatively limited range of equalitarian sentiments, differences were found. Table VI (see p. 142) abstracts the five statements judged most characteristic of "equalitarians" and "authoritarians."

A fairly clearcut differentiation of behavioral patterns emerges in a comparison of the extreme statements. The mean rank of the five statements most characteristic of equalitarians is 5.7, of authoritarians, 22.7. A rank order correlation between the mean rank assigned to each statement by the judges and the discriminatory power of each of the 31 items among the two groups of counselors is reported as being .44. It appears that the children's evaluation of counselors' behavior is positively related to the counselors' scores on the A-E scale, the more authoritarian on the scale being evaluated as more authoritarian in behavior.

In a study of differences between students in an elementary psychology course at the University of Minnesota who volunteered for a "personality experiment" and non-volunteers, Rosen[20] utilized the F scale as one measure of personality. The 62 students who volunteered had an item acceptance mean of 2.97[21] on the F scale.

---

[18] Throughout this chapter, all scores on variations of the F scale will be given as item means. This is to equate scores on tests of various lengths. Normally, the F scale is scored along a seven point continuum with 4.0 being the theoretical neutral point. Lower scores represent individuals rejecting more authoritarian statements than are accepted, scores greater than 4.0 indicate greater acceptance than rejection.

[19] The A-E scale has six alternative responses; scores range from 1 to 6.

[20] Rosen, E., "Differences between volunteers and non-volunteers for psychological studies," *Journal of Applied Psychology*, 1951, 35, 185-193.

[21] These calculations are based on Table 4, p. 190, *op. cit.*

TABLE VI

STATEMENTS CHARACTERIZING "EQUALITARIAN" COUNSELORS

(9)[a] She has a quiet group that pays attention and has fun.
(3.5) She always helps you when you need it in learning something new and seems very glad to do it.
(5) She explains how to do something to your group and then leaves the rest up to you.
(9) You don't want to do what your group is supposed to but she gives you a special job or makes you like it.
(2) She asks you what you want to do at the beginning of a period and lets you do what you want.

STATEMENTS CHARACTERIZING "AUTHORITARIAN" COUNSELORS

(21) She talks to you like you were a baby.
(19.5) When you have done something wrong or been bad, she sends you to the front porch.[b]
(30) You do what she asks you to because she will punish you if you don't.
(24.5) She talks to you like she is mad at you.
(17) You don't do what she asks you to because you like to make her mad.

---

a. The numbers before each item indicate the average rank order assigned to the statement by five psychology and sociology instructors (31 statements).

b. This enigmatic consequence of wickedness is not elaborated in the original reference.

Seventy-two students in the class did not volunteer. Their F scale item mean score was 3.56. This difference in means is reported as being significant at the .001 level. It is noted, "Male and female volunteers evidenced significantly less of the conventionalism, authoritarianism, power preoccupation, and tendency to projection measured by this scale." It is not clear whether this statement is based upon a comparison of items hypothesized as falling in these clusters by the Berkley investigators or whether this is intended as a summary statement of differences of high and low scorers on the F scale as a whole. However, the greater reluctance of the high scorers on the F scale to participate in such experiments is in conformity with the anti-intraceptive and anti-scientific bias found in the California "highs."

Two studies contain data concerning the ability of individuals with differing F scale scores to make accurate judgments of others.

Christie[22] reports on the judgments made by 182 recruits in basic training as to who was best liked by peers in the platoon of which the judge was a member and by the non-commissioned training personnel supervising the platoon. The judgments consisted of making each recruit estimate which three of his peers would be most frequently named as best friends by other members of his platoon and which three would be best liked by the non-commissioned training personnel. Accuracy of these judgments was determined by comparison with the actual choices made by peers and superiors.

It was found that accuracy of the two sets of judgments were negatively correlated (−.24, significant beyond the .01 level). Those individuals who were more accurate at estimating judgments of peers toward other recruits tended to be less accurate in estimating attitudes of the non-commissioned training personnel. In examining possible reasons for this negative correlation the scores made by the recruits on an abbreviated form of the F scale were correlated with each set of judgments. The correlation between F scale scores and accuracy of judgment regarding peers' preferences was found to be −.30 (corrected for attenuation); with accuracy of judgment regarding superiors, +.10 (not significant).

This finding indicates that individuals scoring relatively low on the F scale were more sensitive to the interpersonal relationships among their peers than were the high scorers. It cannot be maintained, however, that the former were more accurate social perceivers in general since they were not as accurate when judgments were made about the preference of superiors. It is impossible to determine from the data whether the high scorers were in actuality better able to predict the rankings of the non-commissioned personnel because they were more sensitive to authority figures or whether they tended to evaluate other recruits upon the same basis as the non-coms. An analysis of men preferred by the training non-coms indicates that they tended to be either those who were actively cooperating in training or those who actually were doing poorly but were trying to do well to the limits of their ability. It may well be that high scoring recruits evaluated their peers from a similar frame of reference and attributed their own standards to the non-coms

---

[22] Christie, R., "Some determinants of the accuracy of social judgments among Army recruits." Unpublished paper read before the Eastern Psychological Association, March, 1952.

(in part correctly, in this case). If this is true, accuracy of judgment would be unrelated to accuracy of social perception.

Returning to the more traditional subjects of psychological investigation we find that 276 undergraduates in an introductory psychology course at Ohio State University were given the F scale (28 items) and 30 items selected from the Minnesota Multi-phasic by Scodel and Mussen.[23] The twenty-seven highest with an item mean acceptance on the F scale of 4.62 (our calculations) and the twenty-seven scoring lowest with an item mean acceptance of 2.38 were selected for further investigation. Each high scorer was paired with a low scorer and the two were required to spend twenty minutes together in a discussion in which they were free to discuss any aspect of radio, television, or the movies. All other topics of conversation were banned.

Each pair was separated at the end of the twenty minute period and each participant was told that he was to engage in a role playing experiment. He was to be given some tests and was to respond on each test item as he believed his former partner would answer. The F scale and the 30 Minnesota Multi-phasic items were then given to be answered according to these stipulations.

Scodel and Mussen predicted upon the basis of their interpretation of *The Authoritarian Personality* that the low scorers would be more accurate in estimating the responses of the high scorers than the reverse, since they expected a greater amount of projectivity of own attitude on the part of the latter. The findings bear out this hypothesis. The high scorers' item mean score when taking the F scale in the role playing simulation of actual low scorers was only .18 lower than their own actual score, this difference not approaching significance. The low scorers apparently compromised when they simulated high scorers; although they were able to break from their own scores to a significant extent, the simulated item mean for high scorers was 3.56, which in actuality is slightly over half way between their own item mean score of 2.38 and the high scorers' one of 4.62.

Neither group was significantly able to simulate the scores of the other group on Minnesota Multi-phasic items although the low scorers did better than chance on four of the thirty items in contrast to only one such case on the part of the high scorers.

---

[23] Scodel, A. and Mussen, P., "Social perceptions of authoritarians and non-authoritarians," *The Journal of Abnormal and Social Psychology*, 1953, 48, 181-184.

The preceding four studies are alike in that they utilized some behavior other than another attitude scale or report of own beliefs or activities and related it to scores made on some variation of the F scale. The subjects investigated came from varied socio-economic strata and their reactions were obtained in both natural and artificial situations. All of the evidence indicates congruity with the theoretical formulations related to authoritarianism stressed in *The Authoritarian Personality*. Counselors accepting authoritarian statements were judged to have behaved in a punitive and condescending manner to social inferiors, high scorers were reluctant to serve as experimental subjects reflecting anti-intraceptiveness, low scorers tended to be better at estimating preferences of peers and high scorers those of superiors which suggests differential preoccupation with the role of authority, and high scorers tended to attribute their own attitude to others to a greater extent than low scorers.

The relationship between authoritarianism and various sorts of self-reported political behavior is explored in other studies. As in the previously cited studies a variety of F scales were used; however, the variable to which these are related is not clearly an independent measure. They may best be regarded as instances of the *reliability* of the F scale rather than its validity.

Milton[24] reports that 390 students at the University of Tennessee were given the F scale (version unspecified) and immediately after completing it were asked to select one of six names of candidates preferred as the next president of the United States. This was done during the early stages of the Republican National Convention in 1952. Milton's findings were:

TABLE VII

AUTHORITARIANISM AND PRESIDENTIAL PREFERENCE

Aspirant	Number Choosing	F scale Item Mean Score
Taft	56	4.18
MacArthur	36	4.15
Russell	16	3.86
Kefauver	101	3.71
Eisenhower	158	3.67
Stevenson	23	3.09

---

[24] Milton, O., "Presidential choice and performance on a scale of authoritarianism," *The American Psychologist*, 1952, 7, 597-598.

The above rankings have a degree of face validity, especially when it is considered that they were gathered before the presidential campaign. However, the six men were ranked for "authoritarianism" (author's quotes—not otherwise explicated) by 18 faculty members. A rank order correlation of .73 was found between the authoritarianism attributed to aspirants for candidacy and the F scale scores of students preferring each man.

Another relevant study is reported by Mussen and Wyszynski.[25] They administered F and E scale items to a sample of 156 University of Wisconsin undergraduates in conjunction with other questions designed to uncover political interest or apathy. No relationship was found between political participation or apathy and response to either scale.

This result is not surprising; the F scale presumably measures fascistic potential rather than political behavior *per se*. Participation and apathy might be related to any sort of political ideology. There is no reason to suppose that authoritarian undergraduates might be either particularly apathetic or active.

What makes this study provocative, however, are the results found on ten projective questions. These seemingly yield a different picture of political apathy. According to the authors, the following statements are characteristic of apathetics' responses to these questions:

(1) An inability to recognize personal responsibility or to examine or accept own feelings and emotions.
(2) Vague feelings of worry, insecurity, and threat.
(3) Complete and unchanging acceptance of constituted authority (social codes, parents, and religion).
(4) Relative absence of responses emphasizing self-expression, ego-strivings, and satisfactions of warm interpersonal relationships.

With the possible exception of the second summary statement, the picture that emerges is, as the authors note, strikingly similar to the portrait of the authoritarian depicted in *The Authoritarian Personality*. In searching for an explanation for the lack of differences on the F scale between the two groups, Mussen and Wyszynski consider such possibilities as the sophistication of the sample and living in a university setting where the social norms are liberal. Despite

---

[25] Mussen, P. H. and Wyszynski, A. B., "Personality and political participation," *Human Relations*, 1952, 5, 65-82.

these qualifications it remains intriguing that response to questions relevant to authoritarianism and political activity yielded no relationship whereas the latter were related to more projective measures of authoritarianism.

In a study conducted with 963 individuals sampled so as to represent the population of Philadelphia, Sanford reports, "We have data showing that authoritarians are not highly participant in political affairs, do not join many community groups, do not become officers in the groups they become members of."[26] In illustration, those individuals who report themselves as non-voters and non-participants in political affairs (n = 96) have an item mean score on the Sanford-Older A-E scale of 3.76, those who report themselves as voters but not otherwise politically active (n = 793) have an item mean of 3.45, and those who are both voters and politically active (n=58) have a mean of 3.16.[27] In evaluating this finding it is difficult to know how much weight to assign to authoritarianism as an independent variable. Political participation is positively related to such indices of socio-economic status as income and education. F scale scores are negatively related to indices of socio-economic status (see IV below). Since socio-economic factors are not held constant in Sanford's study we are unable to determine to what extent the negative correlation between authoritarianism scores and political participation are independent.

Evidence as to the relationship between F scale scores and high school activities are presented by Gough.[28] A negative correlation of −.27 was found between F scale scores and the number of extracurricular activities participated in among a sample of 271 Minnesota high school seniors. The correlation between the F scale and intelligence scores in the sample was −.43 and F scale scores also correlated −.37 with social status as measured by the American Home scale.[29] It is unjustifiable to equate high school extra-cur-

---

[26] Sanford, F. H., *Authoritarianism and Leadership*, Stephenson Brothers, Philadelphia, 1950, p. 168.

[27] Ibid., Table 37, p. 160.

[28] Gough, H. G., "Studies of social intolerance: I. Some psychological and sociological correlates of anti-Semitism," *The Journal of Social Psychology*, 1951, 33, 237-246. Gough's manuscript was accepted for publication prior to the appearance of *The Authoritarian Personality*. The "E-F" scale mentioned by him is identical to the Form 60A F scale utilized by Christie and Garcia. In his tables the "E" scale is equivalent to the usual F scale.

[29] Ibid., Table 1, p. 241.

ricular activities with adult political behavior; however, it is suggestive that F scale scores correlate negatively with both.

In two of the three studies negative correlations between F scale scores and various types of participation in group activity were found. In Mussen and Wyszynski's report no such relationship was found although replies to projective questions did indicate that the politically apathetic tended to display behavior more akin to the authoritarian syndrome. In both Sanford's and Gough's studies more heterogeneous populations were used and the effects of intelligence were uncontrolled. Whether the relationship found would still hold if intelligence were partialled out is a moot point.

Whether individuals high in authoritarianism tend to be less politically active than those low in authoritarianism probably depends upon the sorts of political activity possible in a given setting and the nature of the social pressures operating to favor or restrict such activity. The individual's degree of authoritarianism presumably operates in the determination of the type of ideology favored and no definite statement can be made as to the degree of activity. However, it appears likely that the *intensity* with which beliefs are held might be related to actual behavior. Dombrose and Levinson[30] compared individuals in the lowest quartile on the E scale with those in the second lowest. It was found that the individuals extremely low in ethnocentrism favored much more militant measures to combat discrimination against minority groups than those individuals in the next quartile who were not so extremely anti-ethnocentric.

At least the incentive to participation is perhaps related to the degree of extremeness with which authoritarian beliefs are held. We might reasonably expect a curvilinear relationship between authoritarianism (as measured by the F scale) and political participation under conditions in which equal opportunity for political participation was possible. This relationship would presumably exist most clearly when other factors influencing participation such as education were held constant.

In the few studies which have been reported the F scale is significantly related to various other measures of behavior indicative of authoritarianism. It may tentatively be concluded that it does tap a meaningful behavioral dimension. Despite the statistical sig-

---

[30] Dombrose, L. A. and Levinson, D. J., "Ideological 'militancy' and 'pacifism' in democratic individuals," *The Journal of Social Psychology*, 1950, 32, 101-113.

nificance of the results, however, the magnitude of the relationships reported is not strikingly large. It may be that even more clearcut indications might be found if more precise measures of other types of authoritarian behavior were taken, especially in carefully controlled situations. Future research upon the interactions of high and low authoritarians in situations involving different status relationships appears especially called for in view of the findings to date.

III

The focus of attention in the previous discussion has been upon the meaning and validity of the F scale as a measure of authoritarianism. This initial emphasis was designed to clarify the most ambiguous and original of the scales used by the California and subsequent investigators. The content of the F scale appears closely related to the ideology of political fascism; the reports available on social behavior of individuals accepting these items indicates that they behave in a manner which is characteristically authoritarian.

In a sense, the present chapter has so far been working backwards since the conceptual formulation of authoritarianism was founded upon the study of individuals who admitted ethnic prejudice. Two major points made in *The Authoritarian Personality* regarding ethnic prejudice need to be reviewed in the light of more recent findings. The first is the stress placed upon the interrelatedness of prejudices against various ethnic outgroups. The second and more important point is the relationship found between ethnocentrism and various personality characteristics, particularly those supposedly captured by the F scale. Recent research appears sufficient to illuminate this relationship from varied perspectives.

The authors apply the term ethnocentrism to a general rejection of outgroups and reification of ingroups. Their definition is:

> "*Ethnocentrism is based on a pervasive and rigid ingroup-outgroup distinction; it involves stereotyped negative imagery and hostile attitudes regarding outgroups, stereotyped positive imagery and submissive attitudes regarding ingroups, and a hierarchical, authoritarian view of group interaction in which ingroups are rightly dominant, outgroups subordinate.*" (p. 150, italics in original.)

The concept of ethnocentrism is not a new one; indeed, the authors acknowledge theoretical precursors dating back to Sumner. It has long been noted that individuals prejudiced against one ethnic outgroup also tend to be prejudiced against others, this knowledge antedating the construction of the first Bogardus scale. What is especially interesting is that relatively little attention was focused upon this fact prior to *The Authoritarian Personality*. Stagner, it will be remembered, included prejudice toward minority groups as a manifestation of fascistic ideology and did not break it down into different ways of being prejudiced against the same and different groups. Others of his subscales (such as nationalism) may be regarded as reification of the ingroup.

Ethnocentrism as developed in *The Authoritarian Personality* is an interesting concept in a historical sense. Although it was implicit or taken for granted in much of the earlier research, no previous investigator appears to have faced it squarely and developed its implications systematically.

Logically embodied in the concept of ethnocentrism are a number of subsidiary corollaries:

(1) individuals should reject a given minority group *consistently* on a variety of dimensions (social distance, disparagement of abilities, etc.);

(2) individuals should *consistently* reject members of *all* ethnic outgroups;

(3) individuals who reject ethnic outgroups should *reify* ethnic ingroups.

In the original investigations of anti-Semitism the authors of *The Authoritarian Personality* constructed five subscales. These were that Jews were personally offensive, socially threatening, that attitudes toward Jews as a group were discriminatory, that Jews were too seclusive, and finally that Jews were too intrusive. No claim was made for the subscales being statistically or contentwise independent. (p. 62). Inter-correlations among these five subscales ranged from .74 to .85 indicating a generality of prejudice which led to acceptance of logically incompatible items on the part of prejudiced subjects (Table 8 (III), p. 75).

Another indication of consistent rejection of Jews on different sorts of measures of prejudice may be found in a study by Morse and Allport.[31] Three measures were used. The first was a measure of *hostility* determined by the most extreme statement (as rated inde-

---

[31] Morse, Nancy C. and Allport, F. H., 'The causation of anti-Semitism: An investigation of seven hypotheses," *The Journal of Psychology*, 1952, 34, 197-233.

pendently by 50 judges) accepted of twelve alternatives in response to seven hypothetical situations, such as reaction to increasing numbers of Jewish business leaders in the community. A second measure was that of "anti-locution" derived from a scale permitting degree of agreement or disagreement with six adjectives describing Jews (half of the adjectives were favorable and half were unfavorable according to judges' ratings). A third measure of *aversion* was obtained through eliciting agreement or disagreement with a statement indicating a desire to move away from a Jewish person (presumably in a social situation).

The correlation coefficient between hostility and ascription of unfavorable adjectives to Jews (*non* "anti-locution") was $+.635$, between hostility and aversion $+.635$, and between non-anti-locution and aversion $+.42$. In short, individuals who displayed hostility toward Jews in hypothetical situations also tended to apply disparaging adjectives to Jews in general and did not desire physical proximity to Jewish persons.

A more direct attack on the problem of interrelatedness of various expressions of prejudice was made by Campbell and McCandless.[32] The Campbell Xenophobia Scale was given to 179 college students selected to represent a cross-section of the student population at San Francisco State College. The scale contained 125 items, each of which could be accepted or rejected on a four point scale. Blocks of 25 items referred to English, Japanese, Jewish, Mexican, and Negroes in parallel statements. On the 25 items referring to each minority group five each were in the areas of *affection, blaming, capability, morality,* and *social distance.*

Data are presented in the form of inter-correlations among the five indications of prejudice for all five of the groups. These range from $+.70$ (blame and capability) to $+.87$ (affection and social distance).

The available evidence appears to substantiate the finding in *The Authoritarian Personality* that individuals who react negatively to Jews in a particular fashion also tend to be negative along other dimensions. Further, the study by Campbell and McCandless indicates that this rejection along a multitude of dimensions is a general characteristic of prejudice. If a given ethnic group is disliked, the actual form in which prejudice is expressed appears to be gen-

[32] Campbell, D. T. and McCandless, B. R., "Ethnocentrism, xenophobia, and personality," *Human Relations,* 1951, *4,* 185-192.

eralized to the extent that logically inconsistent statements about the group will be made and accepted as long as they are hostile.

A second point in the consideration of ethnocentrism as a workable concept is the question as to the generality of prejudice toward different ethnic minorities. The intercorrelations among the subscales of the E scale are not presented in *The Authoritarian Personality* except for the initial Form 78. Here the correlations between anti-Semitism, prejudice against Negroes, and "Minorities" (minor political parties, certain religious sects, foreigners, women, Japanese, Okies, criminals, undesirable elements, Filipinos, zootsuiters, insane, and inherently incapable people) (p. 106) ranged from .74 to .76 (Table 6 [IV], p. 113; Table II [IV], p. 122).

Again, the article by Campbell and McCandless affords the best available systematic comparison.[33] The correlations between prejudice toward Japanese, Jews, Mexicans, and Negroes range from .66 (Jewish and Mexican)[34] to .75 (Mexican and Negro). The correlations for the English and the other four ethnic groups are lower and range from .32 (English and Negroes) to .47 (English and Jews). All of these correlations are far beyond the one per cent level of confidence and indicate that prejudice toward one ethnic minority is related to prejudice toward another. Other studies have, of course, yielded similar results.

Prothro,[35] on the other hand, in testing a sample of 383 Louisiana middle-class adults found the correlation between attitudes toward Negroes and Jews to be only .49 (using the Grice-Remmers generalized attitude scale). The Sartain-Bell revision of the Bogardus scale was also given. In investigating possible reasons why this correlation was lower than that reported in *The Authoritarian Personality* he noted that the distributions of scatter diagrams were strongly heteroscedastic and that the relationships were essentially triangular. Prothro notes:

> "The person in our sample who was favorable toward the Negro was rarely unfavorable toward other groups. We might justifiably consider such persons democratic, nonethnocentric. The person in our sample who was antagonistic toward other

---

[33] Campbell, D. T. and McCandless, B. R., *op. cit.*

[34] This is the writer's interpretation of Table 1, p. 191, *op. cit.* There appears to be a misprint in the title of the ninth column in the table.

[35] Protho, E. T., "Ethnocentrism and anti-Negro attitudes in the deep South," *The Journal of Abnormal and Social Psychology*, 1952, 47, 105-108.

groups was rarely favorable toward the Negro. We might consider him anti-democratic, ethnocentric. Highly ethnocentric persons and persons low on ethnocentrism are probably found in the South as elsewhere. Yet it must not be overlooked that there are many Southerners who are anti-Negro though not otherwise ethnocentric."[36]

In general it appears that the person who is prejudiced against one minority group will also be prejudiced against others. However, situational factors which select one group as an especial target of animosity for historical or economic reasons may lead to expressions of prejudice toward the culturally selected target of animosity without concomitant hostility being directed toward other ethnic groups.

The third consideration in regard to the definition of ethnocentrism is the reification of ingroups in conjunction with the rejection of ethnic outgroups. A "patriotism" subscale was included in the original (Form 78) E scale. Although some individual items might be interpreted as falling in the "minorities" cluster, e.g., disparaging remarks about Mexicans, Germans, Japanese, European refugees, etc., (Table 3 [IV], p. 108) they may also be broadly considered as reflecting patriotism of the professional variety. This "patriotism" scale correlated .69 with anti-Semitism, .83 with the Minorities subscale and .76 with the Negro subscale.

Morse and Allport[37] report a much purer test of the "patriotism" hypothesis. They used six questions designed to test the "national involvement" of their subjects. All of the statements utilized appear to reflect directly such a dimension; each statement could be accepted or rejected along a six point scale.

The correlation between hostility scores toward Jews and national involvement was +.50. Somewhat lower but suggestive (significant at the .05 level) correlations were found between national involvement and the anti-locution and aversion measures employed. The entire analysis by Morse and Allport is too complex to summarize in the present context, but in partialing out the effects of other hypothesized causal variables they found that significant relationships still held between national involvement and hostility toward Jews.

---
[36] Ibid., p. 107.
[37] Morse, Nancy C. and Allport, F. H. *op. cit.*

Another variable tested by these authors was that of differential loyalty to Americans. Three situations were presented in which a group was in trouble. The three groups were defined as "foreigners" under one set of testing conditions and as Americans under another. Greater willingness to help Americans rather than other groups was considered as a measure of loyalty to Americans. This factor correlated positively with the three measures of prejudice toward Jews and the relationships were generally significant with other variables partialed out.

It thus appears that there is some reason for assuming that the "patriotic" items on the M subscale of the E scale are part of a reification of ingroup dominance. However, it is unclear to what extent such reification applies to smaller functional ingroups rather than to such comprehensive terms as the nation and other Americans. Only one of the final E scale items refers to "one's own family"; the other items referring to the ingroup have "America" as the referent (Table 19 (IV), p. 142).

The research results to date indicate that the concept of ethnocentrism is supported in that (1) individuals who display one form of prejudice toward a specific ethnic minority or minorities also tend to display other forms of prejudice, (2) prejudice toward one ethnic minority is usually (although not invariably) accompanied by prejudice toward other ethnic minorities, and (3) that the ethnic ingroup is reified to the extent that patriotic and nationalistic sentiments are related to rejection of ethnic minorities. It should be emphasized that the above are general findings; ethnocentrism is by no means uni-dimensional and we do not know the discrete dimensions of prejudice. We can accept ethnocentrism as a working concept with the understanding that it cannot yet be defined with absolute precision.

Let us now consider the relationship between the two major scales developed by the California investigators: the F and the E scales. There is no point in listing all the investigations in which these two scales have been administered to various samples. Countless college students have been exposed to them; undoubtedly there may be colleges whose students have escaped being tested but the writer knows of none where the scales have not been administered at one time or another. Although most of these investigations have not been published it appears safe to assume that in no case was a negative correlation found between the two scales. The roughly twenty studies of the relationship between the two scales with which the author is familiar have invariably yielded significantly positive correlations.

The E and F scales (or modifications thereof) have been given to samples of college students in various parts of the United States, to representative samples of communities in geographically diverse areas, to high school students in various areas, and to samples of adults characterized by heterogeneity in certain attributes. The correlations obtained range from approximately $+$ 0.30 to 0.85, the range determined both by the number and kind of scale items utilized as well as the relative heterogeneity of the samples tested.

Hyman and Sheatsley[38] have previously indicated that the method utilized in constructing the F scale was one which might lead to enhanced correlations between it and the E scale. In addition, they noted that certain items on the two scales were practically interchangeable. An additional factor which might lead to spurious correlation between the two scales is the identical format of items in which acceptance is always related to authoritarianism and ethnocentrism and rejection of the items to equalitarianism and tolerance. In other words a set to accept or reject items irrespective of content might account for part of the correlation. It is therefore a matter of some importance to determine if the universally positive correlations between the two scales are artifacts or if they reflect a genuine relationship.

The most precise answer to the above considerations may be found in the study by Campbell and McCandless.[39] In addition to the Campbell Xenophobia scale which was constructed independently of the E and F scales and which tapped only prejudice against various ethnic groups, the full E and F scales were also given. The correlation between the F and E scales was .73, between F and Xenophobia 0.60 (these are uncorrected for attenuation, corrected they are 0.77 and 0.62 respectively). One is led to conclude that in this case (and probably most others) the correlation between the E and F scales reflects an accentuation of the "true" correlation between relatively "pure" ethnic prejudice and those personality factors tapped by the F scale. Despite this degree of spuriousness, *it should be emphasized that the F scale is still highly significantly correlated with prejudice toward ethnic minorities per se.*

---

[38] See the preceding chapter.
[39] Campbell, D. T. and McCandless, B. R. *op. cit.*

A study reported by Srole[40] also contains relevant data. A sample of 401 individuals in Springfield, Massachusetts were given a five item abreviated form of the F scale and were also given a social distance scale, the referent for the latter being unspecified minority groups. A correlation of approximately $+ 0.39$ between the two was found.[41] In this case there is no possibility of a spurious correlation since the social distance scale was devised independently of the F scale and the mechanics of answering are quite different.

A different approach was taken by Cogan.[42] Among a series of thirteen attitude scales administered en bloc to college classes were two relevant to the present discussion: *hypersubmission to authority* and *rejecting outgroups*. Cogan's definition of authoritarianism was narrower than that embodied in the F scale. All items in the hypersubmission to authority scale refer directly to authorities (policemen, teachers, etc.); acceptance of the items indicates a servile attitude toward the explicitly authoritarian referents. The rejection-of-outgroup scale specified only Jews and Negroes as referents.

The Pearsonian correlation between the two scales was $+ .26$. Although modest, the correlation is significant, indicating that even an extremely narrow (a logical rather than psychological) definition of authoritarianism still supports the Berkeley findings. Of further interest in Cogan's report is a factor analysis of all thirteen sub-scales. After a blind rotation one of the factors which emerged was dubbed "authoritarianism personality dimension" and contained the hypersubmission to authority scale cited above. Another factor which emerged was entitled, "paranoid ethnocentrism," which contained the rejection-of-outgroup scale. These two factors correlated $+ .26$. Inspection of the other scales indicates that the authoritarianism personality dimension was considerably different from that tapped by the F scale. This is the most probable reason for the relatively low correlation between factors.

---

[40] Srole, L., "Social dysfunction, personality and social distance attitudes." Unpublished paper read before the American Sociological Society Meeting, 1951.

[41] This figure represents the writer's calculation of a coefficient of contingency — based upon a recombination of Srole's tables — which was converted to a Pearsonian approximation.

[42] Cogan, E. A. *The Interrelationships Among Social Attitudes as a Function of Personality Variables.* Unpublished doctoral dissertation, University of California at Los Angeles, 1951.

Cogan's factor of "paranoid" ethnocentrism appears upon closer inspection to be more descriptive than truly pathological. The items reflect a suspicion of and hostility toward others. Other statistical and nonstatistical findings, however, indicate an affinity between a lack of such hostile tendencies and lack of prejudice. An examination of the cluster analysis reported by Christie and Garcia[43] indicates that the lowest correlation between any of the seven F scale clusters in the California sample and the E scale is .15, between the cluster entitled "Fatalism" and the latter. The content of the fatalism cluster indicates that the external factors controlling human destiny are all powerful (people born with urge to jump from high places, earthquake or flood will destroy the world, astrology can explain a lot of things). This somewhat somber outlook apparently is passively accepted as the natural state of affairs since the other item falling in the cluster refers to the fact that books and movies should concentrate on themes that are entertaining or uplifting instead of unpleasant (small wonder!).

In short, the content of the cluster indicates a conviction of the inevitability of dire happenings. However, such acceptance appears tempered by a sense of futility at trying to do anything about the situation and an escape from prolonged consideration of it. From this standpoint the relatively low correlation with the E scale might well be interpreted as indicating that prejudice is similarly accepted as inevitable; there is no reason therefore to reject prejudice or on the other hand to vent aggression against minority groups because they are responsible for the generally deplorable state of the world. Such an interpretation is tenuous and speculative; however, the Southwest City clusters hint that a similar relationship holds in that sample. Of the eight clusters found the two with the lowest correlation with the E scale (again .15) included the one entitled, "Voluntary Acceptance of Censorship." The latter consisted of two items, one that it was essential for teachers or bosses to outline what is to be done and the other the item relating to the preferred pollyannish content of books and movies.

Turning to another facet of the problem, Ackerman and Jahoda[44]

---

[43] Christie, R. and Garcia, J., *op. cit.*
[44] Ackerman, N. W. and Jahoda, M., *Anti-Semitism and Emotional Disorder*, Harpers, New York, 1950.

report on forty case histories of individuals who were psychoanalyzed in New York. They note, "In this broad range of diagnoses and vague symptoms, however, one type of disturbance becomes conspicuous through its absence. None of the cases manifested a genuine, deep *depression*." (italics in original). Parenthetically, it might be noted that the reason depression was conspicuous by its absence is the general observation among the psychoanalysts from whose files the case histories were obtained that depression was perhaps the most common syndrome among those individuals who sought and continued analysis.

It is suggestive that the empirically derived statistical clusters on presumably normal populations indicate that the lowest correlation between them and the E scale is among those which reflect what appears to be a highly passive orientation toward the world. Whether this passive and nonpunitive orientation is related to the clinical syndrome of depression among more acutely disturbed individuals is problematic; however, it is clear that a nonaggressive attitude toward the world in general is involved.

This evidence is in accord with the relevant material in *The Authoritarian Personality*. Chapter XXII, "Psychological Ill Health in Relation to Potential Fascism: A study of Psychiatric Clinic Patients" contains a methodologically impeccable analysis of differences between high and low scores on the E scale in a sample of psychiatric clinic patients. In summary, it is noted, "The most common single symptom characteristic of low-scoring men and women was neurotic depression with feelings of inadequacy." (p. 964). This contrasts with the summary statement regarding high scorers, "Rigidity of personality and the tendency to use countercathective defenses seem to be characteristic of both high-scoring men and high-scoring women." (p. 964).

Another approach to the personality characteristics of anti-Semitic high school students was made by Gough.[45] The anti-Semitism scale developed by the California investigators was given to a class of 271 high school seniors. The forty highest and the forty lowest scorers were selected from this sample. An item analysis of the Minnesota Multiphasic Personality Inventory was undertaken upon these two subsamples. Of the 550 items in the Minnesota Multiphasic Inventory, the 47 which differentiated between the two subsamples

---

[45] Gough, H. G., "Studies of social intolerance: II A personality scale for anti-Semitism," *The Journal of Social Psychology*, 1951, 33, 247-255.

at or beyond the five per cent level were selected. These items were then given in conjunction with other scales to a new class of 263 high school seniors. Two criterion subsamples from this group of 38 extremely anti-Semitic and 38 non-anti-Semitic students were selected and it was found that 32 of the 47 items differentiating the original groups also differentiated the criterion groups. These 32 items were combined into a Pr (prejudice) scale. This correlated .49 with the AS scale in the first senior class and .45 with the AS scale in the second senior class. Correlations with the F^{46} scale were .46 and .43 respectively.

An inspection of the items by Gough suggested a number of factors characteristic of the more prejudiced students. According to Gough these were: anti-intellectuality, a pervading sense of pessimism and lack of hope and confidence in the future; feelings of cynicism, distrust, doubt, and suspicion; a diffuse misanthropy and querulousness; a hostile and bitter outlook which verged on destructiveness; a grumbling and discontented evaluation of their current status; a rigid, somewhat dogmatic style of thinking; a lack of poise and self-assurance; and an underlying perplexity related to a feeling that something dreadful is about to happen. Gough summarizes his inspection of the differentiating items by saying:

"The overall picture which emerges from these item clusters is one of a harassed, tormented, resentful, peevish, querulous, constricted, disillusioned, embittered, distrustful, rancorous, apprehensive, and somewhat bewildered person. The syndrome is almost paranoid in its intensity, but is not equatable to paranoid for it lacks the excessive circumstantiality and self-deluding aspects of the latter. Nevertheless it is clear that a set of characteristics such as those listed must be quasi—or near—pathological in its distorting and incapacitating implications for personality."[47]

In view of the preceding discussion regarding the apparent incompatibility of depression and prejudice, the findings on the Depression subscale of the Minnesota Multiphasic by both Gough and the California investigators are of interest. Contrary to what might be expected in light of the previous discussion, Gough found a positive correlation of +.16 between the AS scale and the Depression scale (the sample being the 271 students in the first high school

---
[46] See footnote 28.
[47] Gough, H. G., op. cit., p. 253:

class tested). The California investigators similarly found among the Langley Porter Clinic subjects who had taken the Minnesota Multiphasic, that those scoring high in Ethnocentrism scored higher on the Depression subscale than did those scoring low on the E scale. This was especially marked in the case of the male subjects. In attempting to determine why the low scoring subjects who appeared clinically depressed were not depressed as measured by a standardized test, the 60 items in the Depression subscale of the Minnesota Multiphasic were examined and categorized. Twenty-three of the items were considered as referring:

"to the kind of feelings reported by our low subjects, these were:

1. Signs of inferiority feelings, easily hurt, unhappy, self-criticisms.
2. Opposition to cruelty and aggressiveness, lack of extrapunitiveness.
3. Submissive reactions in social situations.
4. Admission of uneasiness in social situations.
5. Lack of energy, and work inhibition.
6. Rejection of religious ideas (possibly).

"The other 37 items referred to: impairment of mental functioning and of body functions; brooding and "worrying;" perception of the environmental forces as threatening or mistreating the subject; and general expressions of "not feeling well," "don't care about anything." Many of these items, pertaining as they do to very vague and nonspecific ideas, are clinically more consistent with *anxiety* or with anxious rumination of the more obsessive-compulsive variety than with neurotic depression." (pp. 916-17, italics in original).

Three of the 32 items from the Minnesota Multiphasic Inventory which Gough found to be related to anti-Semitism deal with admission of uneasiness in social situations; "It makes me uncomfortable to put on a stunt at a party even when others are doing the same sort of thing," "In school I found it very hard to talk before the class," and "I refuse to play at some games because I am not good at them."[48] None of the other items appear to bear any close relationship to the other five categories believed characteristic of neurotic depression by the Berkeley investigators.

It would appear from the preceding discussion that statements about the relationship between personality factors as measured by

---

[48] Ibid, Table 2, pp. 251-52.

general scales or inventories and prejudice are of dubious validity. The acceptance of *any* statement indicative of neurotic or psychotic tendencies does not necessarily imply that statements indicative of prejudice toward minority groups will also be accepted. Less than six per cent of the items on the Minnesota Multiphasic were found to differentiate between those high and low in anti-Semitism by Gough. He also gave the Maslow Security-Insecurity scale to the initial class of high school seniors and found that it correlated only + .09 with the AS scale. However, as Gough has demonstrated it is possible to isolate items which are correlated with anti-Semitism and construct a scale which does tap those personality tendencies which are related to prejudice.

Available evidence confirms rather than runs counter to the speculations of Ackerman and Jahoda in accounting for the lack of cases of depression among the psychoanalytic cases characterized by anti-Semitism:

> "But the qualitative insight gained from the study of all cases leads us to believe that the absence of depression in the material is more than an accident due to the limited number of cases. For the existence of an anti-Semitic reaction presupposes a tendency to blame the outside world rather than one's own self, and, dynamically, such a tendency is in contradiction to the self-destructive features of a genuine depression. It would seem that when the focus of punitive tendencies is directed back towards the self, the basis for anti-Semitic aggressions no longer exists."[49]

Two studies contained reports on the relationship between Rorschach protocols and prejudice. The first of these by Reichard[50] was conducted with fifteen college women who scored in the upper quartile of the California E scale and fifteen women from the low quartile. These were apparently part of the sample studied and reported in *The Authoritarian Personality*. The Rorschach protocols of these two subgroups were scored and compared. Of 49 comparisons of various categories of responses, only one, the number of movement responses, proved to be significant, this at the .02 level. (One such difference would be predicted by chance with this many comparisons). A further examination of the differences led to the selection of six Rorschach signs as characteristic of the prejudiced

---

[49] Ackerman, N. W. and Jahoda, M., *op cit.*, p: 26.

[50] Reichard, Suzanne, "Rorschach study of prejudiced personality," *American Journal of Orthopsychiatry*, 1948, *18*, 280-286.

students, these being (1) less than 20 responses, (2) less than three movement responses, (3) less than five color responses (of any sort), (4) less than three original responses, (5) less than fifteen per cent definitely bad responses, and (6) no fabulated combinations.

Twelve of the 15 prejudiced subjects showed four or more of these signs in contrast to only three of the 15 unprejudiced students (this difference is significant at the .01 level of confidence). Reichard's cautious summary indicates that in contrast to the unprejudiced subjects the prejudiced subjects showed less interest in thinking, less capacity for empathy and insight, were less productive mentally, less responsive emotionally, less original, and tended to be more inhibited and compulsively over-meticulous. Expected differences in the areas of stereotypy, conformity to group thinking, and overt anxiety did not emerge. Reichard believes that the Rorschach test has limitations in the study of prejudice because it is a method of studying structure rather than dynamics and it is the latter which is important in understanding the genesis of prejudiced attitudes.

Aside from the general congruence of Reichard's findings with those in *The Authoritarian Personality*, two cautions are in order. First, at least two of the differentiating signs are related to intelligence and there is reason to believe that even among a college population a modest negative correlation between intelligence and acceptance of prejudice exists.[51] The second is that almost any test or scale can be given to samples differentiated by an external criterion and some items on the test will usually be accepted by more of one sample than another. Before any assurance can be maintained that these items are reliable differentiators it is necessary to cross-validate them on a new sample and re-examine the relationship between them and the external criterion.

A more extensive development of Rorschach scoring for authoritarianism by Himmelhoch has been alluded to.[52] Two subgroups of 30 each were drawn from the extreme quartiles on both the E and F subscales in a sample of 160 New York University students. An inspection of group Rorschach protocols indicated that the employment of traditional Rorschach categories did not significantly differentiate between the two subgroups. In consequence,

---

[51] See Section IV following.
[25] Himmelhoch, J., *op. cit.*

Himmelhoch turned to the ideational content of the Rorschach responses and proceeded to develop a new scoring system based upon hypotheses regarding the differences between those high and low in prejudice. These served as guides in the empirical comparison of differences between the two groups. Seventy-five indicators were finally prepared and only those which discriminated between the two groups at the .05 level or better were retained. Subsequent revisions were designed to achieve greater discrimination, brevity, and theoretical adequacy. The final form utilized the responses to only five of the ten Rorschach cards and a protocol could be scored in less than 10 minutes.

Six subscales were utilized: (1) identification with male self-figures, (2) identification with female self-figures, (3) identification with other figures, (4) hostility tensions, (5) status tensions, and (6) sensuality tensions. All six subscales differentiated significantly between high and low scorers in the original population; the sensuality tension subscale was most discriminating and the identification with female self-figures least.

A new sample of 30 students was given the E and F scales and the group Rorschach test. Prior to the scoring of the questionnaires two raters independently used Himmelhoch's Rorschach "Self-Acceptance Scale" and another rater (a professional Rorschach worker) independently scored the Rorschach protocols utilizing conventional scoring. She was instructed to categorize the subjects in degree of ethnic prejudice as inferred from the Rorschach. The scores on the questionnaire were then computed and correlated with the Rorschach scores. The correlations between the E scale and the two independent ratings using the modified Rorschach scoring technique were .74 and .76 respectively. No significant relationships were found between the evaluations of prejudice on the basis of conventional Rorschach scoring procedures and E scale scores.

It might be reasonably concluded that a somewhat similar state of affairs pertains to the relationship between the Rorschach and ethnic prejudice as was previously noted in discussing personality inventories. Apparently, most of the scales when utilized in their customary fashion display at best a slight and tenuous relationship to prejudice. However, prejudice is related to certain aspects of personal functioning tapped by such measures and it is possible to develop new modifications of the scales which correlate significantly with measures of prejudice.

These findings substantially corroborate the contention of the Berkeley investigators that there is a relationship between certain aspects of personality and ethnic prejudice. They utilized ratings of clinical interviews, results on the Thematic Apperception Test, projective sentences, and psychiatric case records in demonstrating the relationship. Although their results are impressive, a note might be added in regard to their findings which are not covered in their discussion and which indicate that they might have presented an even stronger case.

Material is presented in Part II of *The Authoritarian Personality* on the intensive analysis of the clinical interviews of 80 subjects selected from the larger sample. Of these 41 had been tested on the earliest version of the E, F, and PEC scales (Form 78), three on the intermediate Form 60, and 34 on the final Form 45.[53] The subjects were selected for interviewing shortly after taking the questionnaire (p. 25). Those who took the Form 78 were interviewed during the first five months of 1945, those taking Forms 40 and 45 from November, 1945 to June, 1946 (p. 21).

Although it is not specifically stated it appears that the ratings were made after the collection of all the interviews. The raters were able to make more accurate judgments as to the ethnic prejudice of subjects who had taken the Form 45. A number of reasons might be advanced as possible explanations for this difference. The following table indicates the relationship between the number of "pure" and "mixed" cases and the percentage of correct judgments made by the raters. A "pure" case is an interviewee who scored in the same extreme quartile on the E, F, and PEC scales; a "mixed" case one who scored in different quartiles on the differing scales. It would appear a reasonable hypothesis that individuals who were consistent in their ideology as indicated by scale scores consistently in the same quartile would be more readily identified by a consistency of personality in their clinical interviews. Since the interviewees who received the Form 45 were 65 per cent "pure" cases in contrast to

---

[53] These figures are obtained by comparing the identification of the subjects in Tables 1 and 2 (IX), pp. 296-297, with the form of the scale given to the groups from which they were selected as determined from Table 1 (I), pp. 21-22. It was impossible to determine the form taken by two of the subjects (M 44 and F 70) since the samples from which they are drawn are not listed in the initial table of groups tested by questionnaires. It is assumed that F 75 listed as coming from a "PW" group is actually from the professional women's group identified as "RW."

only 37 per cent of those receiving the Form 78 the improved predictability hypothetically might be attributed to this sampling difference.

TABLE VIII

PER CENT OF CORRECT JUDGMENTS AS TO
INTERVIEWEES' ETHNIC PREJUDICE

Questionnaire Taken by Interviewee

	Form 78	Form 45	Totals
Pure Cases	80 (n = 15)	91 (n = 22)	86 (n = 37)
Mixed Cases	77 (n = 26)/78	92 (n = 12)/91	82 (n = 38)/84
Totals	(n = 41)	(n = 34)	(n = 75)

Table VIII indicates that the raters did practically as well on the mixed cases as on the pure ones. This leads us to look elsewhere for an explanation. It does not appear to be attributable to sex differences on the part of the interviewees (34 of 40 males were correctly rated, 33 of 40 females) nor to differential numbers of interviews from the two samples on the part of the two raters (p. 328). The most likely answer is that the interview protocols collected on the subjects interviewed at a later date (and who took the Form 45) were more complete. An indication of this may be found in the discussion of discriminating scoring categories on the interviews, "The fact that the categories were generally somewhat more discriminatory in the case of the men than in the case of the women may be accounted for by the fact that most of the men were interviewed at a later stage of the study and that therefore *their records were more complete.*" (pp. 335-36, italics not in original).[54]

The reason why interviews collected later in the study were more complete is not clearly explained in *The Authoritarian Personality*. It appears likely, however, that there was a constant interplay between questionnaire results and the more clinically oriented techniques. For example, in describing the construction of the F scale, it is noted that, "Available for the purpose was the following material: . . . and by far the most important, material from the interviews and the Thematic Apperception Tests." (p. 225) Apparently

---

[54] Although this may explain why accuracy of identification improved over time, it does not explain the lack of difference between "pure" and "mixed" cases. A possible explanation will be found in Section V.

the results of a given questionnaire were used to refine the scoring procedures for various clinical measures, results from the latter were utilized in conjunction with item analysis of the scales to refine the next version of the scale, etc. The progressive refinement led to increasingly greater accuracy in isolating—on the basis of material not explicitly referring to ethnic groups—those who were prejudiced. The authors were so busy improving their instruments that they never finally came to the point of freezing them and then cross-validating them on a new sample—with the apparent exception of the material on projective questions.

The combining of the results of the earlier interviews with the later ones does the authors a disservice since the inclusion of the earlier ones in the totals hides the fact that the later blind ratings of interview protocols discriminated nine out of ten subjects as to membership in high or low quartiles on a scale measuring ethnic prejudice.

Upon the basis of available data, it may be concluded that the general point of view regarding the relationship between personality characteristics and ethnic prejudice developed in *The Authoritarian Personality* has been substantiated by subsequent research. Inasmuch as the Berkeley investigators did not cross-validate their findings and since no one has replicated their clinical scoring techniques it is not clear exactly how right they are. What might be termed the lowest common denominators of the personality attributes of the prejudiced person, among the samples studied, at least, are a relatively low level of mental functioning (probably partly due to low IQ and partly due to inadequate utilization of actual capacity), a hostile view of the social world and a degree of fear of the physical one, an inability to release successfully emotional affect in interpersonal relations, and an inability to accept oneself. These are uncomfortable people in an unpleasant and unpredictable world.

The above statements err on the side of caution. But one must be cautious with the place of facts in a world of values. The presence of a relationship between certain aspects of personality and ethnic prejudice does not mean that the latter can be completely predicted or explained in terms of the former. The writer would estimate that the "true" correlation in middle-class American samples between those aspects of the personality captured by the F scale and prejudice toward minority groups would range somewhere between + .50 and + .60.⁵⁵ If true, the coefficient of determination would account for roughly a quarter or a third of the total variance. It remains for future research to determine whether more refined personality measures will permit more accurate estimates of prejudice or whether the social scientist may most profitably look for other presumed causal concomitants of ethnic prejudice.

IV

The relationship between the cultural sophistication of a subject and the nature of his response to a question or scale item is a highly complicated matter. Through long experience, social scientists have come to be especially sensitive to this factor. Consistently high correlations between attitudinal dimensions and years of education, scores on intelligence tests (based largely on what is learned in school), and various other socio-economic criteria have been found.

Although the authors of *The Authoritarian Personality* realized that their sample was relatively homogeneous with regard to the complex of variables making up its essential middle-class nature, they deemed it wise to add a chapter (VIII) on "Ethnocentrism in relation to Intelligence and Education." The general emphasis is upon the low although consistent negative relationship between indices of high socio-economic status and ethnocentrism. The difficulty of interpretation is revealed in the sentence, "It is not clear which is more important: that the correlation is greater than zero, or that it is at best not far from zero." (p. 287). This summary statement fits neatly with the material presented; however, it may be questioned whether it can be applied to a wider range of groups as is implied when the authors say: "In addition, it is not likely that such sampling factors have distorted to any appreciable degree the relationships among the variables of ideology, personality, and group membership under investigation." (p. 288).

By holding education relatively constant the authors have been able to demonstrate relationships between the misanthropic *Weltanschauung* captured by the F scale and the more specific anti-

---

⁵⁵ Higher correlations reported on the E and F scales for some samples probably reflect a slight spuriousness due to the correlated item selection in their construction. Lower ones have usually been found when an abbreviated F scale or crude measure of prejudice was used.

168 The Authoritarian Personality

minority prejudices tapped by the E scale. When E scale or F scale scores are adduced to have low correlations with high socio-economic status for the general population or to have low intercorrelations in all socio-economic groupings it is important to examine the relevant material.

In few studies are investigators able to give subjects standardized intelligence tests although they usually can obtain such scores in the rare instances in which they have been given to the samples. In three cases in which the samples studied had routinely been given tests it is possible to compare the correlation between the *range* of intelligence sampled and F scale acceptance. Since various tests have differing standard deviations the comparisons in the following table have been based upon the standard deviation of the test given.

TABLE IX
THE RELATIONSHIP BETWEEN RANGE OF INTELLIGENCE SAMPLED AND F SCALE SCORES

Investigator	Sample	N	Intelligence Measure	Approximate Range in Standard Deviations[a]	Correlation: IQ and F scale
Adorno, et al[b]	Maritime School Men	342	AGGT	2.5	—.20
Adorno, et al[c]	Employment Service Veteran Men	104	Otis	4.1	—.48
Christie[d]	Army Recruits	182	Aptitude Area I	4.4	—.48

a. Calculations made by the writer.
b. Data obtained from Table 1 (VIII), p. 282.
c. Data obtained from Table 2 (VIII), p. 283.
d. Christie, *op. cit.*

What is of pertinence in the preceding table is the increased correlation found between intelligence measures and F scale scores as the range of intelligence measured increases. If the relationship is linear, it might be expected that in the population as a whole with a range from roughly —3.0 to +3.0 standard deviations (a range of six S. D.s) the correlation would approach —.60. Such an interpretation would appear to be in disagreement with the point of view expressed in *The Authoritarian Personality*. In referring to the correlation of —.48 between IQ and F scale scores found in the "Employment Service Veteran Men" the following evaluation is made: "Further study is required to determine whether or not the *r* of —.48 is spurious or exceptional." (p. 284). The present interpretation is that the correlation found is *neither spurious nor exceptional;* it simply reflects the statistical truism that the greater the range of ability sampled the more likely correlations between one attribute and another can be demonstrated in those cases where a relationship exists.

It is somewhat simpler to obtain years of education than IQ. Most field research takes advantage of this fact so that a crude measure may be obtained by ascertaining the number of years of schooling of a respondent.

Most studies utilizing the F scale have been conducted on educationally homogeneous samples. It was possible, however, to utilize material from four unpublished studies to determine the nature of the relationship between education and acceptance of F scale scores in more heterogeneous samples. (See Table X, p. 170).

Apparently a sizable negative correlation exists between education and acceptance of F scale items. In Rokeach's and Srole's studies, each of which was based upon one community, an identical negative correlation of —.45 is found. Recruits who were homogeneous in regard to age and sex but came from varied communities in the northeastern United States showed a slightly larger negative correlation between education and F scale scores of —.48 (which was identical with that found between intelligence scores and education as cited in Table IX). The largest negative correlation (—.54) is that estimated for the most hetereogeneous sample, a representative nationwide one. This correlation might have been greater if better F scale items had been used (Two of the five items are not in any version of the F scale reported in *The Authoritarian Personality;* these two have a lower correlation with education than the three genuine F scale items). The consistency of these findings suggests that the relatively low relationships between intelligence and education and F scale scores found by the California investigators are a function of their primarily urban middle-class samples. When relatively homogeneous populations are tested, differences among sample members along the dimensions of homogeneity cannot be expected. In such cases it is more appropriate to relate ob-

TABLE X
THE RELATIONSHIP BETWEEN EDUCATION AND F SCALE SCORES FOR EDUCATIONALLY HETEROGENEOUS SAMPLES

Investigator	Sample	N	Correlation Education and F
Rokeach[a]	Adults, East Lansing, Mich. Obtained in area sample.	86	—.45
Srole[b]	White Christian bus riders in Springfield, Mass. Selected by "modification of the probability sampling method."	397	—.45[c]
Christie[d]	Caucasian inductees in infantry basic training. All men entering training in a given week were selected. Fairly representative of young males in northeastern United States.	182	—.48
NORC-ADL[e]	Representative nationwide sample.	1266	—.54[f]

a. Rokeach, M. Personal communication.
b. Srole, L. *op. cit.*
c. This correlation represents an estimate based upon the writer's computations of Srole's data.
d. Christie, R. *op. cit.*
e. The basic data are presented in Table 4, p. 94. Mr. Paul Sheatsley kindly made the necessary marginals available for analysis.
f. This estimate was arrived at in a rather involved manner. The following steps were taken:
(1) A contingency coefficient of -.24 was computed from the basic data; this represented the *average* correlation of each of the five items with education.
(2) This was converted to a Pearsonian correlation of -.34.
(3) The average inter-item correlation was approximated by solving the equation for partial correlation by inserting the value of .13 for the average inter-item correlation with education held constant (the value of .13 was taken from *The Authoritarian Personality*, p. 261). In this case the partial correlation was known, what was solved was the inter-item correlation in the NORC-ADL sample.
(4) Using the approximate values of each item correlating -.34 with education and +.25 with one another, the correlation of all the items (as a scale) with education was determined by using Thompson's Pooling Squares technique. Dr. John Harding called this technique to the writer's attention.

tained differences to dimensions along which the sample varies. This partially accounts for the fact that personality differences in relation to differential F scale scores were the ones most obvious to the authors of *The Authoritarian Personality*.

Several problems remain, however. First, education is, of course, related to many things besides F scale scores. Older people tend to be less educated than young because of progressively greater opportunities for education; individuals in lower economic strata are less likely to have the opportunities to be motivated for or to obtain education; there are differences in innate intelligence which set ceilings on the amount of education which can be absorbed; there are differential opportunities for education related to geographic areas within the United States; etc. A legitimate question is therefore the extent to which education or intelligence *per se* can be viewed as *independently* related to acceptance of F scale items. No definitive answer can be given. The closest approximation may be determined from the data available on recruits who were homogeneous in age and sex. A partial correlation between intelligence and F scale scores with years of education held constant yields a correlation of —.20. An identical correlation may be obtained between years of education and F scale scores with intelligence held constant.

It will be remembered that in Table IX the correlation between IQ and F scale for the Maritime School Men was —.20. The description of this group indicates that socio-economic background was relatively homogeneous; it is highly probable (although no data are given) that they were fairly homogeneous educationally. Again the sample is composed exclusively of young males. The correlation of —.20 between IQ and F scale scores (with education, sex, and age assumed to be held relatively constant due to sample characteristics) lends support to the relationship found in the sample of recruits. With other variables held constant it appears relatively safe to guess that the correlation between education (or intelligence) and F scale scores will be in the neighborhood of —.20.

A second problem which is of importance is the generalization of the organization of beliefs found in one homogeneous sample to other samples which are also homogeneous but differ in the basis of homogeneity. More specifically, does the relationship between the E and F scales reported on predominantly middle-class samples also apply to samples less culturally sophisticated? The only available approximation to an answer derives from an analysis of Srole's data. He used an abbreviated F scale (five items—unspecified) in conjunction with a social distance scale of five items which referred to minority group members by indirection (however, spontaneous remarks by the respondents during the interview referring directly to minority group members also affected the classification of the respondent along the social distance scale). Holding education constant respondents were dichotomized as to acceptance of F scale items and trichotomized along a social distance continuum (acceptive, ambivalent, and rejective of minority groups).

For Srole's college educated group the correlation between the F scale and prejudice is approximately $+.44$ (an estimate of the Pearsonian correlation from the contingency coefficient computed from a recombination of his tables). This group was presumably the most similar to the sample studied by the Berkeley investigators. The lower correlation than is usually attained by use of the E and F scales may be a result of the different measure of prejudice involved or an abbreviated F scale.

Srole's most different group—the "low education" group composed of those who had less than twelve years of education—yields according to present calculations a correlation of $+.24$. However, this presents a problem in interpretation because five-sixths of the low education group were high authoritarians in Srole's dichotomization as contrasted with forty-two per cent of the college group. It is difficult to know how much reliance to place in the magnitude of the relationship when the sample was so overwhelmingly on the authoritarian side of the dichotomous break. An indication that the true correlation in the sample might be higher is indicated by the fact that a calculation in which the marginals in the low authoritarian group were multiplied by a constant to equate it artificially in size with the high authoritarians led to a table which yielded an approximated correlation of $+.32$. The group intermediate in education, the high school graduates, had an estimated correlation of $+.40$ between the F scale and prejudice. This leads us to suspect that there is a significant correlation between F scale scores and prejudice in lower-class samples although it appears to be less than that found in middle-class samples. Future research directed specifically toward this point is needed, however, before such a conclusion is accepted as final.

One point appears well established. Scores on the F scale vary inversely with various measures of cultural sophistication. How can this finding be best understood?

One obvious explanation would be an extension of the theory of the genesis of authoritarianism advanced in *The Authoritarian Personality*. Differences in child-rearing practices and early sociological environment are known to be associated with socio-economic status.[56] Ericson's data indicate that lower-class children are breast and/or bottle fed longer than middle-class children, they are fed more at will than middle-class children, and bowel and bladder training is begun later (although there were interestingly enough *no* differences in the age at which the training is completed).

Ericson notes, "Middle-class children are probably subjected to more frustrations in the process of achieving these learnings and are probably more anxious as a result of these pressures than are the lower-class children. Lower-class families tend to be more permissive than the middle-class families in the training of their children in all areas."

In relating these findings to the family structure hypothesized to lead to high authoritarianism it is well to recognize that the scoring categories were not directed toward such specific data as the age at which toilet training started but were wisely directed toward the "climate" of the familial setting. In the coding of interviews a "high" father was categorized as *distant,* a *moral-model, pseudo-masculine* (worked his way up, a "success"), *hardworking provider.* A "high" mother was categorized as *sacrificing,* a *moral-model, restricting,* "*Sweet*," *pseudofeminine.* In addition to these individual attributes of parents it was characteristic for children of "high" parents to deny parental conflict, to report discipline for violation of rules, and to report that discipline was "overwhelming" (Interview Scoring Manual: Conceptions of Childhood Environment, pp. 358-359).

The general family constellation described seems to be one in which rather extreme demands might be made upon the infant in the areas of early weaning, toilet training, and discipline.[57] Upon the basis of available data such demands related to high authoritarianism appear much more closely related to middle-class child-

---

[56] Ericson, Martha C., "Social status and child-rearing practices." In Newcomb, T. M. and Hartley, E. L., *Readings in Social Psychology,* Holt, New York, 1947.

[57] In Else Frenkel-Brunswik's chapter the point is made that the warmness and closeness of interpersonal relations are the important variables rather than such factors as time of weaning and of toilet training. With this point the writer is in complete accord. It is suspected, however, that maternal warmth and comfort lead to less strictness in imposition of feeding and toilet training schedules. In other words, the general aura of warmth and affection is the crucial variable in the early environment and premature attempts at training normally reflect an absence of such a general atmosphere.

rearing practices than to those of the lower-class. If the determinants described as relating to high scores on the F scale in *The Authoritarian Personality* were the *only* determinants it would appear a reasonable hypothesis to postulate that a *positive* rather than a *negative* correlation might be found between cultural sophistication (as indicated by IQ and education) and acceptance of F scale items. However, the evidence indicates that the opposite is true. This leads to a consideration of the possible reasons for the differences.

The only person to treat this matter systematically has been Srole[58] and the relevance of his contribution should be carefully considered. Srole was interested in the relationship between anomie (following Durkheim's definition of the term) and prejudice. He constructed an anomie scale designed to tap the internalized counterpart of external social dysfunction, disorganization, demoralization, and group alienation. Some 30 items were initially pretested and five were finally selected as an anomie scale. The results are reported as indicating that there was a positive relationship between positive responses to the anomie scale and to the abbreviated F scale used (writer's calculations indicate the correlation approximates $+.58$). He also reports that a latent structure analysis indicated that the anomie scale tapped a fairly unidimensional continuum and that the anomie and F scales used comprised separate latent structures, i.e., tapped different dimensions. Srole's primary point was that among less educated sample members the relationship between anomie and prejudice (as measured by his social distance scale) was predominant; among highly educated sample members similar to the subjects reported in *The Authoritarian Personality* the relationship between authoritarianism and prejudice was most important.

Srole's findings neatly fit with a plausible explanation for the markedly negative relationship between measures of cultural sophistication and F scale items. It has been previously indicated that the meaning of the F scale items is not universal among geographically different samples equated in terms of socio-economic criteria. It appears equally likely that their meaning would vary among populations of varying sophistication. Inasmuch as many of the F scale items are semi-projective there appears good reason to assume that the referents would differ among individuals drawn

---

[58] Srole, L. *op. cit.*

from different social backgrounds whose experience with the symbols embodied in the F scale are quite different. The statement, "There are two kinds of people in the world: the weak and the strong" might have quite different implications for those whose class membership places them among the "strong," i.e., middle-class, and the "weak," i.e., lower-class. It is a reasonable hypothesis that those in a favorable hierarchical position are not as aware of the discrepancy in freedom of action or of their own privileges as those who are constantly faced with the reality of status differences. In illustration, only 35 per cent of a cross-section of officers during World War II agreed with the statement, "If enlisted men have to observe curfew, officers should too." In contrast, 84 per cent of the enlisted men agreed with the statement.[59]

Anyone familiar with lower socio-economic groupings can scarcely be unaware of the fact that there is realistic justification for their view that the world is indeed junglelike and capricious. They have no relatives or friends with the power to intercede successfully when they are rightly or wrongly accused of legal offenses. Even relatively minor figures in the hierarchy of power are identified with omnipotent forces—police officers are referred to as "The Law" (at least in the Southwest)—and there is always the possibility of being arbitrarily accused of some offense and having no recourse.

The acceptance of an item referring to people prying into personal affairs may reflect paranoid tendencies among middle-class respondents; it may be reality based among lower-class individuals who are the first to be questioned by police, social workers, and other functionaries of the social structure.

It is a tenable hypothesis that a basic reason for the greater acceptance of F scale items among members of lower socio-economic groupings as contrasted with middle-class individuals is related to the reality of the referent in the items. Such an interpretation is even more plausible for Srole's anomie scale since it reflects social dysfunctioning. (According to our calculations the correlation between educational level and anomie in Srole's sample approximates $-.36$.)

If membership in various educational strata is closely related to the degree of acceptance of F scale items, it might be expected that membership in face to face groups would be even more important. It is necessary at this point to return to *The Authoritarian Personal-*

---
[59] *The American Soldier,* Vol. 1, Adjustment during Army Life, p. 374.

ity for two reasons. First, the discussion regarding the relationship between group membership and individual ideology in that volume strongly emphasizes the lack of importance of group membership as a factor in the determination of individual ideology. Secondly, the best available data upon the relationship between face to face group membership and the interrelatedness of attitudes may be found in its tables.

The explicit definition of group utilized in *The Authoritarian Personality* is spelled out:

"The term "group" is used in the widest sense to mean any set of people who constitute a psychological entity for any individual. If we regard the individual's conception of the social world as a sort of map containing various differentiated regions, then each region can be considered a group." (p. 146)

Thus all persons whose fathers are reported as being "Labor (skilled and unskilled)" (Table 20 (V), p. 205) are lumped under the rubric of a group. Again, in discussing the political self-identification of the respondents, the authors refer to such a category as "Wilkie (sic) Republicans" (Table 12 [V], pp. 188-89) as a group. In relating political group membership to E scale scores, the authors conclude, "These intra- and intergroup variations suggest that group membership is not in itself the major determinant of ideology in the individual." (p. 189). It would indeed be surprising if group membership as defined in these broad terms proved to be related to ideology in other than a tangential way.

A rescrutiny of some of the data in *The Authoritarian Personality* utilizing a more generally accepted definition of groups and group membership indicates some interesting relationships. We shall follow Newcomb's definition for the sake of clarity. He defines a group as consisting of two or more persons who share norms about certain things with one another and whose social roles are closely interlocking.[60]

In a first approximation at teasing out the possible relationship between group membership and ideology, the relationship between the E and F scale scores for the fifteen "groups" (actually these are composed of a mélange of classifications, aggregates, and groups) on which both sets of scores are available was examined (Tables 12 (V), pp. 188-89 and 12 (VIII), p. 266). A scattergram indicated that the mean E and F scores for each group were posi-

---

[60] Newcomb, T. M., *Social Psychology*, New York, Dryden, 1950.

tively correlated; a rank order correlation of +.40 was found between the two measures. Many of these "groups" were college classes; it might roughly be assumed that they shared some norms but it is impossible to be specific about the interlocking social roles of say 140 women in a public speaking class or 110 San Quentin prisoners drawn from the prison population.

In an effort to discover more precisely the relationship between group membership and ideology, the scores for one of the 15 "groups" (which was actually a classification in Newcomb's terminology) were broken down. The "group" of 154 "Middle-Class Women" is actually a composite of six face to face groups which displayed strikingly different degrees of ethnocentrism.

TABLE XI
FACE TO FACE GROUP MEMBERSHIP
OF "MIDDLE-CLASS WOMEN"*

Group	N	E Scale Mean
Suburban Church Group	29	5.23
Upper Middle-Class Women's Club	36	5.05
Parent-Teachers' Association	46	3.13
Unitarian Church Group	15	2.32
League of Women Voters	17	2.06
Labor School	11	1.20
Total	154 Mean	3.64

* Taken from Table 15 (V), p. 194. Groups are reordered in descending magnitude of E scale means.

The above table indicates that there is relatively little overlap in E scale scores between the Suburban Church Group and members of the Labor School. The F scale means are not given for the face to face groups listed in the preceding table. However, "Middle-Class Women" as a whole have a mean of 3.62 on the F scale (Table 12 [VII], p. 266) with a standard deviation of 1.26. The correlation between E and F is .83 (Table 10 [VII], p. 263). This indicates that it is statistically impossible for the ranking of the six groups on the F scale to vary markedly from their ranking on the E scale.

An approximation of the congruence of rankings can be made. The six face to face groups can be broken into four groups upon the basis of mean acceptance of E scale items. The Suburban Church Group and the Upper Middle-Class Women's Club do not appear to differ significantly in their acceptance of ethnocentrism. An obviously significant difference exists between these two groups and the Parent-Teachers' Association. A difference which appears to be significant exists between the latter and the next two groups, the Unitarian Church Group and the League of Women Voters (the difference between the last two does not appear significant). Finally, the Labor School members are significantly lower on the E scale than the other groups (their mean of 1.20 is only .20 above the absolute minimum of 1.00; this means that the standard deviation in this group is extremely small).

Since there is a correlation of .83 between the E and F scales for the entire sample of Middle-Class Women it appears to be statistically impossible that any reversals in rank on the E and F scales might occur among the previous four groupings based upon E scale means.[61] It is possible, however, that there could be a reversal of rank on the E and F scales among the pairs in the first and third groupings alluded to. The following table indicates the hypothesized *maximum* discrepancy in rankings possible and the *lowest possible* rank order correlation between the six groups on the E and F scales.

TABLE XII
HYPOTHESIZED RELATIONSHIP BETWEEN GROUP MEANS ON E AND F SCALES

	True E scale Rank	Hypothetically Most Discrepant F Scale Rank	D	D^2
Group 1				
Suburban Church	1	2	1	1
Upper Middle-Class Club	2	1	1	1
Group 2				
Parent-Teachers' Association	3	3	—	—
Group 3				
Unitarian Church	4	5	1	1
League of Women Voters	5	4	1	1
Group 4				
Labor School	6	6	—	—

$$\rho = 1 - \frac{6 \Sigma D^2}{N(N^2-1)} \quad\quad \Sigma D^2 = 4$$

$$\rho = 1 - \frac{6(4)}{6(36-1)}$$

$$\rho = 1 - \frac{24}{210}$$

$$\rho = 1 - .114$$

$$\rho = .886$$

---

[61] The writer has attempted to set up hypothetical distributions which would violate such an assumption but (at least upon the basis of trial and error) was unable to do so.

Thus, the lowest hypothetically possible correlation between mean E and F scale scores for the six face to face groups of Middle-Class Women is +.886 and it may be unity. A similar procedure was utilized in estimating the lowest probable correlation among Middle-Class Men (three face to face groups) and Working-Class Men (four face to face groups). The lowest rank order correlation hypothesized as possible among these face to face groups is + 1.00 and +.80 respectively.

These considerations lead us to suspect that there is a marked relationship between membership in *functional* groups and the degree to which seemingly diverse attitudes are interrelated. This point was clearly made a decade and a half ago:

"Interrelated attitudes are rarely individual affairs, but are largely borrowed from groups to which we owe strongest allegiance. Individual variations such as age, sex, and various personality characteristics have much to do with the nature of the groups with which one becomes affiliated, and with the degree of permanence of such affiliations. Individual experiences, whether of accidental or occasional nature, on the one hand, or those occasioned by family membership or residential community, on the other, are also instrumental in determining group membership. This is by no means to deny the importance of purely psychological factors. But such experimental evidence as is available has led us to the conclusion that the latter are effective largely through their power to select this rather than that group affiliation, to react to it with greater or less intensity, and, to some extent, perhaps, to modify it. *The social psychology of attitudes is the sociology of attitudes illuminated by an understanding of the psychological factors which determine individual susceptibility to group influences.*" (Italics by the present writer).[62]

In view of the material indicating differences in acceptance of authoritarianism among individuals from various socio-economic levels and differing geographic locales and the high degree of interrelatedness of authoritarianism and ethnocentrism manifested as a concomitant of face to face group membership, it appears that the quotation cited safely applies to authoritarianism and ethnocen-

---

[62] This is the final paragraph in: Murphy, G., Murphy, Lois B., and Newcomb, T.M. *Experimental Social Psychology*, Harpers, New York, 1937 (Revised Edition).

trism. This point of view seems at variance with that expressed in *The Authoritarian Personality*:

> "Even if factors of personality did not come explicitly to the fore at particular points in the interviews with these two men, the conception of personality would be forced upon us by observation of the *consistency* (italics in the original) with which the same ideas and the same modes of thought recur as the discussion turns from one ideological area to another. *Since no such consistency could conceivably exist as a matter of sociological fact* (italics *not* in original), we are bound to conceive of central tendencies *in the person* (italics in original) which express themselves in various areas." (p. 56)[63]

Interrelatedness of attitudes among face to face group members appears related to at least two groups of factors; the selective ones affecting initial entry into and continuing membership in the group and, secondly, the dynamics of group functioning which lead to ideological conformity among its members. A major contribution of *The Authoritarian Personality* has been the illumination of initial personality predispositions for affinity with groups of varying ideological orientations.

Although it appears plausible that a given individual in the Suburban Church Group may not have been consciously aware of the attitudes toward authority and ethnic groups of the other members when she entered the group it appears highly unlikely that there would have been a marked initial discrepancy in such attitudes among her and the other group members. Such a group would be composed of women residing in a specific geographic locale who had similar socio-economic standing, were probably of fairly similar age, etc. Under such conditions it is highly probable that membership might have been solicited on the part of the group and that this was done upon the basis of assumed ideological compatibility inferred from similarity of ascribed characteristics of the potential group member and themselves.

Quite a different set of factors appear operative among those "Middle-Class Women" who attended the California Labor School. These women who presumably came from varying sections of a large metropolitan area obviously did not attend because it was the nearest social club. Prior to attendance a choice to do so was

---

[63] The two men referred to are "Larry" and "Mack" whose case histories are followed through the pages of *The Authoritarian Personality*.

made. It appears a reasonable hypothesis that certain ideological proclivities which were not satisfied by their membership in other groups led to such a choice. The relationship between personality variables and ideology indicate that in some cases personality variables play a greater role in the selective process of affiliation with groups (California Labor School) than others (Suburban Church Group).

We do not know, of course, the scores on E and F scales for the members of the groups cited at the time of initial entry into the group. It is therefore impossible to ascertain from *The Authoritarian Personality* what effects continued membership in a face to face group would have upon individual attitudes. Data are available on one face to face group in which individuals were tested at the time of initial entry into the group and later after an approximate six week period of interaction. These were 32 members of a summer workshop in intergroup relations reported by Levinson and Schermerhorn.[64] From first to second administrations the standard deviation on the E scale dropped from 0.82 to 0.71, on the F scale from 0.96 to 0.90 (it is possible that the drops might have been greater if both distributions had not had an initial mean well below the theoretical one with some individuals obtaining the lowest possible absolute score of 1.00 upon the initial administration of the scales). Although the findings are in the expected direction it is hazardous to generalize to other face to face groups since the decrease in variability is not statistically significant, the workshop group was transitory and the group had many other unique characteristics.

The point of special relevance to our inquiry is that Levinson and Schermerhorn believe that the drop in scale means which was found was "... primarily a reflection of a genuine inner change in convictions rather than mere mechanical conformity to workshop pressures."[65] Inasmuch as the drop in means occurred largely among initial high scorers who became more similar to other workshop members, the increased congruence manifested (as indicated by the decreased standard deviations) on the second administration of scales is also a reflection of the assumed inner changes.

---

[64] Levinson, D. J. and Schermerhorn, R. A., "Emotional-attitudinal effects of an intergroup relations workshop on its members," *The Journal of Psychology*, 1951, *31*, 243-256.

[65] Ibid., p. 256.

In evaluating data relevant to the relationship between group membership and ideology it appears reasonable to conclude that the generalizations made in *The Authoritarian Personality* fail to do justice to either the influence of broad social factors or membership in face to face groups upon ideology. What is illuminated, however, is the importance of individual personality characteristics in those instances in which selective identification with groups occurs.

V

With few exceptions, most social scientists agree that the interaction between persisting personality characteristics and the requirements of any given situation cannot be predicted unless the relevant dimensions of both sets of variables are known. A legitimate reason for disagreement arises when general statements are made as to *which* is the more important. In *The Authoritarian Personality* we find a primary emphasis upon the characteristics of the person rather than the contemporary situation.

"According to the present theory, the effects of environmental forces in moulding the personality are, in general, the more profound the earlier in the life history of the individual they are brought to bear. The major influences upon personality development arise in the course of family training as carried forward in a setting of family life." (p. 5-6).

"The present research seeks to discover correlations between ideology and sociological factors operating in the individual's past—whether or not they continue to operate in his present." (p. 6)

Two sections in *The Authoritarian Personality* deal with family structure and childhood environment of individuals differing in manifestations of ethnic prejudice when adults. In Part II, "Personality as Revealed through Clinical Interviews" retrospective accounts of childhood environment elicited from 45 high scorers and 35 low scorers are reported in conjunction with other interview material. In Chapter XXII (pp. 891-970) the intake interviews of 59 patients in a psychiatric clinic were rated for (among other items) "spontaneous mention of unhappy childhood and family relations." These are the data which appear most directly relevant to examination of the hypothesis concerning the importance of early childhood experiences upon adult personality.

In both cases the data regarding childhood experiences were obtained retrospectively from the interviewees themselves. It is

Authoritarianism Re-examined

tenuous to assume that the reports of childhood would completely agree with either the accounts of other individuals in different roles who were exposed to the same situations or with what actually had occurred from 15 to 40 years before. However, since differences do occur in *reports* of what happened which are related to the amount of prejudice on the part of individual respondents one can assume that there are grounds for belief that the early childhood experiences may have systematically differed. If the preceding sentence errs on the side of caution, there is good reason for it. A careful scrutiny of the interviewing and rating procedures raises a number of methodological questions which have implications for the validity of the reported differences, leaving aside the question of what the reported differences mean in terms of *actual* early environmental influences.

An initial problem concerns the individuals who were selected for interviews. The safest procedure to guarantee that the individuals selected as "highs" and "lows" were representative of the populations tested would have been to select them randomly from the first and fourth quartiles on the E scale. Inasmuch as testing went on over a long period of time it would have been impossible to obtain subjects for interviewing half a year or so after they had been tested. Under these circumstances it would have been most feasible to select randomly the interviewees from the upper and lower quartiles of each sample tested. There are two clear cut indications that this was not done. The first was the deliberate selection (for reasons which are not made clear) of certain interviewees who were high or low on E but mixed on F or PEC alluded to previously. The second indication is that different proportions of various groups were selected for interviews. No representatives of most groups tested were interviewed; of those from which interviewees were drawn the percentage of respondents selected for interviews varied from 23.0 (12 of 52 women) in a public speaking class at the University of California to only 0.6 per cent (two of 343 men) of a school for merchant marine officers' training.[66]

---

[66] More accurately, only two interviews were utilized in the analysis. At least seven men from the merchant marine school were interviewed according to the quotations in Part IV: M 1225 a, p. 610; M 1229 m, p. 624; M 1230 a, p. 629; M 1206 a, pp. 650 and 725; M 1223 h, p. 690; M 1214 b, p. 694; M 1230 A, p. 701. Since different code numbers are used to identify interviewees in Parts II and IV it is impossible to determine which of these, if any, were included in both analyses.

Hyman and Sheatsley have pointed out the unrepresentative nature of the total sample.[67] The above data indicate that the sample of interviewees is not representative of the larger sample from which they are drawn. In addition, it is not clear to what extent the sample of interviews utilized in the systematic analysis described in Part II of *The Authoritarian Personality* is representative of the total interview sample.

The preceding considerations indicate that any generalizations made about ratings on the sample of 80 interviewees may be affected by unknown sampling biases within an original unrepresentative sample. It is difficult to know with what certainty the findings represent an overestimation or underestimation of differences between persons high and low in prejudice.

Another important consideration in relationship to the interviews is the method of rating. It has been noted previously that the raters did better on the interviews obtained from individuals who had been selected from the groups which took the later forms of the scales, i.e., Forms 40 and 45. There is no doubt that the raters could determine with a high degree of accuracy from the interview protocols (from which all reference to ethnic groups or political material had been deleted prior to the ratings, (p. 327) the standing of the interviewees in the appropriate extreme quartile on the E scale. However, it should be noted that scores on the individual rating categories were *not independently derived* for each category. The interviews lasted from one and half to three hours (p. 301); it appears impossible that all the questions asked in the interview schedule could be thoroughly covered (p. 306-325). As is stated, "Not all the questions could be asked of all subjects, but an effort was made to cover all the major points with each interviewee. A relative preponderance of the ideological or clinical aspects was found to exist in accordance with the background of the interviewer." (p. 301) It is obvious that the interview protocols were not standardized. In addition to the usual variation among interviewers which might affect comparability there was a high degree of freedom in the formulation of questions on the part of the interviewer. This is a perfectly valid procedure—indeed in exploratory studies in which good interviewers are available it is highly desirable—but it should be noted that ratings derived from noncomparable material are not amenable to statistical treatment based upon independ-

---

[67] See the preceding chapter.

ence of categories. In fact, by presenting comparisons based upon incomplete data, the authors may have weakened the true magnitude of the relationships studied.

Evidently because of the lack of direct evidence bearing upon each category of the interview scoring manual, each rater was allowed to utilize the material from any portion of the interview in making a given rating. "The rating of the interviews was done for each of the categories separately. The score for the category in question, however, was obtained in a synoptic rather than a piecemeal fashion. The major source for the assignment of a score was the clinical part of the interview, but evidence was utilized from any part of the interview which might be brought to bear on each category." (p. 327) This procedure is legitimate if the findings are interpreted in accordance with the procedure utilized. However, the subsequent analysis of individual categories is based upon the frequency with which the categories appear in the interviews of subjects high or low in prejudice. This is legitimate only if it can be demonstrated that in the rating, the raters were not affected by the total content of the interview.

An analysis of the categories correctly assigned as indicated in Tables 1 (IX) and 2 (IX), pp. 296-97 indicates that in the majority of cases the raters were able to make correct evaluations on slightly better than four out of five ratings (80.2 per cent). A correct rating of a category meant that the individual who actually was low in prejudice was judged as making the response congruent with the hypothesized response which a typical individual low in prejudice would make. Similarly, highly prejudiced respondents tended to answer in the fashion hypothesized for such individuals.

According to present calculations, each respondent was rated on 42.99 of the 60 odd separate categories (the number varied for men and women). The average interviewee should therefore have been rated correctly on 34.48 ratings and wrong on 8.51 ratings. The hypothetical distribution can be found by the binomial expansion $[80(.8R + .2W)^{43}]$. It is virtually impossible for any interviewees to be incorrectly classified if the scoring categories are independent (the entire expansion is somewhat tedious but it requires checking of only a few crucial points to establish this fact). However, 13 of the respondents were in actuality incorrectly categorized by their summated scores on individual ratings. In these 13 cases both the summated ratings and the overall intuitive impression of the rater were in error, in the other 67 cases the summated ratings and the intuitive impressions of the interviewers were correct.[68]

It is extremely puzzling to find that a single item allows for correct prediction in 80.2 per cent of the cases but that 43 items taken en masse leads to only 83.75 per cent prediction. An average increase of only 3.55 per cent in predictive ability when the entire range of ratings is used in contrast to a single rating simply doesn't make statistical sense.

In resolving this apparent paradox it is well to examine the individual cases more carefully. When this is done it is found that of the 67 individuals intuitively and compositely judged correctly an average of 40.16 ratings were correctly assigned and only 4.04 categories were incorrectly assigned. However, of the incorrectly judged subjects the mean number of categories scored in the correct direction is only 4.60 but the number scored in the objectively wrong direction is 30.80. In short, when the raters were good, they were very, very good but when they were wrong they were horrid.

As might be suspected from the preceding data the plotted distribution of judgments is markedly bipolar. In Fig. 1, the number of categories scored incorrectly for each subject has been sub-

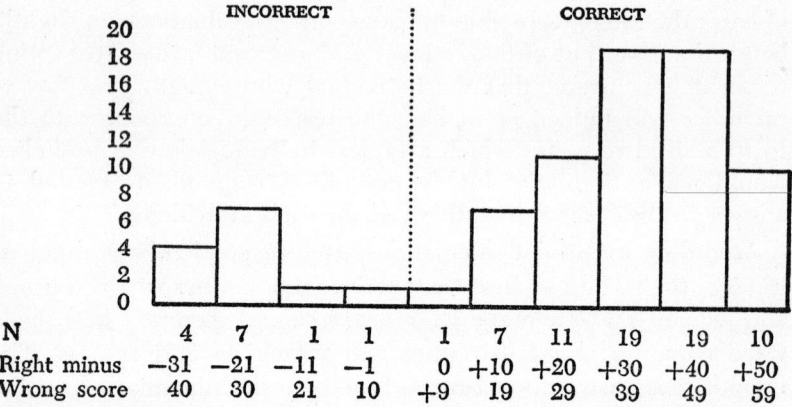

FIG. 1. *Distribution of individuals scored correctly and incorrectly by mean number of correct scores (right minus wrong).*

[68] In the text (p. 472) it is stated, "There is only one subject, F 72, among the 80 interviewees for whom there is a discrepancy between the two values. In her case the composite score (H) is correct; the over-all intuitive rating (L) is incorrect." According to Table 2 (IX), p. 297, F 72 was scored as "High" on 17 categories and "Low" on 26. Unless the table is in error it would appear that the composite score of the subject is "Low" and that there are *no* cases in which the composite score and the intuitive score varied.

tracted from the mean number of categories correctly scored. One possible explanation, of course, is that the individuals who were misjudged actually were "rigid lows" and "equalitarian highs." In this case the relationship between personality and ideology would run directly counter to that found in the other 67 cases where personality-wise lows manifested liberal ideology and the personality-wise highs manifested prejudice and political conservatism. There are two arguments against such a possibility. The first is that it simply appears impossible that such a sample could be collected by either accident or design. Although we do not know how individuals were selected from the larger questionnaire sample for interviews, it seems highly unlikely that the procedures used could have selected so few individuals who were indeterminate and were not clearly "high" or "low" on the scoring categories. The second and most compelling argument is related to the discussion in Section III of the "pure" and "mixed" cases. We would expect the mixed cases who are characterized by incongruent attitudes in various areas to be similarly mixed in terms of the type of answers given in the interview. Table VIII in Section III indicated insignificant differences in the percentage of correct categorization of interviewees among "mixed" and "pure" cases.

It therefore appears highly unlikely that the bipolarity can be traced to the idiosyncrasies of the subjects. Let us examine in more detail the rating procedure.

The most plausible hypothesis is that in making many of the complex and subtle ratings, the raters were influenced by their overall impression of the individual. They knew that each interviewee was either high or low on the E scale and they knew the categories which were hypothesized as distinguishing between "high" and "low" scorers. In many cases a casual remark made by the subject might well have been interpreted in one fashion if the subject were assumed to be a "high" but an opposite interpretation would be put upon it if he were assumed to be a "low" (and it might be noted that this procedure probably led to more correct than incorrect interpretations).

A scrutiny of the data on interrater argreement on nine subjects (Table 7 [IX], p. 330) strongly indicates that raters' overall impressions were important in scoring specific categories. On the seven subjects whom both raters intuitively rated correctly, there was a median difference of only 1.1 per cent in the proportion of "high" ratings assigned to each protocol. This is amazingly close agreement for such difficult ratings. However, on the two subjects on whom there was disagreement, the proportion of "high" ratings assigned by one rater was 70.4 and 72.2, the other rater assigning 31.1 and 27.2 per cent (high) ratings to the *same two subjects*. The first rater intuitively judged the two subjects as high on the E scale; the second could not make up her mind on one and rated the other as low.

If, as the preceding data indicate, the individual ratings were colored by the intuitive impressions of the raters, the statistical comparisons made between highs and lows upon the basis of nonindependent categories are meaningless. The magnitude of the differences between highs and lows is artificially enhanced by an indeterminate amount.

Returning to the major focus of interest, the importance of early childhood experience upon adult ethnic attitudes, it may be noted (Table 1 [XIII], p. 469) that the differences found in the area of "Parents and Childhood" are much less clearcut than such areas as "Attitude toward People" and "Attitude toward Present Self." An examination of Table 2 (X), (p. 362-363) indicates that of 27 separate statistical tests of significance on "Concept of Childhood Environment" only four significant differences were found (three at the .05 level and one at the .01 level). Inasmuch as the differences tested are hypothesized to be spuriously inflated by the rating procedure it is impossible to place any reliance upon the statistical significance of the results.

One other factor related to the childhood environment of the subjects is a source of ambiguity. In the interview schedule an entire block of questions was devoted to sociological aspects of the family background (p. 313). However, no data are presented upon this portion of the interview so it is impossible to determine what differences, if any, were found. These might well have shed further light upon the genesis of authoritarianism.

The second source of primary data is to be found in Chapter XXII, Psychological Ill Health in Relation to Potential Fascism: A Study of Psychiatric Clinic Patients, pp. 891-970. Here methodological queries are excluded by impeccable procedure. The initial psychiatric interview of the patients in the sample was analyzed for spontaneous mention of unhappy childhood or family relations (although criticism of parents on the basis of either past or present attitudes is included it appears relatively safe to consider the material as pertinent for testing the early environment theory advanced by the authors). The subjects were randomly selected from clinic patients and from 85 to 90 per cent were actually obtained.

Two raters evaluated each of seven areas, one of which was the mention of childhood or family. They agreed on 90.7 per cent of the cases in the latter area. In addition, control raters were used (some of these not being highly trained) for each of the seven areas. The control rater on childhood and family agreed with one of the independent raters on 94.9 per cent of the cases. It is abundantly clear that the ratings on spontaneous mention of unhappy childhood or family are highly reliable and that the questions raised in regard to the rating of interviews are not relevant to the data on psychiatric clinic patients. Data presented (Table 11 (XII), p. 933) indicate that one of the overall rater's evaluation of unhappy childhood or family relations correctly identified individuals as to E scale standing in 68.6 per cent of the cases. The control rater evaluations in this area correctly identified 63.6 per cent of the individuals as to E scale score (Table 12 (XXII), p. 934).

The striking feature about such findings (in addition to the methodological safeguards) is that an extremely brief initial psychiatric interview, routinely administered by a person presumably unfamiliar with the later utilization of the protocol for research purposes, is sufficient for the prediction of an individual's membership in the high or low quartile on the E scale in roughly two cases out of three. If more extensive information relevant to early childhood environment had been obtained it might be anticipated that the proportion of correct predictions would have been greater.

As far as can be determined, no studies following *The Authoritarian Personality* have afforded a check upon the relative importance of childhood experiences versus adult experiences in the etiology of ethnic prejudice or of their relative influence upon the personality characteristics of the prejudiced as contrasted with the unprejudiced.

Despite the misgivings regarding the statistical significance of the results presented in *The Authoritarian Personality* it is clear that: (1) ethnically prejudiced individuals report different childhood experiences than individuals who are not prejudiced and (2) there is reason to suppose that the self-reported differences or evaluations have some relationship to reality.

There also exists a paucity of research testing the effects of situational factors as determinants of authoritarianism. In the studies cited in reference to socio-economic correlates of authoritarianism, it is impossible to determine whether the causal factors were primarily operative early in the life history of the individual as postulated by the authors of *The Authoritarian Personality* or whether more recent social factors were more crucial.

A study which indicates that relatively brief situational factors may be of relevance is reported by Levinson and Schermerhorn.[69] The members of a summer workshop were 32 "predominantly middle-class, white, Protestant, female, teachers and social service personnel." The workshop lasted for six weeks and was largely devoted to lectures and discussions on "Intergroup Relations" which were primarily concerned with ethnic groups. The subjects were given an abbreviated F scale (20 items), a modified E scale (20 items), the PEC scale (5 items), and an abbreviated RC (Religious Conservatism) scale of 5 items at the start of the workshop and again during the sixth week.

On all scales except the PEC, there was a drop which was significant at the five per cent level. The mean drop per item on the E scale was .30; on the F scale .36. It is of interest that the drop on the E scale which was presumably most relevant to the workshop's function was less than that on the F scale.[70]

Another point of possible importance is that it was *not* those individuals who were presumably most receptive to the social climate of the workshop who changed the most. A comparison of the half of the sample who were initially lowest on E with those who in the upper half indicated that the drop on the E scale was .07 and .53 respectively, on the F scale the corresponding drops were .17 and .55. It is impossible to evaluate these results precisely because the initial means for the two groups are not given and it is obvious that those scoring low on the E scale didn't have an equal opportunity to decrease in ethnocentrism because of being closer to the minimum possible score. Despite this, it is still provocative that the

---

[69] Levinson, D. J. and Schermerhorn, R. A. *op cit*.

[70] To a certain extent, the larger drop on the F scale may be an artifact of the scaling procedure. A range of from 1.0 to 7.0 was possible on all scales. The initial mean on the F scale was 2.95, on the E scale 2.19. It was therefore possible to drop more on the F scale. Actually, (our computations) the drop on the F scale was 18 per cent of that possible, on the E scale 25 per cent.

amount of change could not have been predicted upon the basis of initial scores—when subjected to a social climate in which ethnic tolerance was the social norm, those relatively high in initial acceptance of ethnocentric and fascistic statements changed more in the direction of the social norms than did those who were initially presumably more receptive to the ideology of the workshop.

A change in the opposite direction, i.e., greater acceptance of F scale items is reported by Christie.[71] Six items were taken from the F scale (these were ones which had previously proved useful in an item analysis of data on different populations) and were administered during individual interviews to each of 182 inductees both prior to and after six weeks of infantry basic training. There was no significant shift for the population as a whole over the six week period despite their immersion in a military setting which might be characterized as authoritarian. However, it was possible to isolate subgroups within the sample. Sociometric ratings were available on each subject from both peers and the non-commissioned training officers directly in charge. Four subgroups were isolated:

(1) Those recruits more liked than disliked by both peers and non-commissioned personnel.

(2) Those recruits more liked than disliked by peers but more disliked than liked by non-commissioned personnel.

(3) Those recruits more disliked than liked by peers but more liked than disliked by non-commissioned personnel.

(4) Those recruits more disliked than liked by both peers and non-commissioned personnel.

Other analyses indicated that common interests and background were influential in being liked by peers. The non-commissioned personnel tended to like those men who were doing well in training or who, although not doing well in training, did not tend to create disruption or extra work.

Of the four groups, all but the first showed only chance fluctuations on the F scale from the first to second administrations. The first group (55 men), however, showed an item mean increase of .19, this being significant at the .05 level of confidence.

These men, liked by both peers and non-commissioned personnel, were characterized by their peers as performing well in train-

---

[71] Christie, R., "Changes in authoritarianism as related to situational factors," *The American Psychologist*, 1952, 7, 307-308 (abstract).

ing, and other data indicates that they served as both formal (squad leaders) and informal leaders in training. They may therefore be viewed as functioning relatively successfully in their roles as soldiers in a hierarchically structured social organization with both implicit and explicit authoritarian values. Additional support is given to this interpretation by the finding that those members of this group who received more mentions as doing well in training shifted the most toward higher F scale scores.

There are several points of interest in comparing these men with the results of the Levinson and Schermerhorn study. Those men who became more authoritarian were initially slightly below the group mean on the F scale. In other words, knowledge of initial F scale standing could not have been utilized as a predictive device in isolating those individuals who were to increase in authoritarianism. In the workshop group, those who changed the most were initially the most authoritarian; in the Army study the reverse is true. The differing systems of roles in the two situations must apparently be invoked to understand the difference in direction of shift. Presumably in the Levinson and Schermerhorn study the workshop emphasis on equality in intergroup relations established fairly democratic group norms. Also it must be noted that membership was voluntary and individuals presumably had fairly strong motivation to come in the first place. However, all of the recruits were inductees and were in military life without having strong motivation (at least not strong enough to volunteer). Under these conditions, the sample as a whole did not shift in acceptance of authoritarian statements. However, those men who performed well in the military role and were accepted by peers and superiors for reasons unrelated to initial F scale scores did become more authoritarian.

In both of these studies, situational factors were of demonstrable importance. In neither was it possible to use the F scale as an independent personality variable and obtain meaningful results. At least this is true if it had been (naively but reasonably) hypothesized that individuals higher in authoritarianism would respond more appropriately to an authoritarian situation and that those lower would respond most appropriately to a democratic situation.

We are left at an impasse. The material in *The Authoritarian Personality* indicates that personality factors related to early life history are of importance but we cannot accept the assumptions underlying the statistical treatment; we do not know how important they are. Similarly, the two studies reporting change in F scale scores are not completely satisfactory since we do not know enough about the early histories of the individuals who shifted in accordance with the role demands of the two situations.

A final answer as to the relative importance of personality and situational factors does not appear imminent; indeed it appears not unrelated to the nature-nurture problem in this respect. However, the final report by Else Frenkel-Brunswik on the study of prejudice in children and the results of current experimentation on the effects of roles with varying degrees of involvement in an authoritarian hierarchy upon shifts in authoritarianism should lead to greater knowledge of the relevant variables.

VI

Any treatment of the implications of the research reported in or inspired by *The Authoritarian Personality* must either be cursory or take as many pages as that monumental volume. The present account of necessity falls prey to the former alternative. The writer has been both stimulated and frustrated by the necessity of evaluating veritable mountains of relevant data. As a compromise solution, five areas were selected for evaluation. The selection represents the attempt of the writer to answer queries arising from an attempt to clarify the meaning of more recent research.

The first focus of attention was upon the F scale. An examination of the relevant data indicated that it appeared to tap a political *Weltanschauung* characteristic of formal fascist ideology. However, it did not appear to capture authoritarianism *per se* as displayed in other forms of political ideologies. At least those individuals who were members of or closely affiliated with the Communist Party did not emerge as authoritarian on the F scale. Furthermore, an examination of the relationship between F scale items indicated that the postulated personality variables underlying their acceptance had tenuous but provocative support.

Turning to the empirical correlates of the F scale it was concluded that it did discriminate between individuals who displayed behavior which was authoritarian in interpersonal relations rather than politically. Individuals high on the F scale tended to be condescending toward inferiors, resistant to scientific investigation, more sensitive to superiors than peers, and more prone to project their own attitudes upon others. Although these differences are consistent, they are not characterized by an exceptionally high degree of discrimination between individuals high and low on the F scale.

An examination of the concept of ethnocentrism as defined by the California investigators indicates that available data support the contention that individuals who are antagonistic toward a given minority group in one respect also tend to be antagonistic in other respects. Those antagonistic toward one minority group also tend to be antagonistic toward others although situational factors may introduce complications. Those antagonistic toward ethnic outgroups also reify abstract ingroups such as "America." It is impossible to draw conclusions regarding the relationship between prejudice toward ethnic outgroups and identification with face to face groups upon the basis of available data.

The relationship between ethnic prejudice and certain aspects of personality appears to be well established. Those persons who view the world as threatening and unpredictable tend to be less tolerant of minority groups than those who are more at ease with their social environment. From a different perspective, those individuals who are characterized by extreme passivity toward the world (depressives) appear to have little hostility toward minority groups. The relationship between personality variables and ethnic prejudice is not simple, however. The dimension of authoritarianism apparently cuts across customary personality scales and scoring categories. Although it bears little relationship to more frequently utilized personality variables, it is closely related to certain items on personality inventories which reflect suspicion of others and hostility toward the world.

An examination of the relevant research indicates a sizable negative correlation between scores on the F scale and various measures related to socio-economic status. F scale and ethnocentrism scores also covary among face to face groups. These findings are interpreted as running counter to the general argument in *The Authoritarian Personality* which emphasized purely personality determinants of potential fascism and ethnocentrism and discounted contemporary social influences.

The data presented in *The Authoritarian Personality* relating to the hypothesized greater importance of early environment in contrast to adult experiences in the genesis of potentially fascistic per-

Authoritarianism Re-examined

sons was re-examined. It appeared fairly clear that the rating methods used on interview material enhanced the differences in childhood environment reported by those high and those low in ethnic prejudice. Neither the original data nor subsequent findings are sufficient to prove or disprove the hypothesis. It is clear that prejudiced individuals report different childhood experiences from those who are unprejudiced, and these reports have undoubtedly a basis in reality. Recent studies indicate that changes in authoritarianism (as measured by the F scale) have occurred as a result of experiences in adulthood. It may well be that the problem of the relative importance of early versus late environment is one which cannot yet be definitively answered.

It has been necessary to omit several areas of relevant research from the present chapter. A number of studies upon the relationship between F scale scores and ethnic prejudice among members of minority groups have been made. Here the results substantiate the findings reported on majority group members in *The Authoritarian Personality* and other studies.

Another area of recent interest has been upon the dogmatic liberal or "rigid low." Any attempt to draw conclusions upon the basis of present data is premature.

A host of studies are currently in progress upon the behavior of ethnocentric and authoritarian individuals in controlled laboratory situations. Some of these studies are treated in the final chapter and no review has been attempted in this chapter which was primarily concerned with the social correlates of authoritarianism (social is here used in restricted fashion since laboratory studies with human subjects involve social interaction between the experimenter and subject).

It is a tribute to the vitality of *The Authoritarian Personality* that it has inspired such a tremendous volume of research. Many of the questions which are as yet unanswered or capable of only tentative answers should become increasingly clarified as new data become available. One encouraging trend in recent research is the movement away from studies which merely demonstrate the generality of the relationships between those aspects of personality tapped by the F scale and ethnocentrism toward controlled studies of the varied behavior of authoritarians in interaction with other persons.

One final note should be added. Both the strength and weakness of *The Authoritarian Personality* lie in its basic assumptions which are rooted in psychoanalytic theory. Such an orientation has led to the uncovering of a host of data which in all likelihood would not have been discovered by investigators with differing theoretical viewpoints. Despite some methodological weaknesses in the original research, subsequent findings have been predominantly confirmatory. The original interpretation of the data, however, appears to be weakened by the lack of concern with other theoretical approaches. It is the privilege of investigators to interpret their data as they choose; it is the privilege of others to re-examine the data and suggest alternative interpretations. Whether these alternative interpretations are of greater or lesser validity than those originally made can never be simply determined. Indeed, it is a matter of no great moment. The examination of a given body of data from a variety of perspectives leads to new hypotheses which can be put to an empirical test. It is hoped that the present chapter serves to highlight a few problems which subsequent research will clarify.

HAROLD D. LASSWELL

THE SELECTIVE EFFECT OF PERSONALITY ON POLITICAL PARTICIPATION

*B*EGINNING as a study of prejudice the research program under review in this volume expanded until it became a full scale contribution to the theory of the structure and development of power-centered persons. Ethnic prejudice is described as a form of "hostility toward outgroups," and hence implies willingness to damage the target.[1] Power relations are therefore involved, since the participants expect to impose, or do impose, severe deprivations upon one another. In a politically organized community coercion is handled by law, which means that it is managed according to a system of arrangements both authoritative and controlling.[2] We speak of political participation when we are describing the various roles involved in the making and execution of decisions. Furthermore, there are linkages of many kinds, strong or weak, between the playing of these roles and the nuclear drives of any given personality. This is t' ɔ sphere in which the research on the dynamics of prejudice has made its most distinctive contribution to political science. The performing of certain roles in society is connected with the structure and development of personality.

If the significance of the conception of authoritarian personality is to be properly assessed, we must include an examination of the concept in reference to the scientific study of politics. The present discussion characterizes the state of knowledge and research in the field of political science. In general, political scientists have described many of the roles involved in political participation,

---

[1] Bettelheim, Bruno and Janowitz, Morris, *Dynamics of Prejudice*, Ch. 1.

[2] For a systematic statement of politics see Lasswell, H. D. and Kaplan, Abraham, *Power and Society*, New Haven, Yale University Press, 1950.

without giving major emphasis to personality structure or development. However, the connection between politics and character has been recognized to be a major problem since the days of classical Greek thought.[3]

I

The generalized description of political roles has been most commonly carried out in connection with the study of political parties. This came about for several reasons. It was in the study of political parties that modern political scientists began to write about the facts of effective (as distinct from formal) power in the internal politics of nations, states and localities. The mass organization of modern parties brought into the foreground the role of the "boss" who often operated with no formal authority. Modern trends also directed attention to the tendency of the mass parties possessing a democratic ideology to concentrate power in the hands of a relatively small elite recruited from among the public leaders, the key promoters of organizational activities, and the permanent bureaucracy of the party. The highly decentralized character of party activity in the United States brought the Boss into prominence, while the very centralized Social Democratic parties of Europe, and especially Germany, brought the concentration tendencies into the open. The early work of Ostrogorski and Lowell (among other scholars) gave prominence to the boss.[4] Michels, on the other hand, was the outstanding contributor to the analysis of Socialist party dynamics.[5] The attention of scholars was gradually directed to countries outside Europe where effective leadership was conspicuously informal. The *Caudillo* was a well-recognized role in Latin American politics,[6] and after the 1912 revolution in China the "war lords" came into prominence.[7]

---

[3] See Jaeger, Werner, *Paideia*: *The Ideals of Greek Culture*, Oxford University Press, New York, 1943, especially Volume 2, and Jaeger, Werner, *Aristotle*: *Fundamentals of His Development*, Second Edition, Oxford, 1948.

[4] Ostrogorski, M., *Democracy and The Organization of Political Parties*, Macmillan, New York, 1902.

Lowell, A. L., *The Government of England*, New York, 1908 (Volume 2).

[5] Michels, Robert, *Political Parties*: *A Sociological Study of the Oligarchical Tendencies of Modern Democracy* (E. and C. Paul, tr.), Free Press, Glencoe, Ill., 1949.

[6] Ford, G. S., ed., *Dictatorships in the Modern World*, U. of Minnesota Press, Minneapolis, 1939.

[7] Linebarger, Paul M. A., *Government in Republican China*, McGraw Hill, New York, 1938.

The study of public leaders, bosses, and reformers was expedited in the United States when colleges and universities began to swell the number and size of departments of political science, and when the importance of field research began to be recognized. "Reformers" were much more prominent in this country than elsewhere, and waged a struggle, often on sorely unequal terms, on behalf of efficiency and law enforcement, notably in municipal affairs.[8] Thus the reformer was described as performing a specialized ideological role, while the public leader and boss, on the other hand, were differentiated principally on the basis of public prominence and relationship to formal or effective power. Whether they were public leaders or organizers, reformers were frequently caricatured as fanatics who could never get along with one another. It is true that the talk about personal traits drew more research attention toward the problems of how they got that way; this was typically dismissed with impressionistic remarks unsupported by research, and not intended to stimulate serious investigation.

The study of political parties did, however, direct research interest to the "grass roots." In practice, of course, the most rewarding field investigations were usually made on the grassless sidewalks of a metropolis like New York or Philadelphia. Portraits were drawn of precinct leaders and of the leaders and members of political clubs, the "cogwheels" in the vast party machines.[9]

At the upper levels of party activity public figures were continually being described. Most of this work was done by journalists or historians who made little effort to relate the details of a specific life history to a general theory of political participation. Hence the concepts employed were usually those of a sophisticated layman who brought his commonsense to bear on a problem.[10]

The field of "public opinion" was closely associated with the study of political parties. Public opinion research was stimulated by studies of the "crowd" that were conducted by political conservatives in the hope of discrediting popular government, and also by

---

[8] Munro, W. B., *Personality and Politics*, Macmillan, New York, 1924.

[9] Peel, R. V., *The Political Clubs of New York City*, Putnams, New York, 1935. Merrim, C. E., *Chicago: A More Intimate View*, Macmillan, New York, 1929. Salter, J. A., *Boss Rule: Portraits in City Politics*, McGraw-Hill, New York, 1935. Gosnell, H. F., *Machine Politics: Chicago Model*, U. of Chicago, Chicago, 1937. Forthal, S., *Cogwheels of Democracy*, William-Frederick Press, New York, 1946.

[10] A recent exception: Gosnell, H. F., *Negro Politicians, The Rise of Negro Politics in Chicago*, U. of Chicago Press, Chicago, 1935.

lawyers and judges who had to face the problem of what to do about group acts in violation of public norms, often in a large gathering where emotions were wildly stirred.[11]

As nationalistic and proletarian movements grew in scope, they gave occasion to examine "collective movements." One result was to influence political leadership studies by emphasizing the "nonrational" factors in the interplay between the public figure and the audience.

The "agitator" or "revolutionary" became a subject of increasing interest under the impact of social protest movements; such "nonrational" elements in conduct as "suggestibility" (associated with hypnosis) and the "unconscious" were utilized as explanatory concepts (originally stressed by philosophers and literary men.)[12]

Throughout these decades the "bureaucrat" continued to be a figure of public ridicule and complaint.[13] But little serious research was undertaken on administrative types.[14] With the rise of pressure groups and other voluntary associations the "pressure group bureaucracy" began to emerge.[15] The "syndicus" or "permanent secretary" was usually presented as a "lobbyist" and "fixer." The most recent emergent has been the "propagandist" or "public relations" man.[16]

---

[11] Gustave LeBon's many publications on the crowd were written by a "reactionary" for "reactionaries." As Ernst Kris remarks, "translations, except in English and German, were sponsored by Grand Dukes, Ministers of Justice and General staffs. His biography was written by a Japanese Foreign Minister." In "Some Problems of War Propaganda," *Psychoanalytic Quarterly*, 12, 1943, p. 388. Gabriele de Tarde is a good example of the jurist.

[12] The volume by the German philosopher Eduard von Hartmann on the unconscious (Die Philosophie des Unbewussten, Berlin, 1869) is an instance.

[13] For the English speaking world Charles Dickens did the classical portraits in *Bleak House* and *Little Dorrit*.

[14] But see Macmahon, A. W. and Millett, J. D. *Federal Administrators; A Biographical Approach to the Problem of Departmental Management*, Columbia University Press, New York, 1939; Merton, R. K. (ed.) *Reader in Bureaucracy*, Free Press, Glencoe, Ill., 1952.

[15] Rosten, Leo C., *The Washington Correspondents*, Harcourt, N. Y., 1937; Key, V. O., Jr., *Politics, Parties, and Pressure Groups*, 2nd Ed., Crowell, New York, 1947; Martin, E. M., *The Role of The Bar Association in Electing the Bench in Chicago*, U. of Chicago Press, Chicago, 1936; Garceau, O., *Political Life of the American Medical Association*, Harvard University, Cambridge, 1941.

[16] Pimlott, J. A. R., *Public Relations and American Democracy*, Princeton University Press, Princeton, 1951. Baker, Gladys, *The County Agent*, U. of Chicago Press, Chicago, 1939. Herring, E. Pendleton, Jr., *Group Representation Before Congress*, Johns Hopkins, Baltimore, 1929.

Effect of Personality on Political Participation 201

Attempts have continually been made to explain the successful military figures of history, and to solve the problem of leadership training in the armed forces.[16a] But little of this was done by political scientists, who tended to restrict themselves to civilian activities, and to veer away from the direct examination of specialists on violence even in civilian society. Hence policemen, on the side of law and order, and murderers, on the other, were either neglected or left to forensic medicine and criminology.

Although the literature of political science includes a very considerable body of generalized description of political role playing, political participation was at no time the main scholarly interest in the field. Departments of political science put the accent on the political philosophy, public law and comparative government.[17] Although academic political science in the United States has gone farther as a specialized discipline than in Europe, the growth of the subject as a behavior science has been retarded by several factors. The neighboring discipline of economics, for example, developed much farther, thanks to the relative absence of these factors. The members of an economics department could study the market without conducting a rear guard action with colleagues who specialized on "economic philosophy" or economic "public law." In departments of political science the specialists on "political philosophy" (often called "political theory") were historians of past writings on the "state." Possessing a voluminous and dignified tradition they were so weighed down with the burden of genteel erudition that they had little intellectual energy with which to evolve original theory for the guidance of either science or policy. Academic economists were fortunate enough to have a less voluminous and a less dignified inheritance. And they were comparatively unencumbered with legalism. Hence they dealt with questions of policy in a less formalistic framework. More of their energy went into the construction of theoretical models to guide empirical research. In contrast with economics the systematic evolution of political theory was left in a curiously stationary condition. Hence empirical work in political science received a minimum of constructive aid from scholars formally responsible for political theory. This led to a damaging schism between the great corpus of general tradition and

---

[16a] An excellent perspective is Vagts, A., *A History of Militarism; Romance and Realities of a Profession*, Norton, New York, 1937.

[17] See Haddow, Anna, *Political Science in American Colleges and Universities, 1639-1900*, Appleton, New York, 1939.

empirical studies. The latter were too likely to be both parochial and noncumulative.

II

In the light of the foregoing, it is not surprising that researches of the kind appearing in *The Authoritarian Personality* have been almost entirely absent in political science. Systematic research on political participation has played a subordinate part and much of the empirical work has been conducted at a low theoretical level. The study of political roles has not been planned or extended to the consideration of the total personality structure of the politician, or its developmental history.

The research on "the dynamics of prejudice" provides a working conception of the power centered person. This is obtained by examining all of the situations in which an individual participates during a given period of time. In each situation the problem is to describe the degree in which the person seeks to impose himself on others by the use of coercive measures. Anti-Semitism is a prejudice, "a pattern of hostility in interpersonal relations which is directed against an entire group, or against its individual members; and fulfills a specific irrational function for its bearers."[18] The point of stressing the irrationality of the hostile attitude is that more than superficial opinions are meant. A nuclear, not a peripheral, function must be performed in the personality system as a whole. (In classifying a given opinion as irrational a convenient operational index is persistence "when exposed to facts.") Before a specific pattern can be linked to the nuclear structure of a personality, all situations in which the person participates must be methodically described. If we demonstrate that the person maintains a relatively constant level of hostility in all circles, or that he has a periodically recurring cycle of such attitudes, a fundamental characteristic of the personality is established. In short, the personality includes a level (or a cycle) of demand to give expression to destructive impulses. The implication is that the identity of the target is much less significant than the inner rhythms of the personality system. Not only Jews, but Negroes; and not only ethnic groups but other social groups may be used as targets, such as nations, political parties and pres-

---

[18] Ackerman, N. W. and Jahoda, Marie, *Anti-Semitism and Emotional Disorder; A Psychoanalytic Interpretation*, Harper, N. Y., 1950, p. 4.

sure organizations. The research on prejudice evolved the conception of the authoritarian (power centered) personality by weaving together several lines of investigation. Since the research did not sample the active elite of government or parties, a gap remains between the conception of the authoritarian personality and the demonstration that such personality factors exercise an important selective effect on the choice of the roles of particular interest to political scientists.[19]

This demonstration needs to be made, since political scientists usually evince a considerable degree of scepticism about the possibility of arriving at a useful conception of the impact of personality on politics. Is politics, after all, a homogeneous activity? In the United States many tens of thousands of persons are public officials and employees in county, town, city, state and federal services. "Politics" includes the committees and staffs of political parties, of hundreds of nationally organized pressure groups, plus commentators and reporters connected with public media of information. When we consider all nations of the world it is clear that a total figure for government and party personnel would be big. If we were to add an estimate of all who have been connected with government at all times and places, the grand total would run into many millions. How can a common denominator be found for world conquerors like Alexander the Great and plodding clerks in local government?

If we bear in mind the distinction between "conventional" and "functional" definitions, the search for common elements does not seem absurd. We are using the term "politics" in a conventional sense when we include all the personnel of government departments and agencies. A functional conception, on the other hand, affirms that the most important decisions in a community are "political," whether they are made by individuals who are in or out of government in the conventional sense. In some communities a great contrast is to be found between the conventional structure of decision

---

[19] An example of an elite study of a national legislative body is Ross, J. F. S., *Parliamentary Representation*, Yale University Press, New Haven, 1944; of an administrative structure, *Representative Bureaucracy* by J. Donald Kingsley, The Antioch Press, Yellow Springs, O., 1944; of a Court, *The Judges of The Supreme Court, 1789-1937; A Study of Their Qualifications* by Cortez A. M. Ewing, U. of Minnesota, Minneapolis, 1938. See The Elite studies in course of publication at the Standard University Press in *The World Revolution of Our Time* (Hoover Institute and Library).

making and the functional structure. The important decisions may be made by party bosses, or by the heads of business corporations, trade unions, churches, or other unofficial organizations. In order to locate the functional political elite it is necessary to investigate the making and execution of actual decisions, and to discover whose voice is controlling. Typically we find that there is a predominance of power, composed of group leaders and groups, who determine the result during any given period.[20] In periods of crises, at least, it is plausible to believe that roles in the decision making process, functionally defined, tend to be played by personalities who attach great value to imposing themselves on others. If this hypothesis is to be verified by future research, the conception of authoritarian personality will contribute a great deal to refine the theoretical model of the *homo politicus* to be investigated.

This is true not only in the "cross sectional" sense, but developmentally. By locating significant factors in the formation of the authoritarian personality in the family, the probable nature of the link between early life and adult years has been clarified. It appears that the crucial questions deal with the intensity and the timing of anxiety. The work of Else Frenkel-Brunswik, in particular, points toward some dynamisms which can be found in the early lives of at least some of the infants and children in all conceivable cultures. It should be possible to specify with increasing precision what is meant by repressions that are made "too severely, too suddenly or too early in life."[21] Under the provocation of these factors it appears that the specific dynamisms are invoked that characterize the "authoritarian personality." The emphasis is upon the formative influence of obsessional-compulsive patterns. These patterns reduce anxiety by holding destructive impulses in check, which is a result that depends upon the repetition of simplified modes of thought and expression. A particularly convincing result is the report of testing the capacity of children to endure ambiguity, which brought into the open a wide range of latent differences in the ease with which children were able to cope with situations where instructions for the performance of various tasks were left vague. Anxious chil-

---

[20] For example, Stephen K. Bailey, *Congress Makes a Law: The Story of the Employment Act of 1946*, Columbia U. Press, New York, 1950; David M. Truman, *The Governmental Process*, N. Y., Knopf, 1951; Stein, H. (ed.) *Public Administration and Policy Development*, Harcourt Brace, N. Y., 1952.

[21] *The Authoritarian Personality*, Harpers, N. Y., 1950, p. 480.

Effect of Personality on Political Participation 205

dren were unable to endure the uncertainty, and were manifestly ill at ease. Other youngsters could carry on quite comfortably under the same circumstances.

When we relate these findings to previous work we are impressed by the confirmation given to the theoretical tools of psychoanalysis, especially to the closeness of the connection between compulsiveness and the internal disciplining of incompletely repressed hostility (explosive or continuing rage).

Something more than the picture of anxiety disposed of by compulsiveness is needed if we are to evolve a usable theory of the power centered man. Such a man must be able to adopt politically significant roles. This does not mean that these roles must be highly influential. But there must be at least a minimum degree of motivation and capability for entering into continual social relationships. Hence our working theory of the political man needs to distinguish him from persons who fail to attain the minimum level of participation. Two marginal types are of interest, the isolated psychopath and the extreme neurotic (or psychotic) who withdraws into fantasy.

The isolated psychopath who migrates from one job to another, and from one human contact to the next, is not included in a useful conception of the political man because of insufficient continuity of participation in the decision making process of the community. The psychopath, like the power centered person, is hostilely oriented toward people. As a thug he may gain momentary ascendancy over others, but this soon vanishes. In the extreme cases such a person cannot operate with confederates because of inability to control his destructive impulses.

The best insight that we have into the formative factors in the making of a solitary outlaw comes from the story of "incorrigibles," especially by Aichhorn, Redl and their associates.[22] In the Detroit experiment with "children who hate" the subjects were youngsters who had been exposed to an extraordinarily severe and continuing sequence of rejection by the human beings with whom they had been thrown. Speaking generally, the difference between these children and those who develop into politicians (even in our modest definition) is in the sphere of identification. From the earliest days the children who hate receive insufficient emotional support and in

---

[22] Aichhorn, August, *Wayward Youth*, Viking, New York, 1935; Redl, Fritz and Wineman, David, *Children Who Hate*, Free Press, Glencoe, Ill., 1951.

consequence feel everlastingly alone in an unresponsive and actively hostile world.

Even the elementary degree of success that we have stipulated for the political man requires something more than the naked assertion of will. It is necessary to put the self forward as an exponent of values shared by others. The ideology of the established order is a storehouse of symbols on which the active politician can draw in putting himself forward as the spokesman of party, faction, nation, neighborhood, region, religion, or any other group. Counter-ideologies are available when the politician's stand is in opposition to the regime. This identification of the self with common perspectives can be made by many persons on a spontaneous basis that involves no conscious calculation of special advantages to the self, and no significant demands on the unconscious level to exploit the bond of association. But the power oriented person is not given to quick and unpremeditated responses. His egocentricity is too great, so that he takes a detached and objective position toward the bonds of sentiment. (Egocentricity is here taken to mean that the person organizes his demands and expectations in reference to the primary ego. This is the "I" or "me," not the "we" that comprehends family or other groups.) If the egocentric is not to become an isolated psychopath or to withdraw entirely into fantasy, other features of the personality must permit the individual to engage in continuing activity with others. In some cases it is possible for the individual to participate in politics, even with success, for some time before displaying tendencies toward withdrawal, or forms of conduct that provoke society to exclude him from the ordinary social process. This applies to the psychopathic characters who function adequately save for occasional crackups.[23] It also applies to some of the victims of severe paranoid processes, whether of the grandiose or persecutory kind.

III

When we bring the various lines of evidence together that have been gathered in the research on prejudice and other investigations, it is possible to outline a workable conception of the power-centered person. A general proposition is that *the accent on power rather*

---

[23] Vivid cases showing the occasional crackup are in Cleckley, H., *The Mask of Sanity,* Second Ed., Mosby, St. Louis, 1950.

Effect of Personality on Political Participation 207

than some other value in the social process has come because limitations upon access to other values have been overcome by the use of power. In the broadest sense, therefore, power is a defense. Individuals turn to it in the hope of overcoming low estimates of the self when appraised in terms of any or all values. When non-power values fail to remove deficiencies, hope is focussed upon power. And when the expectation is accepted that other values depend on power, the pursuit of power looms larger in the personality system. When we try to account for the component of the self on whose behalf power is sought (and especially the primary ego), one general proposition appears to be that extreme egocentric fixation reflects an environment that provides meagre emotional support during early years.

The following interrelated propositions sum up a theory of the developmental history of the power-centered person:

Political personalities come into being by the use of power as a defense against threatened or actual loss of values.

Expectations: The value position of the self is regarded as low either on the assumption of actual or of threatened loss. Non-power values are appraised as likely to be unsuccessful means of defending and improving the position of the self. The use of power, on the contrary, is viewed as comparatively successful.

Demands: Success fosters the demand to use power or to pursue power as a major goal.

Identifications: The boundary of the self depends upon the indulgences received from the environment during early years. Egocentricity is most pronounced when early support is weakest. In all cases a basic minimum of support is essential to keep the individual alive and active.

Skills: The person possesses the aptitudes for acquiring the skills by which at least a minimum degree of participation can be acquired in the decision making process.

The data gathered in the research on authoritarian personality development confirms the formative significance of the Oedipal phase. This is the period in which the relations of the child to family authority undergo relatively rapid and decisive crystallization. It is a time when the physical and personality development of the child has prepared him to expand his activity. He is on the verge of moving outside the immediate ken of his nurse-protector, thereby enlarging the scope of his mobility and independence. At this point a conflict breaks out between the tendency to stay in the older and safer grooves of conduct, and to launch out beyond them. The conflict betrays itself in many ways, notably by shrinking from new opportunities, and remaining closely attached to key figures in the primary circle. In this period the Oedipal conflict must be resolved, or distortions of growth occur.

When the conflict is successfully resolved by the child a new set of goals is adopted in place of the demands for immediate body contact and for continual protection and supervision; and also in place of the destructive demand to annihilate the rival. The new goals implicate a wider context of human beings in time and space. Specifically, they include the copying of adult patterns of conduct and the sharing with playmates of the subculture of children that stays in touch with though distinct from the world of adults. Directing energy toward progressive goals of this kind the child is able to hold his destructive tendencies in check and to forestall acute internal crises of anxiety in which guilt and fear predominate. Once the Oedipal phase has been successfully surmounted the personality has achieved a major consolidation, and is able to acquire the culture of the community at an accelerated rate.

Failure to arrive at a smooth solution of the Oedipal conflict fosters deviation, especially in relations involving authority. One frequent response is to become utterly timid, submissive, and compliant in dealing with authority figures. Among boys this may go to the point of renouncing the male role, and of remoulding the self as an effeminate object. But another alternative is rebelliousness. Youngsters are rebellious who seize the destructive horn of the dilemma that they dimly sense, and assert themselves aggressively in order to keep down their impulses to make a total submission to authority. The latter alternative is unconsciously interpreted as including the sacrifice of masculinity. There are many degrees of rebelliousness, such as a continual display and threat of force, taking a chip-on-the-shoulder attitude, indulging in outbursts of rage without warning, and attacking indirectly by means of tale bearing. The picture of chronic rebellion presented by some of these children may seem to bracket them with the incorrigibles noted above. But the hostility of the rebel differs from that of the child who has failed to receive enough affection to build up a loved image of the self. The rebellious child is able to achieve a rather satisfactory positive identification with at least one member of the primary circle, but at the Oedipal phase is unable to sustain or achieve this relationship to the authority object. From this group come these "pretty boy" gunmen who succeed in captivating a great many people, and in maintaining relatively stable relation with a gang (which typically has the structure of a band of rebellious brothers who are in league against "law and order").

The egocentricity associated with these rejections of authority attitudes comes partly from failure to complete the self by incorporating the authority figure, and partly from the heightened ego-awareness that comes from interpreting the world entirely as struggle. Since images of authority include the threat or use of disciplinary measures, the fact of struggle in the world is implied in all authority symbols. But when the images of authority are not adopted as part of the self, the isolated and hostile child perceives the world as a battle ground. This fosters the political personality, who construes the social process as a vast arena of conflict.

It should be pointed out that rebellious attitudes toward authority exist in all degrees and that they may be modified or overcome in later years. More and more authoritative roles are pushed upon an individual, and a large part of the flow of gratification begins to come from performing these functions in family, business, party, or other association. Where age is a respected image, the passage of time produces a certain ascendancy over younger and less experienced members of the community. Specific targets of early animosity may fade away, and new targets may seem less overwhelming. It is worth remembering that later growth processes tend to cure earlier deficiencies. Hence fixations along the line of development are not necessarily immutable.

Also there is evidence that personality maturation may proceed over long time periods. This is indicated, for example, in the study of criminal careers conducted by the Gluecks.[24] They reported the life history of individuals who seemed to outgrow their early troubles with society. Although the environments to which they were exposed differed in no discernible way from other criminals, these persons appeared to take themselves in hand and execute a series of intimate and professional adjustments that integrated with the community. By contrast, many showed no tendency to mature. The disintegrative features so prominent in early life continued without letup.

---

[24] Glueck, Sheldon and Eleanor, *Criminal Careers in Retrospect*, Commonwealth Fund, New York, 1943.

For many problems it is necessary to push beyond the Oedipal phase to earlier years. There is evidence that some personalities develop self-generating cycles of hate as a result of early traumatic incidents occurring which are elaborated at the Oedipal and adolescent phases of development. Such a cycle is particularly obvious in the case of highly egocentric personalities who make little attempt to clothe their naked demands in terms that can be shared by others. Thus the "rebel without a cause" described by Richard Lindner, whose recurring acts of destructiveness were traced to a personality rhythm evolved early in life.[25]

The interpretations advanced by Mrs. Klein have been particularly influential in the study of human destructiveness, of which the demand for power is a partial expression. According to Mrs. Klein's account the infant is threatened by inner conflicts of such intensity that paranoid and depressive states are not infrequent. Infants and children seek outside support against the misery of such crises, and are able to develop a strong and consistent self system only when the persons in the primary circle act dependably, and provide genuine security.[26]

There is a sense in which it is meaningful to say that power activities begin at the very threshold of life. The behavior of infants is strikingly "all or none." They are very much asleep, or very quiet, or very noisy. When something goes wrong, the whole organism goes storming into action. The growth of discrimination and the graduation of responses are achieved but gradually. The "movement storm" of the infant appears to be the functional counterpart of the adult's use of the most severe sanctions at his disposal for the purpose of imposing his will upon others. In this wide perspective we can say that all men are born politicians and some never outgrow it.[27]

Our developmental theory of the power centered personality began with the experience of deprivation, which means anxiety,

---

[25] Lindner, Richard M., *Rebel Without a Cause, The Hypnoanalysis of a Criminal Psychopath*, Grune & Stratton, New York, 1944.

[26] A proposed application to political science is by R. E. Money-Kyrle, *Psychoanalysis and Politics: A Contribution to the Psychology of Politics and Morals*, Norton, N. Y., 1951. See forthcoming studies by Elliott Jacques.

[27] This remark is put in context in Lasswell, *Power and Personality*, Norton, New York, 1948.

misery, and discomfort. Since all human beings undergo varying occasions and intensities of anxiety, it will be necessary to make our hypotheses more specific if they are to assist in the search for significantly distinctive episodes. This calls for a clearer conception of the place of power in the social process as a whole.

For many purposes it is convenient to conceive of the social process as human beings interacting with one another and utilizing resources. The various gratifications that people seek in these interactions can be classified in broad categories of preferred events (values). The specific patterns of shaping and sharing are "practices," which constitute "institutions." In comparing the adult patterns of one community with another, we may take eight categories of values and institutions, as follows:[28]

Value	*Institutions* (examples)
Power	Government, political parties, pressure groups.
Wealth	Industries specialized to the production and distribution of goods and services.
Respect	Social class discriminations.
Well-being	Agencies for the care, treatment and prevention of disease, accident, death.
Enlightenment	Mass media of communication; special information services; civic training.
Rectitude	Churches and other bodies specialized to declaration of standards of right and wrong.
Affection	Families, friendship groups, patterns of devotion to secondary groups like nations.
Skill	Vocational and professional associations: methods of creation and standards of aesthetic appraisal.

The examples are from our own culture, and use the conventional names of institutions. Although the eight value terms are kept constant for the purpose of comparing all current or historical societies, the specific practices comprising the institutional pattern

---

[28] The social process as sketched here is utilized by Myres S. McDougal and the present writer in examining the interplay of law, science and policy. For example, McDougal, "A Comparative Study of Law for Policy Purposes: Value Clarification as an Instrument of Democratic World Order," *Yale Law Journal*, 61, 1952, 915-946.

may vary greatly from one place (and time) to another. The value categories are not intended to be a list of "instincts" or "drives" found among all people everywhere. Nor are they intended to suggest that every person, or every community, has the same rank order of values. All of these points are to be ascertained by the appropriate methods of research. In our civilization research work in the social sciences is specialized in rough approximation to the eight values. Power, for instance, is the frame of reference for political science, international relations and law; wealth is the field of economics; respect is the reference frame for sociologists of social class and caste; well-being is the problem area of medicine and public health; enlightenment is the province of students of communication (e.g., press, radio-television, film) and civic education; rectitude draws upon the sociologists of comparative criminal law and religion; affection is the domain of specialists on the family and upon identification with large groups; skill is the field of the sociologists of the professions, and of specialization on the history and theory of aesthetic standards. Institutions include patterns in which the expectations, demands and identifications of the participants are important, and patterns in which operating routines are most prominent. For the study of the first set of patterns it is increasingly common for the psychologists of personality and of collective processes to be involved. By contrast, the study of technical routines draws much less extensively upon psychologists. In political science, for example, psychologists cooperate most easily with specialists on political parties, pressure groups, public opinion, and personnel administration; and have least in common with those who compare systems of public law and legal philosophy. In the study of the roles involved in political participation, and connected with comprehensive theories of political structure and development, it will be necessary to foster the cooperation of psychologists and political scientists on an ever-widening front.[29]

---

[29] Charles E. Merriam was the most potent figure among political scientists in bringing about an enlarged conception of the field. See his *Systematic Politics*, U. of Chicago Press, Chicago, 1945, that undertook to bring together the viewpoints expressed during the previous twenty five years. The relative uniqueness of American political science is indicated in the UNESCO volume, *Contemporary Political Science: A Survey of Methods, Research and Training*, Paris, 1950. Among jurists Jerome Frank is an outstanding innovator (*Law and the Modern Mind*, Coward-McCann, N. Y., 1930). See further, Almond,

In seeking to connect pre-adult development with the playing of adult roles, we can look at pre-adult dispositions in reference to adult values and institutions. It is practicable to explore the balance of indulgence and deprivation in the interpersonal relations of individuals at various ages. Key questions become: Is deprivation in terms of one value more likely than others to precipitate adjustment in terms of power? What are the "severe" and "mild" indulgences and deprivations in terms of each value?

Well-being: In any community we expect to be able to discover the prevailing patterns of chastisement that are invoked by parents and nurses in dealing with children, by children in dealing with one another, and by children in seeking to cope with older people. The degree of "severity" can be appraised according to community perspectives.

Affection: We also expect to find in any community that evidences of affection may be withheld as disciplinary measures in the three sets of relations mentioned above (adult-child, child-child, child-adult).

Rectitude: In our culture, especially, we are prepared to find standard patterns of deprivation in terms of "bad" ("naughty," etc.).

Respect: Ridicule (with associated gestures) is a pattern of deprivation employed from very early years.

Wealth: Denial of access of objects and services (the rudimentary equivalent of wealth) is usually part of standard disciplinary measures.

Skill: The acquisition of skill may also be interfered with (such as stopping various forms of play).

Enlightenment: Also there are denials of enlightenment, as when curiosity concerning the body is not gratified; or what goes on in the parents' room.

Power: Of course power is involved in all these relations when they are regarded as severe.

G. A., *The American People And Foreign Policy*, Harcourt, N. Y., 1950; DeGrazia, Sebastian, *The Political Community: A Study of Anomie*, U. of Chicago, Chicago, 1948; Riesman, David, *The Lonely Crowd*, Yale University Press, New Haven, 1950; *Faces in the Crowd*, Yale U. Press, New Haven, 1952; Ranyard West, *Conscience and Society*, Emerson Books, N. Y., 1945.

In referring to "deprivation" as a precipitating incident in the ultimate development of a power-centered person, we must distinguish between the perspectives of the individual who is being studied, and the consensus that may prevail in a given cultural situation. It is adverse estimates of the "self by the self" that appear most likely to precipitate efforts at active defense.[30] Although the consensus of the group (of parents or children) may be nearly complete about the classification of a given act of discipline, we may discover in the concrete case that the target of the alleged deprivation does not perceive it as such. Our hypothesis relates to *deprivations from the standpoint of one who regards himself as deprived*. In general the hypothesis affirms that *deprivations of deference values are of the greatest significance as occasions of active defense*. More specifically, this applies to *rectitude, respect* and *affection*. Deprivations in terms of well-being, wealth, opportunities to develop skill, or the gratification of curiosity (enlightenment) are of minor importance unless they occur in a context of guilt, ridicule, or loss of love. The hypothesis does assert that severe losses of any value give rise to defenses in terms of power. Thus low estimates of the power position of the self emphasize the significance of obtaining power. The general hypothesis refers to such traumatizing circumstances as severe guilt connected with masturbatory tendencies, or an episode in which the child is held up to ridicule (possibly because of alleged physical or mental defect), or rage at being displaced in the home by a step-parent or another child.

Since the sense of being deprived is not always followed by active defense, it is necessary to explain when the situation is met affirma-

---

[30] Bettelheim and Janowitz take as the fundamental factor in "hostility among outgroups" the feeling of the hostile individual "that he has suffered deprivations in the past." *Dynamics of Prejudice: A Psychological and Sociological Study of Veterans*, Harper, New York, 1950, Ch. I. In this connection I have suggested that it is not useful to introduce the fact of conscious hostility into the definition of prejudice. In a "perfect" caste system the slave-serf may be aware of no hostility against the master-lord, and vice versa. We can take the influence of hostility, conscious and unconscious, as a research problem, rather than seeking to dispose of it by definition. Also the term "outgroup" slurs over the question of the factors which enable the lowly individuals in a caste system to repress all demands for equality in the name of the primary ego and all doubts about inherent inferiority. See "Personality, Prejudice and Politics" in *World Politics*, 399-407.

tively, rather than with hopeless passivity. Let us formulate the hypothetical explanation in these terms: *If active defense is to occur, the deprivations must not be so overwhelming that self-confidence is destroyed.* Otherwise we are likely to see withdrawal into fantasy. Confidence in the self is sustained by *the expectation that a better value position is possible; and that this possibility depends in part upon the taking of active measures by the self.* If some optimism about the future position of the self is not maintained, the response may be more final than when there is withdrawal into fantasy, since the individual may turn his aggression against the self and commit suicide. Such an act is an act of power, but is the greatest possible contradiction of an active, continuing search to attain a more favorable position in the social process.[31]

When efforts at defense are active, they are not necessarily in terms of power. As indicated above, one hypothesis is that *if deprivation is conceived as having been in terms of power or by means of power, the probability that power will be used is increased.* Attention is then focussed upon power. But *measures in kind may not be employed if in the past non-power methods have not succeeded.* Reliance upon seduction, flattery and bribery may be expected to get results. *The chances of invoking power are increased if success followed the use of power* under similar circumstances (especially in the recent past).

The foregoing re-statement of the developmental theory of the power-centered man is an expansion of the conception of the political man in terms of *private motives displaced upon public objects and rationalized in terms of a common good.*[32] We now speak of power demands in the primary circle as being directed to secondary circles and justified in terms of common values. (We have substituted less "clinical" terms for "displacement" and "rational-

---

[31] An ambivalent conception of the self can arise, for instance, by incorporating the mother's ambition for achievement, while interpreting the conditional affection of the mother as indicating something basically unlovable about the ego.

[32] My formulations of the political personality (and various sub-types) can be found in *Psychopathology and Politics*, U. of Chicago Press, Chicago, 1930; *Politics: Who Gets What, When, How*, McGraw Hill, New York, 1936 (Ch. 8); *Power and Personality*, Norton, New York, 1948. The first two volumes are reprinted in *The Political Writings of Harold D. Lasswell*, Free Press, Glencoe, Ill., 1951, together with a new analysis of *Democratic Character*.

ization," and we use "defense" of the self against low self-appraisals.) It is clearer that the "public objects" are the institutional patterns of power in a given social process.

Reliance upon active defense against deprivation rather than withdrawal, isolated aggression, or suicide has been accounted for by reference to the self confidence surviving from past success, and to current exposure to less than overwhelming deprivation. The resort to power instead of non-power values has been related to the comparative success of power in previous circumstances of a kind confronting the individual in the current situation. Finally, the comprehensiveness of the self-system has been related to the support received from the early environment. Where support is deficient, the characteristic outcome is egocentricity. More inclusive self systems depend upon the attainment of positive identification with figures in the primary circle.

IV

The conception of the "authoritarian personality" is in some ways too general to provide a developmental model of *homo politicus*. It does not sufficiently distinguish between the inner conflict that is resolved by active role playing, rather than by withdrawal, isolated aggression, or suicide. It does not deal explicitly with aptitude and opportunity factors affecting the acquisition and exercise of roles in the social process. The connection between the nuclear personality and political participation is left in a relatively ambiguous condition.

The reason for this lack of clarity arises because the types of research programs necessary to illuminate the development of political personality have not been organized. The important contributions from the research on the dynamics of prejudice give an indication of what can be accomplished when research teams having interrelated though differing skills are brought together. The most promising line of future advance in the study of political man calls for closer cooperation between political scientists and specialists on the various periods of development.

As an indication of how the hypotheses outlined here can be clarified for research purposes, the following table will be considered:

TABLE 1.
THE DEVELOPMENT OF POLITICAL PERSONALITY

PERIODS OF DEVELOPMENT	Environment		Responses	
	Values	Institutions	Kind	Level
Infancy	Power ± (– –)[a] Respect ± (– –) Rectitude ± (– –) Affection ± Wealth ± Well-being ± Enlightenment ± Skill ±	Family ± School ± Government ± (and others conventionally named)	Assertion Submission Hyperaggression Isolated aggression Fantasy Suicide	Conscious (C¹)[b] Available to Consciousness (C²) Unconscious (C³)
Childhood	Schema as above plus PREDISPOSITIONS acquired in preceding period.			
Juvenility	Schema as above plus PREDISPOSITIONS acquired in preceding periods.			
Adolescence	Schema as above plus PREDISPOSITIONS acquired in preceding periods.			
Adulthood	Schema as above plus PREDISPOSITIONS acquired in preceding periods.			

[a] The symbol (– –) indicates areas where severe deprivation is of greatest significance for the development of power-centered values.
[b] See the text (p. 219).

The heading "Periods of Development" serves to indicate the functional divisions of the career line of each subject from birth (or conception) through adulthood. The Hypotheses in *The Authoritarian Personality* and in the present discussion relate chiefly to infancy and childhood (the second being understood as the Oedipal period).

"Environment" refers to the events in the social process of the subject, classified according to values and institutions. The environment during any time slice (short or long) is described as indulgent (+) or deprivational (−) depending upon the way in which it is perceived by the subject. Before the individual has acquired facility in the use of language all current estimates of how the environment is perceived must depend upon operational indices of other kinds (such as the overt act of crying). After language is mastered the perception may be ascertained by retrospective interviewing (with or without the aid of hypnosis or narcotics). The perceptions of any given subject may be related to the consensus that prevails in the culture (or sub-culture) about the usual interpretation that is given to such environmental patterns (as indulgent or deprivational). In classifying the pre-adult environment the adult patterns of the culture are of primary importance, since the aim of developmental research is to clarify the predispositions of young people who move into the environments provided by the adult world. More concretely, the objective of research on political personality is to discover the selective effect in the choice of adult roles of the nuclear personality evolved in pre-adult years.

It will be noted that "Institutions" are "conventionally" named. This means that the terms in local use are employed to designate the situation in which an interaction is taking place, without attempting to make a functional reclassification according to the predominance of the values actually shaped or shared. For instance, we speak of "family," "school," and the like without stopping to consider whether the situation referred to is, in fact, one in which the dominant values are affection or enlightenment. In the same way, "juvenile court," "reformatory" or "police" are called "governmental" without assessing the degree to which they actually impose or are expected to impose severe deprivations.

Since extreme deprivations in the social process involve power (functionally defined), it is necessary to make a separate category for "severe deprivations" in recording value changes in respect, rectitude, and other provisional classifications. Where the individual is a participant in a group that has an organized decision making process for the control of coercion, power deprivations can take the direct form of exclusion from membership, from voting, from eligibility for office (or losing a nomination, an election, a legislative proposal, an administrative recommendation, a case before a court).

By recording the pattern of indulgence ($+$) or deprivation ($-$) according to " Institution" (in the conventional sense) we intensify our knowledge of the functional significance of the culture patterns current in the situations we are studying.

"Responses" must be described from two points of view, from the standpoint of the participating group, and in terms of the total personality of the specific person. The first describes the act in reference to "roles," and the latter in terms of the nuclear personality. We take it for granted that there may be great discrepancies in the significance attached to the same response when they are assessed from both points of view. It is commonplace to observe that "timid" children imagine that they are acting in a most aggressive manner when, from the standpoint of the play group, they are quite submissive. When we classify the response in reference to the personality, it is necessary to distinguish at least three levels: C^1, which means that the perspective referred to is fully conscious; C^2, signifying that it is not at the center of waking awareness, but that it can be formulated with some effort; and C^3, meaning that the prospective is unconscious (and therefore calls for the overcoming of anxiety before it can become C^1 or C^2).

These distinctions are essential because some of our hypotheses about political personality must be progressively refined in the direction of clarifying the interplay of conscious and unconscious relations. In terms of role analysis, the "isolated aggressive," for instance, does not enter into enduring relations with others. Human associations are typically broken off because of intolerable provocativeness. From a personality standpoint the demand to impose upon others is so intense that skills in political role playing are not acquired or exercised. Our hypothesis explains the intensity of the power demand by regarding it as a defense against early perceptions of the self as a damaged object, unable to obtain even a modicum of indulgence by non-intimidation.[33]

---

[33] In this connection note "the delinquent integration" as formulated by Donald A. Bloch. After pointing out that delinquent activities function to minimize anxiety in interpersonal relations, he suggests that the "specific pathogenic response is that the anxiety produced in the adult by the communication

The "hyperaggressive" response refers to a role that is played in continuing group relationships. It is "bullying" or "provocative" conduct that falls short of provoking the exclusion of the individual from ordinary society. Often it is linked with "submissive" responses toward stronger persons.[34] The personality structure has come to rely on power, and achieves a degree of success by more differentiated behavior than the isolated psychopathic person is able to master.

It will be recalled that our conception of the power-centered adult is made on a comparative basis. Rather than attempting to set up an "absolute" definition, we have specified "relative" accent on power, relative in terms of the community context as a whole or of selected sub-groups within it. Research indicates that in some societies power is not a major value, and that, on the contrary, the use of coercive human relations is kept at a minimum. Nevertheless, when we study such a society, we expect to find that some persons put comparatively more valuation than their fellows[35] on coercing others. Our developmental hypotheses are intended to account for differences of this kind, as well as for the formation of personalities who select from among the more abundant power roles in such a civilization as ours.

By utilizing a multi-valued model in personality and role analysis, we are able to clear the way for a more differentiated consideration

---

from the child of a need — food, play, attention, or what not — is dealt with by totally rejecting the child's need." The world of the delinquent is full of early deprivation, dearth of durable intimacies, and the expectation that the world is composed of "crooks and suckers." *Psychiatry*, 15, 1952, 297-304. The broad hypothesis that those who play political roles, even in the British Parliament, are recruited from delinquent personality types is elaborated in Comfort, Alexander, *Authority and Delinquency in the Modern State*, Kegan Paul, London, 1950.

[34] The "submissive" variation of the demand for power means that the individual emphasizes power by seeking to become dependent upon dominant figures as a means of enhancing one's power position. A break occurs with the dominant figure when the individual assesses the self as strong enough to make a challenge, directly, becoming hyperaggressive by finding a more potent master, or by joining a bloc of allies deemed sufficiently powerful to assert themselves jointly. Where the conflicts arising in a dependency relationship are intense, the individual may find it necessary to withdraw from participation in politics, perhaps into neurosis or psychosis, or even into isolated aggression. A revealing case study of submissiveness and neurosis (at least) is Rees, J. R. (ed.), *The Case of Rudolf Hess: A Problem in Diagnosis and Forensic Psychiatry*, Norton, New York, 1948.

[35] See Ruth Benedict's classical and provocative treatment of the Zuni in *Patterns of Culture*, Houghton Mifflin, New York, 1934.

of these connections than has been applied in the past. For instance, to what extent are the politicians who are active in a given context at a given time recruited from power-centered persons? To what extent do they come from personalities whose dominant value is wealth, respect, rectitude, or some other value?

It is tempting to suggest that politicians tend to be recruited—self-recruited—from power-centered personalities in all forms of government and in all periods of crises (or non-crisis). But this is exceedingly doubtful. Consider the United States, which can be described as a great (indeed a giant) power in the arena of world politics, possessing relatively democratic institutions so that the active decision making elite in government is selected by procedures in which a large part of the community is involved and must be taken into account. When we study the Presidents, for example, we are impressed by the strength of many values in their careers, whether we are thinking of Washington, Jefferson, Jackson, Lincoln, the Roosevelts or Wilson. Only by the most fanciful kind of oversimplification can we classify these men—even Jackson—as consumed by passion for power, and utterly ruthless in its acquisition or exercise. The following hypothesis is more likely to be verified by further research than its opposite: *The leaders of large scale modern politics where comparatively free institutions exist are oriented toward power as a coordinate or secondary value* with other values, such as respect (popularity), rectitude (reputation as servants of the public good), and wealth (a livelihood). Even if these leaders are power-centered relative to many of their fellows, the degree of concentration on power is far short of the images of the political man that make of him a wolf man (*homo lupus*).[36] The Bosses are more likely to be concerned with personal wealth than with power as their goal value.

---

[36] Psychiatrists have noted so many points of resemblance between tyrannical political figures and paranoia, paranoid schizophrenia, severe psychoneuroses with paranoid coloring, and paranoid character that they have often made diagnoses instead of demonstrating how the pathological processes were interrelated with the development of the total personality structure and the playing of political roles. This is one reason why the direct contributions made by psychiatrists to the analysis of politics and politicians have been of limited utility. An outstanding exception is Heidenhain, Adolf, *Rousseau, J. J., Personlichkeit, Philosophie und Psychose*, in "Grenzfragen des Nervenund Seelenlebens," Heft 117, Munich, 1924. See also Kligerman, Charles, "The Character of Jean Jacques Rousseau," 20, *Psychoanalytic Quarterly*, 237-252; and Engle, Bernice and French, Thomas M., "Some Psychodynamic Reflections Upon the Life and Writings of Solon," *Ibid.*, 253-274.

Another hypothesis may be put forward to apply to the same kind of society: *Intensely power-centered persons tend to be relegated to comparatively minor roles.*

(a) *This is most likely to be true of persons who attach importance to acting coercively in face to face relations.* Many manual laborers are given to quarrelsomeness and physical combat. The roles permitted to the lower social classes provide many direct outlets for destructive impulses. We find such coercers in the migrant labor force, and in the lower managerial level in charge of groups in construction work, lumbering, mining, harvesting, and the like. They are frequent among longshoremen, top sergeants, truck drivers, policemen, firemen, and athletes. We find personally aggressive individuals among those who have failed at a white collar activity, or whose careers have been much more modest than they had expected.[37] As we move up the ladders of modern industrial society the number of links with other human beings that must be maintained is a factor in success that reduces the usefulness of arbitrariness, for example.

(b) *It is also likely to be true of those power-centered personalities who rely upon compulsive mechanisms (the "authoritarian personalities").* Compulsiveness sets a limit upon the adaptability of the individual to political participation. Young people with rigid personalities may discover that the ladder of advance in politics is less congenial than the more regular steps provided by standard professions and vocations. Not the top spots, but a circumscribed, prescribed and secure chair in the bureaucracy is the type of role to which they are well adapted.[38] With the re-enforcement of the administrative setting, they are able to keep their destructive impulses from discharging too disruptively in immediate personal relations. The hazards of running for office, or of promoting new projects, put a tremendous strain on the compulsive character.

The rigidity of the compulsive character poses some important questions concerning the recruitment of the active elite in a totali-

---

[37] The recruitment of non-proletarian revolutionary movements is especially significant. See Neumann, Sigmund, *Permanent Revolution*, Harpers, New York, 1942 (Ch. 3 "The Political Lieutenant"); Lerner, Daniel, *The Nazi Elite*, Stanford University Press, Stanford, 1951; North, Robert, *Kuomintang and Chinese Communist Elites*, Stanford University Press, Stanford, 1952.

[38] Otto Sperling reports that he has analyzed twenty bureaucrats and found the majority to be compulsive neurotics. "Psychoanalytic Aspects of Bureaucracy," *Psychoanalytic Quarterly*, 19, 1950, 88-100.

tarian, industrial society. When such a regime is well established, it is typically ridden with terror and threat. Is it necessarily true that persons in authority show less endurance of uncertainty than other types? This seems most unlikely. It is more plausible to believe that persons are best fitted to survive who have relatively few internal conflicts and are comparatively free to make realistic appraisals of the environment. Anxiety ridden persons may be suitable for the niches provided by the hierarchy of administration. But in all probability they are too ready to distort the intentions and capabilities of others to achieve the realistic orientation essential to the upper levels of policy making. In view of these considerations, we state the following hypothesis:

It is improbable that the top leaders of an established totalitarian regime in an industrial society are recruited from "authoritarian personalities." Note that this proposition refers to regimes that have been in power long enough to recruit their own elite from young persons reared under the new system.

Some modern totalitarian parties recruit aggressive young people in order to capture their energy rather than to leave potential opponents outside the hierarchy. Among these youths are sadistic individuals who are cruel to the weak and provocative in dealing with everyone. If they are unable to control the expression of their drives, or lack aptitudes for more complex tasks, they may eventually become prison guards, police torturers, and the like. If their aptitudes are greater, and they can keep the inexpedient expression of sadistic and provocative impulses under control, they may move upward to large organizational responsibilities. Young people who are assertive and rivalrous without being sadistic, and who have the requisite aptitudes, may continue to climb in the hierarchy.

In some cases the training of the elite member is designed to cut all ties of identification with family, friends and other associations, and to create a thoroughly reliable instrument of the party and the regime. The cutting off of early identifications is easy for highly egocentric persons. Complete identification with the party, however, is more difficult for egocentrics, and may be a source of division and therefore of weakness in totalitarian regimes. *But egocentric personalities are likely to rise to high positions in totalitarian regimes if internal conflicts are not resolved by extreme compulsiveness.* It is probable that *a basically healthy personality is essential to survive the perpetual uncertainties of political life.* This means that in the primary circle the infant and child must be able to receive enough love and care from at least one parent (or nurse) to develop a positive image of the self, and to gain experience in giving and receiving affection free of anxiety. It is implied that these top leaders differ in developmental history from the withdrawn, the isolated psychopath, or the rigidly compulsive type. The deprivational traits of the self are intermingled with indulgences, and the underlying view of the world does not conceive of it exclusively as an arena of power.

The final hypothesis for study is this: *All top leaders in democratic or totalitarian regimes (in a non-caste system) tend to be recruited from fundamental personality patterns that are not primarily oriented toward power. A considerable degree of egocentricity in later phases of development is an asset in selecting and playing political roles.*

If hypotheses concerning personality and political participation are to be investigated under the most favorable circumstances, cooperation and timing are important elements in the over-all design of research. Cooperation signifies that teams of political scientists and psychologists should work together. By timing is meant the importance of so arranging teams of research workers that the changing connections of personality and political participation can be described through time. It is probable that the selective effect of various types of personality change as the interrelations change among the roles. In crisis situations, for instance, the agitational role may rise in importance when compared with the judicial role; or the political police role may gain in weight at the expense of other administrative activities. The more power-centered personality forms may gravitate to the new functions at a discernible rate. At the same time, it is likely that the adolescent, juvenile and earlier environmental patterns are being altered. Hence the community may be creating more personalities who value the pursuit of the power potentialities of the situation in which they find themselves. Since the meanings of words are continually changing, the interpretation of what constitutes a role is changing, and tests must be continually re-calibrated through time.

An important pioneer study has been made by John B. McConaughy, political scientist, in close cooperation with psychologists (at the University of South Carolina).[39] The Bernreuter Inventory

---

[39] *American Political Science Review*, 44, 1950, 897-903.

was given to eighteen of 170 South Carolina legislators who were compared with norms obtained for adult males in the state. The political leaders were slightly less neurotic, more self-sufficient, and decidedly more extroverted; but they were only slightly more dominant. The Guildford-Martin Inventory of Factors G-A-M-I-N indicated that South Carolina political leaders have more general pressure for overt activity than the average person. Also, they are decidedly more masculine than the general male population, and are decidedly more self-confident than the average person (and have fewer inferiority feelings). On the Edwards Unlabelled Fascist Attitude Test, the legislators are less fascist than those treated by Edwards. The C-R Opinionaire indicates that South Carolina political leaders are significantly more conservative than the general college population but not much more conservative than the samples of South Carolina population used as controls.

McConaughy's study points the way to a long neglected form of cooperation among scientists that may gradually put our theories to a continuing application (and re-test) through time. By choosing a "legislature," which is part of the conventionally defined power institutions of South Carolina, comparisons are facilitated with other structures of government. Eventually these studies can be extended to business, church, and other institutions (as locally identified). With a richer body of empirical data, functional definitions can be made more operational, and many of the tools developed in connection with the research on the authoritarian personality can receive rewarding application.

ELSE FRENKEL-BRUNSWIK

FURTHER EXPLORATIONS BY A CONTRIBUTOR TO "THE AUTHORITARIAN PERSONALITY"

As THIS IS written, four years have passed since the work on *The Authoritarian Personality* was completed, and more than two years since it was published. In times when thinking and research in the social sciences move ahead as rapidly as is the case at present, this seems not too short a span for a discussion of some of the background, parallel developments, sequels, and implications of our work, both experimental and theoretical.

In the present chapter special emphasis will be placed on material from a separate project on social discrimination in children and adolescents carried out at the Institute of Child Welfare of the University of California at Berkeley.[1] Its distinguishing features are a further exploration of socio-economic indices in their relationship to authoritarianism, a systematic inquiry into children's conception of social roles, a direct clinical approach to the childhood phase and family background of ethnocentric and non-ethnocentric children, and especially the introduction of the experimental approach, notably on such cognitive aspects as "intolerance of ambiguity."

After a brief introduction on the interrelationships of the social and the personality approach in which we will recapitulate and

---

[1] This project was begun in 1944 and was well under way before the study on adults on which *The Authoritarian Personality* is based was completed; it was carried out by a different staff under the charge of this writer. For brief advance reports see Frenkel-Brunswik, E., "A study of prejudice in children," *Human Relations*, 1948, 1, 295-306, and "Intolerance of ambiguity as an emotional and perceptual personality variable," *Jour. of Personality*, 1949, 18, 108-143. More detailed reports will be listed in the proper context.

expand the assumptions underlying *The Authoritarian Personality,* we will review our recent investigations of social correlates of ethnocentrism in children. We will then turn to the results of the exploration of the cognitive aspects of the authoritarian pattern. After presenting recent experimentation along this line, we will bring into the picture a source not hitherto fully examined as to its relevance to our problem, that is, E. R. Jaensch and the Nazi syndrome of personality that has been made explicit in his writings. Except for the fact of its glorification by Jaensch, this ideal shows striking structural similarity to our conceptualization of the authoritarian personality which thus receives support from a source certainly not biased in our direction. We will then proceed to probe into the background of modern personality theory in psychoanalysis and retrace some specific phases of empirical personality research that bridge the gap to the academic tradition. These developments will be followed up in their implications upon further interpretation of the authoritarian personality pattern, with added emphasis upon recent research on the problem of personal bias and values.

SOCIAL AND DEVELOPMENTAL COMPLEMENTATION OF "THE AUTHORITARIAN PERSONALITY"

Authoritarianism is multi-determined, as are all social phenomena. It can be placed in the context of economic, social and political institutions, or it can be viewed in the light of the function it has for different individuals. The two approaches are so closely interwoven that neither can stand alone. The multiplicity of the factors involved does not, however, make it necessary for every single investigator to explore, or in any direct sense "control," all the potentially relevant variables. However, he should avoid the lurking danger — not without precedent in scientific research — of ascribing primary importance to his own major avenue of material evidence.

In our work in *The Authoritarian Personality* we concentrated on the search for correlates of socially relevant attitudes, such as ethnocentrism, in the dynamics of the individual personality. This does not mean that we attempted an explanation of the origin of ethnocentrism or of fascism in general on the basis of, say, the number of immature individuals in a given country or society. Few clinicians, if any, and certainly none of the authors of *The Authoritarian Personality* are inclined to regard psychological factors as the major or exclusive determinants of political or social movements. We have explicitly acknowledged that historical, social and economic factors are crucial determinants of the rise of political movements. Such acknowledgment is the best one can do whenever certain avenues of approach have been omitted from the program as they were in our study. In the introduction to our book we have clearly stated that "broad changes in social conditions and institutions will have a direct bearing upon the kinds of personalities that develop within a society." The two groups of factors are seen to operate on equal footing in that under traumatic socio-political circumstances authoritarian personalities may be brought to the fore and latent authoritarian trends in individuals who otherwise would remain democratic may be reinforced. "Thus under certain socio-economic conditions an entire nation may become inclined to 'escape from freedom'" (p. 486). As was pointed out by Fromm,[2] this was probably the case with Nazism in Germany. There can be little doubt that most traumatic situations are met according to the predispositions of the individuals involved. We have always stressed that the validity of our results is limited to relatively stable circumstances in which there is a choice between alternative ideologies with not too much suggestion or pressure exerted in either of the two directions, and that our specific approach deals with no more than the selection, by the individual, of social attitudes from a variety of more or less institutionalized outlooks offered to that individual in a complex society.

In essence, our work constitutes a shift of attention from the structure and origin to the actual functioning of these institutions and to their influence on man and social behavior; in any such restructuring, psychology will necessarily come to the fore. This is the case even in the domain of more purely sociological work, in

---

[2] An outstanding attempt at integrating psychological and psychoanalytic with socio-political concepts which was of great influence on our work on the authoritarian personality is Erich Fromm's *Escape from Freedom*, New York, 1941. Some of the most important pioneer work along the lines of such an integration has been undertaken by H. D. Lasswell in his *Psychopathology and Politics*, Chicago, 1930.

Further Explorations by a Contributor

the sense that this shift implements a direct approach to the ways in which social processes are experienced. Choice of the approach-via-personality is especially called for when, as is true in our case, objective social structure is taken for granted and constitutes no more than the common background of an investigation centered about finding individual differences in the appeal various elements of a common social background may exert upon varying personalities. It must be remembered that it has never been our aim to generalize from our individuals to the culture as a whole; since we described a variety of fairly distinct personality syndromes existing in one and the same culture, such inference could not even have been justifiably attempted. If our major interest would have been to assess the predilection toward authoritarianism in different societies we would have had to concentrate on a comparative study of the institutions of these societies, and this we did not set out to do.

It proved extremely intriguing to allow ourselves to be guided through the reverberations of social patterns within the most intimate realms of individual life. This we did in some detail regarding political and economic ideologies as experienced by the individual, perception of one's own group as well as of members of outgroups, conceptions of inter-personal relationships in the family unit and the interactions within that unit, and attitudes towards authorities and toward the alleged "underdog." We explored the ways in which people relate themselves to social institutions and to shared norms and values; we investigated their feelings of belongingness, the degree to which they tend to see themselves as conforming or deviating from the norms. We were interested in our subjects' notions of the parent-child relationship and of the relationship to the opposite sex, in their conceptions of the occupational roles they played and the goals and economic aspirations they pursued, and in their religious and social outlook. Thus we extended the clinical or personality-centered approach to issues which have traditionally been the prime concern of the social sciences. Though sociological conceptualization is primarily oriented toward constructs and relationships other than those favored in psychology, there is sufficient overlap to make such rapprochement possible.

Perhaps more strongly than ever, the present writer realized the necessity of combining the sociological and psychological approach when, in an attempt to discuss the outlook of ethnocentric children, she found herself describing attitudes toward the family or the other sex once in terms of the general norms and social "roles" envisaged by the subjects—such as their conceptions of function within the family, of masculinity and femininity—and then in terms of underlying motivation and emotion.

The general prevalence of personality traits among the authoritarians in our sample was in this manner discovered indirectly, through the psychological study of individuals.[3] The role played in our culture by such personality traits as self-alienation, mechanization, standardization and stereotypy, piecemeal functioning, intolerance of ambiguity, lack of individuation and spontaneity, and a combination of irrationality with manipulative opportunism shows the mark of some of the features inherent in the process of industrial mass production and in the machinery by which it operates.

Another of the many possible examples, from our study, of the way in which the functioning of social institutions may be reflected in, and illuminated by, their realization within the individual is given by our investigation of our subjects' attitude toward political figures such as Roosevelt. In contrast to the exclusively personality-centered approach of psychoanalysis, this investigation was not made with an eye on understanding the subjects' attitude toward their fathers, but rather with an eye on socio-political aspects. Yet, we probably would never have been able to understand the range and subtlety of our subjects' attitudes toward Roosevelt had we not been guided by the accumulated and integrated findings of psychoanalysis on attitudes toward fathers, father-substitutes, and father-figures.

In view of the recent stress on direct studies in group dynamics, we should like to add that the life space of the individual personality (in Lewin's[4] sense of the term), when studied in this manner, is seen as revealing not only the individual's interactions with his

---

[3] For cross-disciplinary familiarization with the type of reasoning of which our study of the authoritarian personality was a manifestation see Frenkel-Brunswik, E., "Interaction of psychological and sociological factors in political behavior," *Amer. Political Science Review*, 1952, 46, 44-65; the paper cited is part of the Symposium on Sociological and Psychological Problems Involved in the Study of Social Stratification and Politics held at the 47th Annual Meeting of the American Political Science Association in San Francisco, August, 1951.

[4] Lewin, K., *Principles of Topological Psychology*, McGraw-Hill, New York, 1936.

immediate surroundings but also as reflecting interactions of different social groups.

In our case, the major advantage of the personality-centered approach lies in the fact that it enables us to catch certain subtle aspects of human behavior which are usually bypassed in both purely sociological and in most current social-psychological descriptions. For the same reasons, the approach via personality is the ideal method to give what we call below the necessary "psychological turn" to certain hitherto purely sociological concepts, such as that of marginality of social status.

One of the difficulties in discussions concerning the relative importance of personality vs. situational factors arises from the fact that usually neither of the two terms is sufficiently specified in its appropriate context. "Situations" may be relatively stable or unstable and traumatic; they may be past or present; they may be of a more personal type, more or less specific to the individual in question, or they may be group situations; and the group concerned may be a cultural subgroup such as a specific socio-economic class or the entire nation as in the case of war. By a flexible use of terms, the personality point of view could be subsumed under the situational point of view in that it stresses the importance of relatively early and relatively personal situations in addition to the contemporary situation. Finding such a common denominator would make it easier to realize that the personality point of view fully allows for traumatic situations of a more general socio-political type to supersede the individual components to a greater or lesser extent.

Our basic assumption that political and social attitudes are not isolated phenomena within the individual but are intimately related to what may be considered more personal attitudes, e.g., toward family and sex, has been borne out by fact. Correlations between sexual, emotional, and cognitive outlook, on the one hand, and social and political attitudes, on the other, proved consistently significant. Conventionality, rigidity, repressive denial and the ensuing breakthrough of one's weakness, fear and dependency are but aspects of the same fundamental personality pattern, another manifestation of which is ethnocentrism; and they can be observed in personal life as well as in attitudes toward religion and social issues.

Not only did we find statistically significant relations between social attitudes and personality, but our understanding of social and political beliefs and of religious and ethical ideologies was deepened when woven into the matrix of the total individual. That these attitudes also are woven into the over-all pattern of society had been more widely stressed and was more widely appreciated before our study than were the relationship of these attitudes to the seemingly more remote intimate aspects of our lives.

We should add that the correlations of personality characteristics —conceived broadly to include attitude toward social roles and institutions—on the one hand, with social-political outlook, on the other, were in general higher than those of the latter with gross sociological indices such as income and class membership which had also been incorporated in our study. This does not exclude, of course, the possibility that finer sociological indices will tell us more about the ethnic or occupational locus of our personality types.

Being aware of the influence of the family upon individuals, as well as that of broader social factors upon the family, we should expect variations in these broader social factors to be related to variations in child rearing patterns and in the general mode of living and of perceiving social realities. In fact, in the parallel California study on ethnocentrism in children, we found variations of the authoritarian personality syndrome to be related to parental occupation.

In studying these distributions, the concept of marginality was a most important organizing principle; it already had proved fruitful in the analysis of the interviews in *The Authoritarian Personality*. In the project on children, data on the socio-economic history of the families of the extremely ethnocentric and of the non-ethnocentric children were collected over a period of time. One of the chief purposes in obtaining this material was to see whether the feeling of marginality, which seemed so important to ethnocentrism, is determined by sudden changes in the socio-economic status of the families. The assumption was that loss of status might undermine individual security, whereas a gain in status might lead to a variety of attempts to maintain this gain. This hypothesis has been partially confirmed in that families with a history of privileged socio-economic status seem to be less ethnocentric than families with unstable histories; but instability of status *per se* goes almost as often with ethnic tolerance as it does with ethnocentrism. It was possible to find families perfectly matched so far as socio-economic locus is concerned, yet quite different in their reaction to such locus. Some of the families objectively marginal to the group to which they belonged in previous generations developed rigid defenses against their social recession whereas others apparently utilized their marginality and greater distance to their own culture for creative purposes and for deeper satisfactions. Since it is the subjective feeling of marginality which seems the crucial factor in ethnocentrism and this, in turn, is found to be less related to actual status than to the discrepancy between aspired and actual status, there appears the necessity of giving "a psychological turn" to what was originally a sociological construct. We may take this as an illustration of the interweaving of the psychological and the sociological approach. We also find that sexual or other individual forms of marginality may have the same effect on social and political attitudes as does marginality in the sociological sense.

Further, ethnocentrism appears to be more closely related to the occupational affiliation of families than it is to purely economic factors. In the study of adults it was found that, at least in the majority group, the parents and grandparents of subjects low in ethnocentrism are significantly more frequently from such professional fields as medicine, law, teaching, and the ministry than are those of subjects high in ethnocentrism. In following up this finding in the study on children we found a relatively high percentage of non-ethnocentric families among the small merchants of our sample; perhaps the small merchant in California does not feel basically threatened. There was, however, a relatively high percentage of ethnocentric families among the workers, especially among those aspiring to a higher status. Among other employees we found an even distribution of ethnocentric and unprejudiced families although salesmen, policemen, firemen and their families seem to be more frequently among the prejudiced while bus drivers, accountants, government workers and their families seem to be more frequently among the unprejudiced.

As was the case with the effects of marginality, these relationships, too, can only be explained by a combined psychological and sociological approach. Choosing the occupation of salesman may indicate self-promoting tendencies whereas that of policeman may reveal identification with authority and aggression and poor adjustment to work *per se;* on the other hand, choosing to be a bus driver may be related to enjoyment of this kind of activity as an end in itself and thus to good work adjustment. Work adjustment in turn was found negatively related to ethnocentrism. Of equal importance in the sociology of occupations is that in the pursuit of a certain occupation or social role a selective reinforcement of specific traits appropriate to that role is likely to occur.

Such political attitudes as preference for the Republican or Democratic Party seem to be more closely related to economic factors than to ethnocentrism. Studies in this field apparently warrant the establishment of a rank order of political and social attitudes with respect to their relatedness to economic factors. Ethnocentrism, obviously less directly connected with economic self-interest, leaves more room for personality differenes to come into play. Though it seems highly probable that certain social and political attitudes are closely determined by economic self-interest, it must also be stressed that certain individual or group actions are blatantly against self-interest. In view of evidence which is continually accumulating, it is very difficult to deny that irrationality, distortion of perceptions and projections of hostility and of other thwarted tendencies influence the social scene.

We should like to emphasize that our material seems to suggest considerable variation in verbal or behavioral conformity to the values and norms often assumed to be generally approved. Here again, it is the authoritarian person who apparently tends to judge people predominantly on the basis of their position in the socio-economic hierarchy and of rigidly fixed roles. The liberal tends to exhibit greater distance to these conventional values and at the same time tends to be more integrated as a person.

Let us turn once more to an interesting problem intertwined with that of conformity, that is, the variants of the authoritarian personality pattern from one social class to another. According to *The Authoritarian Personality*, the true conservative and conformist, largely to be found in the higher income groups, must be distinguished from the pseudo-conservative, a psychopathic variant of the conservative pattern found more frequently in the lower income groups. There are many points of similarity between the two types; however, William Morrow, in his chapter on prison inmates, has vividly described the conventionality and conformity of the ethnically prejudiced who have violated legal standards. Viewed from the aspect of personality dynamics, the difference between the upper-class and the lower-class authoritarian may be suspected to lie in the defense mechanisms employed.

In our study of prejudice in children we found that the upper-class authoritarian personality is more likely to repress his hostility; the lower-class authoritarian, on the other hand, will more likely repress his passivity since in his subculture aggression is generally not as inhibited as in the middle and upper strata.

Many of our main findings on the authoritarian personality may be phrased in terms of a dependence of social and political attitudes upon the structure of the defense mechanisms. Since the origin and direction of the defense mechanisms are determined by the particular set of taboos and values existing in a given society, this finding again points to the importance of social factors in the etiology of ethnocentrism.

A detailed phenomenological study of the parents' attitude toward social institutions is also being conducted in our project on children. The type of conformity displayed by parents of ethnocentric adolescents does not always consist in a genuine identification with traditional values. Our previous evidence already pointed to the fact that the authoritarian person has frequently lost his traditional roots and has made an attempt to compensate for this loss by non-functional forced and rigid conformity. We are now in the process of analyzing the various types of distortion and simplification of the meaning of social institutions. It seems that the predominant values are too uniformly and too absolutely interpreted in the direction of power and status. In *The Authoritarian Personality* the status concern of the ethnocentric individuals was emphasized. However, more recent data make it even more evident that this status concern is often quite different from a realistic attempt to improve one's position by effort and by an adequate means-goal instrumentality. The status concern of ethnocentric parents often takes the form of an infantile need for importance, a wish to be close to someone who is strong and powerful.

In order to throw more light on this problem, a detailed inquiry is being made into the goals of these parents as well as the steps which they consider necessary for attainment of their goals. For example, one of our adolescent subjects has a highly prejudiced father, a garage mechanic, who believes that he will become a great inventor. He is preoccupied with finding a powerful and benevolent sponsor who will have confidence in him; but, from what we could gather, he gives very little thought to the anticipated inventions.

An exploration of what Kardiner[5] calls the "primary social institutions" was, furthermore, undertaken by a study of child rearing

---

[5] Kardiner, A., *The Individual and his Society*, New York, 1939.

practices and of interpersonal relations and values prevalent in the families of the children and adolescents studied. In *The Authoritarian Personality* our information on family background, handling of discipline, and childhood events was recruited entirely from the retrospective accounts of adult subjects. In our study of social discrimination in children, these questions were tackled by means of visits to the home and extensive interviews with the parents. We inquired into the attitude of the parents toward the child, their goals or positive ideals concerning the child as well as their negative ideals, i.e., what they did not want the child to become. Furthermore, we collected detailed data on child training such as the handling of discipline, type of punishment used, procedures in weaning, toilet training, and so forth. Data on the family background of the parents themselves were also gathered.

A preliminary inspection of the data supports the assumption made in *The Authoritarian Personality* that warmer, closer and more affectionate interpersonal relationships prevail in the homes of the unprejudiced children; the conclusions concerning the importance of strictness, rigidity, punitiveness, rejection vs. acceptance of the child seem to be borne out by data from the children themselves. Somewhat surprisingly, on the other hand, certain frequently emphasized details of procedure seem to be relatively unrelated to the outcome in which we are interested, that is, to the development of an authoritarian vs. a liberal personality structure. Among these comparatively irrelevant factors seems to be the circumstances of nursing, such as breast feeding vs. bottle feeding and time of weaning, and those of toilet training, such as the age at which it is begun. As an illustration we may refer to the mother of one of our most liberal and creative children who told us with considerable worry how, following the advice of a pediatrician, she had done "all the wrong things" such as starting toilet training very early; however, the obviously very warm and accepting attitude of this mother toward her child seems to have been a much more crucial factor than the concrete techniques used. What seems to count most is the establishment of an intelligible, non-ego-destructive type of discipline.

In the home with the orientation toward rigid conformity, on the other hand, actual maintenance of discipline is often based upon the expectation of a quick learning of external rigid and superficial rules which are bound to be beyond the comprehension of the child. Family relationships are characterized by fearful subservience to the demands of the parents and by an early suppression of impulses not acceptable to the adults.

Since the moral requirements in such a home must appear to the child as overwhelming and at the same time unintelligible, and the rewards meager, submission to them must be reinforced by fear of and pressure from external agencies. Due to the lack of a genuine identification with the parents, the fearfully conforming child does not make the important developmental step from mere social anxiety to real conscience. The liberal parents, on the other hand, showing as they do less anxiety with respect to conformity and thus allowing themselves greater richness and expression of emotional life, provide guidance and support rather than condemnation and thus help the child to work out his instinctual problems. This makes possible the development of higher stages of maturity as well as greater socialization and sublimation of instinctual tendencies.

Let me now turn to the reverberations of the patterns of family life just outlined in the social personality of the children and adolescents exposed to them. Study of these personality patterns was undertaken by means of direct and indirect questionnaires,[6] and especially by means of interviews.[7] It was found that, at least after the age of ten, childrens' personalities tend to fall into patterns similar to those observed in the adults described in *The Authoritarian Personality*. Thus ethnocentric youngsters tend to display authoritarian aggression, rigidity, cruelty, superstition, externalization and projectivity, denial of weakness, power orientation, and tend toward dichotomous conceptions of sex roles, of kinds of people, and of values.

One of the ways in which our study differed from *The Authoritarian Personality* is given by the fact that the interviews included the children's immediate descriptions of the social atmosphere in

---

[6] The results of these tests are being published by this writer jointly with Murray E. Jarvik and Milton Rokeach in a monograph tentatively titled "Ethnocentrism in Youth: Its Measurement and Personality Correlates" (scheduled for publication in *Genetic Psychology Monographs*).

[7] A series of articles on the results of the interviews with ethnocentric and liberal children is now being prepared by this writer and Joan Havel. The first of these articles, "Authoritarianism in the interviews of children: I. Attitudes toward minority groups," has appeared in *Jour. of Genet. Psychol.*, 1953, 82, 91-136.

which they grew up and also referred to the ideals they had formed concerning this social world surrounding them. We investigated their images of the real parents along with their notions concerning ideal parental roles, the role of the teacher, their notions of a "perfect boy" and "perfect girl" and of a "bad boy" and "bad girl," of the "best" or "worst" professions for men and for women, and so forth.

To sketch briefly some of the results on this aspect of our study, we should like to point out that in the ethnocentric child the conception of family life was found to be based on rather clearly defined roles of dominance and submission in contradistinction to equalitarian policies as stressed by democratic-minded children. Prejudiced children consider the major role of figures in authority, such as parents and teachers, to be that of disciplining, controlling and keeping them in line. Thus, the perfect father is described by one of the highly prejudiced boys as one who

> "Doesn't give you everything you want . . . doesn't let you do the outrageous things that you sometimes want."

Other boys in this group say about the perfect father:

> "He spanks you when you are bad and doesn't give you too much money," or:
> "When you ask for something he ought not to give it to you right away," or:
> "Not soft on you, strict."

In the cases where parental roles are described by assertion rather than by negation, the emphasis is on punitiveness, strictness, or on the parents' role as deliverers of material goods. More frequently, however, prejudiced children describe the ideal as well as the real parents in negative terms such as abstention from severe corporal punishment. One of the highly ethnocentric boys describes the perfect father thus:

> "Don't let you get spoiled, punishes you when you deserve it, . . . doesn't get drunk, makes an honest living, loyal to his wife, pays his income tax, not in cahoots with a gang of some sort, . . . don't break the hair brush over a child."

The unprepudiced children, on the other hand, tend to describe the perfect father as companionable and relaxed, and tend to emphasize positive values such as a kind, and gentle disposition. Passages from the protocols of two of the boys in this group follow:

"Will make sure his children get three meals a day, are well-fed and clothed and that they get a lot of play in the air; make sure they do well in school; would help them in their school work; . . . see that his children have lots of friends; see that they mind adults and people in charge; . . . he would take his children out and have a good time with them; . . . my father does."

"He thinks up things for his children to do . . . (activities) . . . wouldn't change his father much."

The bad father emerges in the description obtained from prejudiced children as a poor provider and as someone who does not exert adequate discipline, while unprejudiced children stress lack of understanding, rejection and neglect as his major characteristics.

The pattern of responses concerning the ideal teacher is similar to that concerning the ideal parent. Here are the responses given by two democratic-minded boys:

"Would carefully listen to your viewpoints and explain what's wrong and what's right about it, and let you argue it out instead of flatly telling you you are wrong; should have a fairly good knowledge of nature and foreign languages, be interesting. If she can relate her own experiences in relation to some topic you are studying, it is interesting. Has the personality to keep order in the classroom and not afraid the pupils will dislike her if she does. Should accept a joke but not let it go too far.

"Fair in her attitude toward all pupils, doesn't favor one, explains the lessons and helps you within reason."

Contrast this with the following passage from the protocol of a highly ethnocentric girl:

"Someone that is strict. If she asks for homework, you have to have it done. Most teachers are not strict enough. If the assigned work is not in you should be given a zero. She shouldn't let the class get out of hand."

The fact that discipline is experienced by the ethnocentric child significantly more often as threatening, traumatic, overwhelming and unintelligible is in line with the type of home we have pointed out above as being usually offered this child. It is thus not surprising that the image of the parents acquires for the prejudiced child a forbidding, threatening and distant quality.

The lack of an internalized and individualized approach to the child on the part of the parents and the tendency to transmit mainly a set of fixed rules and customs may be considered as interfering with the development of a clear-cut personal identity and integration in the growing child. While unprejudiced children are more apt to see positive as well as negative features in their parents and can accept feelings of love and hate towards the same persons without too much anxiety or conflict, ethnocentric children frequently seem compelled to dramatize the image of the parents by seeing them once, and openly, as altogether good, and then, and mostly covertly, as altogether bad. These latter children split the positive from the negative sides of their feelings and attitudes rather than becoming aware of their coexistence. This pattern of denial of ambivalence constitutes a break in the integration of personality. The description of the parents in this type of case is often stereotypical and exaggerated, indicating a use of clichés rather than expression of genuine feelings, and the range of responses is rather narrow and without the variations commonly found in the description of real people. Only the more palpable, crude, and concrete aspects are mentioned. The presence and potency of negative attitudes is revealed in responses to questions or approaches which are more indirect. Many of the children in this group who display only glorification and admiration for their parents in direct questioning omit the parents from the list of people they would choose as companions on a desert island. Or in their responses to parental figures on the Thematic Apperception Test they tend to stress only the coercive and punitive aspects of parents.

As is the conception of the parent-child relationship, the notions on sex roles are likewise highly conventionalized in the ethnically prejudiced child. There is a tendency toward a rigid and exaggerated conception of masculinity and femininity. The "real boy" must be "a regular guy" who knows how to fight, is tough and not a sissy, and at the same time does unquestioningly what he is told to do by his parents and teachers. By contrast, the unprejudiced boy tends to stress such values as likeability and real internalization of adult values. He is often considered as a sissy by the other group. There is a "dichotomous" conception of sex roles on the part of the prejudiced children, with the rejection of the more urbane boy and the tomboy girl. In specifying the differential roles of boys and girls, these children tend to take a standpoint best expressed by the quotation, "the best friend of a boy is a boy and of a girl, a girl." While unprejudiced boys tend to maintain that in the company of a girl a boy should talk about the things he likes to talk about—"the same as to another boy," as one of them puts it—prejudiced children tend to stress that girls should act "ladylike" and not assume the manners and privileges of boys. The following are passages from the characterizations of the perfect girl by highly ethnocentric boys:

> "They don't do things like a boy does, but what girls do. They shouldn't be tomboys."
> "Isn't filthy minded, not too rough, not a tomboy."

Both the girls and the boys in the prejudiced group subscribe relatively often to the statement that girls should only learn "things which are useful around the house." In contrast to this, unprejudiced boys do not tend to stress differentiation of sex roles. Witness the following descriptions of the feminine sex role, and of the perfect girl, by three boys in this group:

> "If she likes to do housework, it is good to be a housewife, or she can be a career woman. It is up to her."
> "Well, they've got their rights; they can do it if they like."
> "She's pretty and she's got brains. She's not too scared. She likes dogs."

The element of conventionality in the conception of sex roles is only part of a more general conventionality in the image of self and society as found in ethnocentric children. Good manners, attainment of success and status, self-control and poise are some of the most frequently stressed requirements. In line with this, highly ethnocentric children tend to define the best and the worst occupations predominantly in terms of their appropriateness to status or sex roles or in terms of exhibitionistic self-glorification. Thus the ideal occupation for men is considered by the prejudiced boys chiefly from the angle of prestige and external success in the social hierarchy, while the worst occupation is very frequently defined in terms of inferior or "dirty" work as exemplified by that of a garbage collector or ditch digger. Unprejudiced children, on the other hand, consider as ideal occupations anything that is exciting or interesting or that is liked for its own sake, or an activity for which one is adequately trained, and as a bad occupation something one dislikes or something which is morally weakening (e.g., having too much money). Prejudiced children specify that for women very few occupations are suitable, such as that of secretary; one of the boys expresses the opinion implied by many in his group when, to the question about the worst occupation for a woman, he answers:

"To earn her own living; usually the man does that."

As an ideal occupation for women the unprejudiced children stress qualities similar to those stressed for men. While the prejudiced children, in their responses to the question concerning the worst occupation for women, stress mainly "dirty" work or "hard" work or socially objectionable work like that of a nightclub singer, the unprejudiced children stress work which is disliked or work that may prevent the raising of children and the fulfillment of the essential aspects of the feminine role. The adherence to the delineated norms is likely to be rigid even though it may imply restrictions and disadvantages for their own group. Rigidity is thus set above advantage.

At this point we may return once more to the discussion of the home atmosphere as it must be assumed to underlie to a large measure the development of the attitude patterns just described, and cite further evidence from the literature. In a study by Harris, Gough, and Martin,[8] questionnaires returned by mothers of Minnesota high-school children provided systematic data regarding their beliefs about child rearing practices. An analysis of the responses by the mothers of 36 highly prejudiced pupils and by those of 36 pupils low on prejudice indicated that mothers in the former group tend toward greater authoritarianism and greater rigidity or "fussiness." Further support concerning the importance of family structure and child rearing may be derived from a study by Huffman and Levinson,[9] using a special Traditional Family Ideology (TFI) Scale largely constructed along the lines of the hypotheses employed in our California studies.

In our material, there is one interesting exception to the parallelism between the adolescent and the adult ethnocentric personality. This is given by the fact that it is the unprejudiced rather than the prejudiced child who appears to display the greatest conformity to adults. He or she seems to think it wise to follow the advice of

---

[8] Harris, D. B., Gough, H. G., and Martin, W. E., "Children's ethnic attitudes: II. Relationship to parental beliefs concerning child training," *Child Development*, 1950, 21, 169-181.

[9] Huffman, P. E. and Levinson, D. J., "Authoritarian personality and family ideology: I. A scale for the measurement of traditional family ideology," *American Psychologist*, 1950, 5, 307.

grown-ups and to accept the values of the parents or teachers to the point of frequently becoming a "teacher's pet." This conformity to adult values is based on genuine love and identification with the parents and is to be differentiated from the fearful submission of the ethnocentric child. The latter tends to be alternately submissive and rebellious toward authorities and at the same time is imbued with a "gang spirit" of his own, being "against" adults and against those children who are interested in academic achievement or who are otherwise "different."

In trying to explain this reversal on the basis of general clinical knowledge, we may venture the conjecture that the child who conforms relatively closely to adult standards is at the same time the one who will show independence in adulthood. It appears as if the unprejudiced children generally tend to seek the help of adults in working out their own problems such as aggression and control of impulses, and look to the adult for guidance in the acquisition of scholarship and ethical principles. The typical prejudiced child, however, appears to make much less of an attempt to manage his own impulses and appears to vacillate between a fearful surface submission to authorities and a comparative neglect of social standards. Many of our subjects are in the pre-adolescent stage; it is probable that in the course of adolescence and post-adolescence the unprejudiced child becomes engaged in a struggle for independence.

These results, obtained from interviews and personality tests, are supported by a sociometric test intended to reveal the social reputation of ethnocentric and liberal children. This test contains descriptions of special traits of boys and girls in single sentences; the children are asked to list under each of the items any classmates to whom the description applies.[10] The results to date suggest that unprejudiced children are more frequently considered by their classmates "to act the way grown-ups want them to," as "not to mind being told what to do and not to mind being bossed"; they are the ones "who don't care whether they are the center of attention"; they also are the ones whom "everyone likes" and the ones who are relatively often claimed as "best friends"; but at the same time, the boys in this group are relatively often considered to be "sissies." In the familiar picture of the unprejudiced child, this stresses popularity

---

[10] A brief advance report on preliminary results of this aspect of our testing program has been given by this writer in "Studies of social discrimination in children," *American Psychologist*, 1946, 1, 456.

along with rather quiet, withdrawn and docile aspects. Prejudiced children, on the other hand, are relatively often considered as "complaining" and as "the ones who always want things for themselves and won't help others." All this tends to confirm or round out the results gained with other tests.

In *The Authoritarian Personality* subjects low on authoritarianism tended to describe themselves as having been isolated in childhood and as sexually backward in adolescence. The results of our direct study of children generally tends to corroborate these descriptions from memory given by the adult subjects in reference to their childhood.

While the personality structure of the ethnocentric child is in many ways similar to that of the ethnocentric adult, there are important differences in the over-all picture which shall now be listed briefly.

Whereas the ethnocentric personality pattern seems quite firmly established in the adult, it appears in the child as incipient, or as a potential direction for development. This is indicated by the fact that certain correlations are lower than the analogous ones in adults. For instance, we often find in ethnocentric adults a highly opportunistic, exploitive and manipulative attitude toward other people. The ethnocentric child, however, in spite of showing tendencies in the same direction, still generally seeks more direct satisfaction of his psychological needs. Furthermore, the ethnocentric child is more accessible to experience and reality than the ethnocentric adult who has rigidly structured his world according to his interests and desires. Finally, the child's position as a comparative underdog constitutes a possible experiential basis for his sympathy for other underdogs.

In spite of the differences between the ethnocentric and liberal child, it must be pointed out that with respect to many of the features mentioned above, such as superstition or conformity, children as such seem to have more of a touch of the ethnocentric than of the liberal adult. In turn, the ethnocentric adult may be considered as more infantile than the liberal adult with respect to these features. The older the children are the greater the differences between the ethnocentric and the liberal child. All this seems to indicate that some of the trends which are connected with ethnocentrism are natural stages of development which must be overcome if maturity is to be reached.

Outside of California, the relationships of children's ethnic attitudes to personality factors were further explored by Gough, Harris, Martin, and Edwards[11] who found that Minnesota school children showing the greatest intolerance toward Negroes and Jews also tended to be more constricted, cynical, and fearful, less confident and eager, and more suspicious and generally ethnocentric.

COGNITIVE PATTERNS AND "UNITY OF STYLE"

In setting out, as we did, to combine the resources of psychoanalysis, general psychology, and social psychology, psychoanalytic thought influenced us in our attempt to relate socio-political attitudes to the underlying dynamics of the personality. From general psychology derives a further interest, that in perception and the thinking processes, a topic on which we shall now expand. No experiments along this line were done within the framework of *The Authoritarian Personality*. However, there is one section in the book which concentrates upon cognitive personality organization as based on an analysis of the interviews. A more specific approach to cognitive variables is possible through direct experimentation on perception and thinking. One set of these experiments, using school children as subjects, was undertaken by the present writer and her collaborators as part of the project mentioned earlier in this paper. A shift of research emphasis from the emotional to the perceptual area controls certain social biases which may interfere with the investigation of social and clinical topics. Controversial issues can be delineated and at least indirectly examined in a more neutral context. The experiments have shown that the tendency to resort to black-white solutions, to arrive at premature closure—often at the neglect of reality—and to seek for unqualified and unambiguous solutions which had been found so characteristic of the social and emotional outlook of ethnocentric subjects could also be ascertained in their perceptual responses.

When ethnocentric children were first presented with familiar objects and then with somewhat related but unfamiliar and

---

[11] Gough, H. G., Harris, D. B., Martin, W. E., and Edwards, M., "Children's ethnic attitudes: I. Relationship to certain personality factors," *Child Development*, 1950, 21, 83-91.

ambiguous stimuli, they tended either to cling longer to the original object perceptions or to fall into a spell of haphazard guessing. Concerning another experiment, involving the retelling of a story from memory, a quotation from the writer's paper on "Intolerance of Ambiguity" (see note 1) may suffice; the prejudiced children showed either a

> "clinging to the presentation with little freedom and distance, i.e., a stimulus-boundness in the sense of Goldstein, . . . or a neglect of the stimulus altogether in favor of purely subjective fantasies. It is in this manner that a rigid, cautious, segmentary approach goes with one that is disintegrated and chaotic, sometimes one and the same child manifesting both patterns in alternation or in all kinds of bizarre combinations. As do negativism and distortion in general, both these patterns help avoidance of uncertainty, one of them by fixation to, the other by tearing loose from, the given realities" (p. 126).

Thus, preliminary results support the conjecture that, by and large, such tendencies as the quest for unqualified certainty, the rigid adherence to the given—be this an authority or a perceptual stimulus—the inadequacy of reaction in terms of reality, and so forth, operate in more than one area of personality. It can be demonstrated, further, that such specific forms of reaction as "stimulus-boundness," that is, the pedantic orientation toward concrete detail, tend to occur again and again within an individual in contexts seemingly far removed from each other. Inclination toward mechanical repetition of faulty hypotheses, inaccessibility to new experience, satisfaction with subjective and at the same time unimaginative, over-concrete or over-generalized solutions, all appear to be specific manifestations of a fairly general "intolerance of ambiguity" which holds sway among certain groups of individuals. Among the particular characteristics to which this intolerance of ambiguity seems related, we should like to single out submission to authority, feelings of social marginality, lack of originality, externalization of values, hostility, power-orientation, and rigid social stereotyping.

Since the phrase "intolerance of ambiguity" can be easily misunderstood, a number of clarifying attributes to sharpen its meaning in the present context shall be listed. "Ambiguity" was not intended to indicate undesirable aspects of cognition, such as confusion or inarticulate vagueness; rather it was to stand for the complexity and differentiation which is an essential aspect of the creative process. Accordingly, the following aspects of intolerance of ambiguity were specified: undue preference for symmetry, familiarity, definiteness, and regularity; tendency toward black-white solutions, over-simplified dichotomizing, unqualified either-or solutions, premature closure, perseveration and stereotypy; a tendency toward excessively "good" form (that is, excessive *Prägnanz* of *Gestalt* organization), achieved either by diffuse globality or by over-emphasis on concrete detail; compartmentalization, stimulus-boundness; avoidance of uncertainty as accomplished by the narrowing of meanings, by inaccessibility to experience, by mechanical repetition of sets, or by a segmentary randomness and an absolutizing of those aspects of reality which have been preserved.

It is thus clear that intolerance of ambiguity does not lead to greater consistency in one's outlook or behavior. Real consistency can be based only on an adequate appraisal of many-sidedness, conflicts, uncertainties, differences, and complexities wherever they happen to exist. Perhaps paradoxically this is compatible with the holding of strong beliefs in intrinsic general principles so long as these principles are broadly and flexibly conceived and "alternative manifestations" (see below) are permitted. Rigid adherence to an absolute dogma is a poor substitute for such intrinsically more consistent principles; it constitutes an inadequate attempt to escape lurking chaos, cynicism, and relativism.

A problem in rigidity that is related to the more general problem of the intolerance of ambiguity was investigated by Rokeach.[12] He used a gestaltpsychological thinking problem involving the manipulation of three jars as containers. A mental set was first established by exposing the subjects to a series of problems which could be solved only by a relatively long and complex manipulation of the containers. The subjects were then presented with further problems which could be solved either by maintaining the original set or by using a more direct and simple method. Children scoring extremely high on ethnic prejudice were found to cling more rigidly to the original set than those extremely low on prejudice.

Additional evidence for the association of prejudice and intolerance of ambiguity is provided by Block and Block[13] who found that subjects high in ethnocentrism established a personal norm in

---

[12] Rokeach, M., "Generalized mental rigidity as a factor in ethnocentrism," *Jour. of Abnormal and Social Psychol.*, 1948, 43, 259-278.

[13] Block, Jack and Block, Jeanne, "An investigation of the relationship between intolerance of ambiguity and ethnocentrism," *Jour. of Personality*, 1951, 19, 303-311.

repeated trials on the autokinetic phenomenon more readily than the ethnically unprejudiced. In accounting for their results, however, the authors preferred to theorize in terms of excessive ego control rather than in terms of intolerance of ambiguity.

Further relevant to intolerance of ambiguity in its relation to rigidity and to the abstractness-concreteness problem is a study on young children by Kutner.[14] He found that children scoring low on ethnic prejudice demonstrated awareness of the abstract conceptual nature of the test given, whereas high scoring children exhibited a concrete approach, produced numerous fanciful responses culminating in failure, and tended toward over-generalization and the development of supernumerary "hypotheses." Nonetheless, intelligence as measured by the Kuhlman-Anderson test was found to be unrelated to prejudice; both groups were equally adept with syllogism-type deductive problems. Less well-structured deductive problems, however, led to a significantly greater proportion of failure among the prejudiced as contrasted with the unprejudiced children. Their failures were accompanied by a tendency toward dogmatic conversion of problems to syllogistic form, toward simplification, fractionalism and concretization. On a problem solution test, unprejudiced children showed significantly greater facility in finding correct solution principles than did prejudiced children. Failures are attributed to the development of inappropriate hypotheses, to persistence of perseverative sets, and to the effects of low frustration-tolerance.

The role of rigidity of set or *Einstellung* in the dynamics that lead from frustration to aggression was demonstrated by Christie.[15] He found that "junior high school students who were rated as being most frustrated used the set solution over twice as long as those rated not highly frustrated." Furthermore, "college students who were frustrated after establishing the set, took over twice as long to solve the final problem as did non-frustrated members of the control group." It was concluded that the effects of frustration upon an established set were such that the strength of the set was increased and behavioral rigidity was manifested.

---

[14] Kutner, B., "Patterns of mental functioning associated with prejudice in children," *American Psychologist*, 1951, 6, 328-329.

[15] Christie, R., "The effect of frustration upon rigidity in problem solution," *American Psychologist*, 1950, 5, 296-297. (For a more extended report see the author's University of California Doctoral Dissertation, Berkeley, 1949, bearing the same title.)

In the context of the *Gestalt* law of *Prägnanz*, Fisher[16] has joined this line of research with the use of verbal material and geometric forms. His conclusions are that "Lows showed pronounced tendencies to break the leveling directions of memory changes in time. ... With time, the tendency toward symmetry increased in frequency among the Highs and decreased among the Lows. ... Erasures tended to occur more often when there was less tendency to simplification and symmetry"; that is, they occurred more often among the Lows than among the Highs in the reproduction of geometric forms.

With the use of an esthetic preference test involving a large number of simple-symmetrical and complex-asymmetrical figures Barron[17] has found that subjects preferring the symmetrical figures tend to be less original, less intellectual, less sensual, less internalized, more constricted, more conservative, more ethnocentric, more conformant, and less independent. These findings corroborate in a most satisfactory way the relationships we had established with the variable "intolerance of ambiguity."

Case studies collected by a number of collaborators in our California study of social discrimination in children show in detail the consistency of the children's and adolescents' reactions to perceptual and cognitive tasks with the over-all clinical picture. Thus, one of the boy subjects who showed a great deal of conformity and compliance toward parents and authorities with an occasional breaking through of fits of rage and explosive aggression, tended to display in the perceptual and thinking experiments a generally cautious, restricted and conservative attitude toward the stimulus with an occasional shift toward disintegrated, random behavior when the strain of coping with the task became too great. Unprejudiced children, when blocked, more often tend to wait and reconsider the problem. They tend to have more independence in the

---

[16] Fisher, J., "The memory process and certain psychosocial attitudes with special reference to the Law of Pragnanz: I. Study of nonverbal content," *Jour. of Personality*, 1951, 19, 406-420.

[17] In a somewhat different context, the test is briefly described in Barron, F. and Welsh, G. S., "Artistic perception as a possible factor in personality style: its measurement by a figure preference test," *Jour. of Psychology*, 1952, 33, 199-203. The results summarized here will be reported in Barron, F., "Personality style and perceptual choice," *Jour. of Abnormal and Social Psychol.* (in press); the writer is indebted to Mr. Barron for allowing her to quote from the manuscript.

sense of being able to remain in suspense, whereas prejudiced children more often rush into random activities or give up the problem altogether. More detailed study of cases reveals that some of the prejudiced children perform well on some of the relatively simple or routine perceptual and cognitive tasks in spite of the fact that there are signs of rigidity in their performance; here we are reminded of the frequently-noted technological abilities of the German Nazis. On the other hand, those children in the ethnocentric group who perform poorly are often found to slide into overfluidity and disintegration. The performance of unprejudiced subjects is generally more pliable, tending toward creative flexibility, although there sometimes appears to be complete blockage in the solving of the tasks concerned; the latter frequently seems to be caused by a lack of interest in the aspects of reality involved in the particular set of tasks.[18]

The two subtypes of ethnocentric subjects which were discernible in the performances on the perceptual and thinking experiments, that is, the over-cautious, conservative, compulsive type, on the one hand, and the impulsive, reckless, psychopathic type with inability to delay action, on the other, seem to correspond rather closely to those discerned on the basis of political attitude in *The Authoritarian Personality*. These were the conservative, tradition-bound, conventional "Highs," on the one hand, and the ones who desired, by impulsive and destructive action, to restructure all of society in the hope of gaining prominence themselves, on the other.

The existence of rigid sets and outlooks and of a predilection to use preconceived, dogmatic categorizations together with a certain inaccessibility to new experience could, on the basis of the interviews, be ascertained significantly more frequently in the highly prejudiced individual than in the low-scorer on ethnocentrism. There is a tendency toward dichotomizing which extends from the conception of the parent-child relationship to that of sex roles and moral values, as well as to the handling of social relations as manifested especially in the ingroup-outgroup cleavages. It had further been observed that those scoring high on ethnocentrism tend to

---

[18] These observations are in agreement with results by Roger Brown (personal communication) who found, in a thesis carried out at the University of Michigan, that certain differences in rigidity between groups of ethnically prejudiced and unprejudiced subjects become manifest only when there is ego-involvement in the tasks in question.

concretize or "reify" abstract concepts and to have less pronounced appreciation of the complexity of personal relations, as well as little sympathy with the psychological and social sciences studying these relations.

At the same time, it was stressed, however, that there is a certain distinct sub-type of the unprejudiced personality who exhibits certain similarities to the pattern just described and in whom instead of democratic ideology we find another of its opposites, a left-wing radicalism. Since this sub-variety seems most prominently characterized by signs of rigidity in his personal makeup, it was labelled the "rigid low." The differentiation and subdivision of the major syndromes found in *The Authoritarian Personality*, notably of the low extreme in ethnocentrism, was expanded in a number of separate studies. A study by Rokeach[19] deals with the relation between "narrow-mindedness" and ethnocentrism in college freshmen. The subjects were asked to define a series of religious and politico-economic concepts ("isms"). The quartile lowest on prejudice was found to tend toward abstract rather than concrete definitions but also to favor the type of "reification" definition hinted at previously as a characteristic of extreme "highs." This confirms the hypothesis that reification, as a fallacy of abstraction, "might be a manifestation of dogmatism, which is sometimes present in low prejudiced individuals." In the first of the two reports listed above, Rokeach further stresses the "comprehensive" rather than "isolated" or "narrow" concept-formation technique of the extreme "lows." Also relevant to the problem of subtypes is a study by Dombrose and Levinson[20] who found that the most extreme "lows" tend toward militant programs for the establishment of democratic values whereas moderate "lows" tend toward pacifistic programs. In line with this is the finding of Haimowitz and Haimowitz[21] that therapeutically-induced shifts toward greater racial and religious tolerance occur among those initially classified as mildly rather than strongly hostile or friendly.

---

[19] Rokeach, M., "'Narrow mindedness' and ethnocentrism," *American Psychologist*, 1950, 5, 308, and "Prejudice, concreteness of thinking, and reification of thinking," *Jour. of Abnormal and Social Psychol.*, 1951, 46, 83-91.

[20] Dombrose, L. A. and Levinson, D. J., "Ideological 'militancy' and 'pacifism in democratic individuals," *Jour. of Social Psychol.*, 1950, 32, 101-113.

[21] Haimowitz, M. L. and N. R., "Reducing ethnic hostility through psychotherapy," *Jour. of Social Psychol.*, 1950, 231-241.

The results of the cognitive experiments cited above may be used further to clarify the problem of "unity of style" sometimes posed in personality theory, and especially in German "typology." Chiefly under the influence of psychoanalysis we searched for, and found, in *The Authoritarian Personality* unified themes in the private modes of experience as well as in religion and ideology. A somewhat more complex view emerges after consideration of the cognitive sphere of the personality.

Before offering our own answer to this problem, we should like to insert here a brief summary of some of the views of a psychologist prominent in Nazi Germany, E. R. Jaensch, so far as they are relevant to our problem.[22] There are two reasons why we expand on these views of Jaensch. The first is that he expressed rather dogmatic and oversimplified notions on the style-unity (*Stileinheit*) of the person, with special emphasis on cognitive aspects. The second more general reason is that Jaensch concentrates on a very articulate description of the most desirable personality type from the standpoint of Nazi ideology and that this type shows marked similarities to our description of the authoritarian personality. The fact that Jaensch glorifies this pattern while our attitude is one of reserve, or criticism, adds to the interest of this parallelism. The parallel delineation lends confidence to our interpretation of our results, since they are concurred in by psychologists glorifying the authoritarian personality.

The title of Jaensch's most comprehensive publication on the subject may be translated as "The anti-type." The anti-type is the opposite of the idolized German nationalist or peasant type, which in turn is a sub-variety of Jaensch's more general "integrated" type. Although Jaensch uses extensive and in part rather originally conceived laboratory experiments, they do not go beyond the scope of sensory perception; there is no concern with the motivational and projective aspects of perception. Furthermore, his samples are very small and statistics are of the crudest type, or, more often, completely lacking. Subjects of the groups against whom his criticism is explicitly directed in the more theoretical parts of his writings, such as Jews and "Parisians," are never directly included; rather, two or three "Orientals," such as Turks or Indians, are substituted instead.

---

[22] Jaensch, E. R., *Der Gegentypus*, Barth, Leipzig, 1938.

The anti-type is also called the "S-type," since persons of this type are said to manifest synesthesia, the well-known phenomenon of color-hearing or tone-seeing. Jaensch sees in this phenomenon an indication of the general lack of clear-cut and rigid evaluation of, and submission to, the stimulus, that is, of a tendency toward "loosening" (*Auflockerung*) and "dissolution" (*Auflosung*); hence the adjective "lytic" (dissolving) is also used by Jaensch to characterize this type. In contrast to this, Jaensch considers his ideal type to give unambiguous reactions to stimuli, a feature which he confounds with receptiveness and precision. In the quotation that follows, Jaensch in effect commits himself to the the notorious "constancy hypothesis"—a well known tacit fallacy in older psychological systems exposed by the Gestaltpsychologists whom Jaensch rejects for their theoretical stress on ambiguity.

"To the points of the retina correspond firmly and unequivocally determined locations in the visual space. This coordination between stimulus configuration and perceptual Gestalt is disrupted in the case of the S-type" (p. 37).

The glorification of rigid stimulus-response relationships by Jaensch and the assertion of their predominance in the Nazi ideal fits with our finding that "intolerance of ambiguity" is a frequent accompaniment of ethnocentrism.

A further element in Jaensch's theory is given by an oversimplified version of the doctrine of the "style-unity" of the person. Thus he postulates an essentially homogeneous and direct transfer of specific modes of response from one area of the person to all others; he dogmatically generalizes that the "subjective and unstable" evaluation of sensory stimuli as given by ambiguity carries over into a general lack of firmness and stability of the personality; and he assumes this to be degenerative, morbid, immoral, and dangerous for society. "Liberalism" of every kind—and "adaptability" in general—goes with this lack of strong ties, according to Jaensch.

"The lytic S-type has no firm tie with reality. In fact he has no ties at all. He is the liberalist at large (p 44).... This social liberalism is paralleled by innumerable other forms of liberalism, all of them mentally rooted in the S-type; liberalism of knowledge, of perception, of art, etc."

Rigid control, perseveration and avoidance of differences are an integral part of Jaensch's ideal of discipline. To him, one of the most gratifying experiences is the feeling of "equality of palpable, physical characteristics, . . . uniform, marching in step and column" (p. 337), whereas the anti-type is criticized for his aspiration to some measure of being different in developing his individuality. All this ties in with a questionable notion of masculinity. As we have found, emphasis on an exaggerated ideal of "toughness" goes with repression and rejection of feminine traits in men, and with contempt for women. There is hardly any mention of women in the presentation of Jaensch, and if there is, usually some affinity between women and the S-type is pointed out. According to Jaensch, the struggle between firmness and lack of firmness, between stability and what he calls "lability" is the struggle between the masculine and the "effeminate."

The intellect is considered such a non-virile element. The anti-type is said to have an inclination toward the playful, aesthetic and intellectual. We have actually found this inclination to be present in our adult low-scorers on ethnocentrism but have found little reason for looking askance at it; as was detailed earlier in this paper, a similar trend was found in the separate study on children and adolescents.

The rejection of theory and the general anti-intraceptiveness found in our "highs" is also prominent in Jaensch's version of anti-intellectualism. In his appraisal of science, theory is not considered a necessary detour to better understanding of reality but a subjectivistic leading-away from reality.

" 'Unorganically clapped upon' the unstable basic personality is a rational superstructure (which furnishes to these people a substitute for their lacking firmness and stability, for the dropping out of what is simply and plainly given in the external and internal world, and for the given 'world' altogether). . . . The struggle conducted by the physicists Lenard and Stark in an attempt to dislodge the theory of Einstein by establishing a more concretely oriented 'German Physics' can be understood only from this point of view. It is the struggle for consideration of reality in natural science and against the S-typical inclination to dissolve all reality into theory" (pp. 46, 49).

It will be remembered that recently Soviet writers have attacked Einstein from an anti-theoretical standpoint very similar to that of the Nazis, accusing him of an "idealistic" orientation of his physics.

Intelligence tests, Jaensch further asserts, were invented by the anti-type and thus do justice only to the anti-type. Failure of children of "the best German type" on these tests is ascribed to this disadvantage.

The way in which rejection of ambiguity and anti-intellectualism tie in with racial theory is revealingly illustrated by the following quotations from Jaensch. In the case of racial mixture,

"Nature has to leave . . . everything uncertain and in suspense. . . . The individual at birth may be endowed with nothing fixed and certain, just with the uncertainty, indeterminability and changeability which will enable him to adjust to each of the various conditions of life. . . . The opposite is true if an individual possesses only ancestors who from time immemorial have lived in the North German space and within its population. . . . The characteristics necessary for this life therefore may be safely placed in his cradle as innate, fixed, and univocally determined features."

And then he adds condemningly:

"Among all the higher mental functions intelligence is the most flexible and adaptable" (p. 230 ff).

In discussing adaptability, Jaensch further points out that the anti-type, when engaged in psychology and anthropology, is prone to think in terms of environment, education, intellectual influences and reason while his ideal type will refer to such factors as blood, soil, and tradition. It will be remembered that in *The Authoritarian Personality* the "highs" on ethnocentrism were prone to offer vague explanations of their failures in terms of heredity.

Heterogeneous blood mixture is connected, in the mind of Jaensch, with physical pollution by germs. According to psychoanalytic theory, the idea of pollution and contamination is related to sexual thoughts. In our material fear of germs was one of the more marked characteristics of the "highs." Jaensch also assumes a connection between certain contaminative syndromes and the feminine principle. Fear of illness is also present in his "struggle against the hollowed-out and diseased Christianity of the antitype" (p. 511).

Jaensch's programmatic quest for firmness, unambiguous response, and definiteness is in strange contrast with his endless writings full of intricacies and subtle if bizarre observations. It seems that Jaensch, like our "highs," is struggling for a way out of his own and his culture's unbearable complexity. Reportedly Jaensch was well aware of the presence of the dreaded "anti-typical" features in himself; apparently it is the projections of these features which he fights in his image of the anti-type, much in the way our "highs" fight their own projections in the outgroups. It was one of our findings that in order to maintain a glorified image of oneself and of the ingroup, such tendencies as fear, weakness, passivity, and aggressive feelings against authoritative figures must be kept in a repressed or suppressed state. Thus Jaensch's ideal type can afford even less than the anti-type to keep clear of the confusions involved in the mechanisms of projection and displacement.

Just as in our empirical findings on "highs," the overrigidity of Jaensch's ideal type reveals its affinity to confusion and chaos; and the faithfulness to reality in detail ascribed to this type also reveals its affinity to missing the essence of reality. Hence the unrealistic tendencies to expansion and the gross underestimation of the enemy. Hence it must be somebody else, say, the American, who will be considered unsoldierly and effeminate. Once more, refusal to face conflicts and shortcomings in oneself turns out to lead to a personalized view of other people and of the outside world, resulting in a distortion of reality and eventually in destruction.

This leads us back to a comparison between Jaensch's over-simplified view of "style-unity" and the self-compensatory type of unification tendencies within the person suggested by our data and the experiments that have followed. In spite of the rather consistent recurrence of elements of rigidity in various areas, there is no obvious or simple all-pervasive unity of style in the basic patterns of personality as we have conceived them. In surveying the attitudes which tend to go together in authoritarian individuals, we were faced with the coexistence of rigid perseverative behavior and an over-fluid, haphazard, disintegrated, random approach. This view of personal style thus involves "closeness of opposites," a principle not adequately understood by Jaensch. In my paper on "Intolerance of Ambiguity" (see Note 1) it was pointed out that

> "Lack of distance and too much distance to culture, parents, and other stimulus configurations seem to be more closely related to each other than is either of these to what we may term 'medium distance' from these situational elements" (p. 141).

A related phenomenon seemingly at odds with personal unity concerns discrepancies found in comparing one level of personality with another. Thus we may say that, in our prejudiced subjects, the negative side of the feelings toward parents is repressed without losing its dynamic force, only to be projectively transferred to other objects, such as minority groups. The clinging to definite dichotomies and demarcation lines apparently reduces the conflict on the conscious level but at the same time increases the underlying confusion.

We may rephrase the closeness of opposites, found both within each of the various levels of personality and from one level to another, in the verbal form of a paradox by saying that the authoritarian person tends to be consistently inconsistent, or consistently self-conflicting, in that he combines within himself such traits as: rigidity with extreme fluidity; over-caution with the tendency toward impulsive shortcuts to action; chaos and confusion with control; order and over-simplification in terms of black-white solutions and stereotypy; isolation with fusion; lack of differentiation with the mixing of elements which do not belong together; extreme concreteness with extreme generality; self-glorification with self-contempt; submission to powerful authorities with resentment against them; stress on masculinity with a tendency toward extreme passivity; and many other seemingly incompatible opposites, which thus reveal an intrinsic affinity of style to each other.

The higher-order unity of style given by these pervasive inconsistencies especially found in the authoritarian personality appears to be, as we may conclude, the result of attempts to reduce drastically underlying conflicts and ambivalences as well as cognitive complexities and ambiguities without producing reality-adequate or truly adaptive solutions.

Although most of the "high" ethnocentric subjects tend to combine opposite extremes in the manner described above, that is, tend to show a mixture of too much and too little distance from social or perceptual stimuli, we were able to distinguish sub-types within the "highs" in which one or the other side prevails. In one of these sub-varieties there is a prevalence of control, rigidity, caution and order so far as overt behavior is concerned while the chaotic side is suppressed and becomes manifest only under stress. In the other of these sub-varieties there is a predominance of chaos, fusion and acting out in impulsive action while the ideal of control and rigid order remains to a large extent inactive on the symbolic level of consciously-espoused values.

Both of these sub-varieties of the authoritarian personality pattern must be contrasted with the personality exhibiting a medium degree of flexibility, conformity and order to the effect that existing complexities are not unduly reduced. A kind of self-reconciled consistency is thus achieved which succeeds in managing the inconsistencies of reality at a conscious level rather than allowing them to invade the unconscious and to be lived out deviously and by displacement upon an alternative object or alternative goal. Such concepts as that of the "rigid low," introduced in our book and discussed in the present paper in the context of cognitive patterns, amply testify to the fact that we have not lost sight of the possibility that there may be curvilinear relationships among the various attitudes or traits of personality and that certain sub-varieties of the non-ethnocentric personality likewise exhibit the closeness of opposites that is bound to accompany intolerance of cognitive ambiguity or emotional ambivalence.

Our efforts toward definition of sub-types should further be taken as an indication that our concentration on extremes in terms of ethnocentrism—namely, the extremely "high" ethnocentric individual and the one extremely "low" on ethnic prejudice—has not led us to any questionable dichotomizing or all-or-none classification as seems present in such authors as Jaensch. We have made it clear repeatedly throughout our book that we meant to deal with group trends and statistical syndromes rather than with "types" in the historical absolute sense of pigeon-holing, although we have used the word occasionally for brevity.

In the way of statistical syndromes, however, the authoritarian pattern seems to offer something new in that it cuts across customary forms of classification, including those employed in psychiatry, in criminology, or in the description of social class structure. The authoritarian personality syndrome, by encompassing a previously unexplored combination of areas of investigation, may turn out to have predictive value in certain directions not covered by other existing classifications.

"LATENT" MOTIVATION AND THE "MANIFEST" PERSON

In discussing a joint work such as *The Authoritarian Personality*, what any one individual contributor may have to say will, understandably, depend upon his or her general theoretical and empirical orientation. To my mind, one of the most important features of our

Further Explorations by a Contributor

book in general, and of the interpretation of the interviews in particular, is the further illumination of the relationship between the so-called "latent" and "manifest" layers of personality as first conceived by psychoanalysis. This relevancy is facilitated by the fact that, as in psychoanalysis, our approach to the latent layer is based primarily on the subjects' verbal statements. While our extensive interviews on which many of our interpretations were based certainly cannot compare with the "analytic couch" type of material, depth interpretations were attempted (Chapters IX to XIII). These inferences were deliberately made in a global and intuitive way, and the relationship to the manifest data was by no means always explicit. Judgments of independent raters showed satisfactory reliabilities. A more rigorous attempt in the same direction was made in the study on ethnocentrism in children.

Before the advent of psychoanalysis, the importance of the distinction between overt manifestations and inferred motivational dynamics had mostly been overlooked. This importance is based on the fact that in our culture one's real motivations must quite often be disguised or transformed in order to pass individual and social censorship. In psychoanalysis, the unconscious, irrational, archaic, primitive or deep layer is almost by definition seen as modified or disguised in its manifestations. By the same token, the question of its accessibility to scientific effort arises. In statistical terms, disguise of motivation means that specific observable behavior becomes variable somewhat independently of motivational factors. Still, these underlying factors cannot be verified except by observation of behavior.

Due to this difficulty, we find two major types of inadequacy in approaching the problem of the relationship between manifest behavior and latent motivation. The first of these inadequacies is present in investigators prior, or unamenable, to psychoanalysis who have worked on the basis of a tacit assumption of a one-to-one relation between motivation and behavior. Such a concept of motivation would indeed represent no more than an unnecessary and operationally meaningless duplication without explanatory value. Nothing short of some sort of independent variability would necessitate the introduction of motivation as a separate category to account for the various patterns of manifestation. The second form of scientifically inadequate approach to the problem of motivation is characterized by the introduction of concepts so intangible, or so removed or divorced from behavior, that they become mystic or non-verifiable. For this reason, some researchers in the first group have suggested abandoning the concept of motivation altogether.

A third type of approach would seem to be able to get around these difficulties. It consists of the attempt to establish operationally independent bases for the two strata, motivation and behavior. There may be areas of overlap between the operational indicators for them; in this case the two could be kept conceptually separated by utilizing different segments or constellations of behavioral events. This policy would at the same time preserve their independent variability.

A systematic attempt of this latter kind was made by this writer[23] in a statistical analysis of the interrelationships between motivational and behavioral variables in the framework of a longitudinal University of California Adolescent Study. This attempt shall be reported here briefly because it is relevant as part of the background underlying the studies on the authoritarian personality. A basic assumption was that the introduction of intuitive motivational ratings based on an over-all appraisal of *long range* behavior may give an "independent" approach to motivation and thus resolve discrepancies between apparently diverse overt manifestations in *specific* behavior situations. This may furnish an important lead for uncovering an underlying set of fundamental characteristics of the subjects as brought out in the interpretative over-all ratings. Thus certain forms of overt behavior, e.g., surface friendliness, aggressiveness, and so on, were examined in a wider causal-genetic and dynamic context, and inferences were drawn which go beyond—and often are in apparent contradiction to—the gross phenotypical characteristics.

It turned out that different classes of behavioral expressions statistically not correlated with each other could be related to the same drive as conceived in terms of an over-all interpretation rating and thus could be viewed as "alternative manifestations" of that drive. Drive ratings, though involving more complex and more abstract concepts than do specific-behavior ratings, offer considerable advantages in organizing data on overt behavior in specific social situations.

---

[23] Frenkel-Brunswik, E., "Motivation and Behavior," *Genetic Psychol. Monographs*, 1942, 26, 121-265.

To give an example: Overt behavioral ratings on "exuberance" and "irritability" were found to correlate negatively with one another ($r = -.25$) and thus to be relatively incompatible; however, both of these behavior traits showed some positive correlation (.30 and .42) with ratings on the "drive for aggression." As a result of this statistical pattern, the multiple correlation between aggression and the two diverse behavioral features was found to be relatively high (.73); this means that adolescents considered basically aggressive are likely to be either overtly maladjusted, tense and anxious, or else successful in their overt social activities (say, as leaders), or occasionally both. Constellations of this kind are crucial in operationally establishing the principle of alternative manifestations of a drive.

One of the basic conclusions of *Motivation and Behavior* was that a total score based on summation of specific behavior items does not constitute an adequate basis for inferences concerning latent motivation. Among other things, the realization of this character of motivational constructs and of the fact that they must be based on a synopsis of seemingly conflicting or opposite alternative manifestations supplies a justification for the rather global character of the variables used in the evaluation of the interviews in *The Authoritarian Personality* and in the study on prejudice of children. In our view, the susceptibility to ethnic prejudice itself is but another case of "alternative" behavior; this view can be supported by any of the objective evidence brought forth in confirmation of the original psychoanalytic demonstration of displacement and of related mechanisms of substitution.

Before considering more fully our approach to the latent level, one more line of reasoning must be introduced. It may be linked to a study of the writer dealing with mechanisms of self-deception.[24] Verbal statements of students at the University of Vienna describing their own conduct and ideals were compared with certain crucial aspects of their actual behavior in which the underlying motivation could be assumed to be relatively close to the surface. It was hypothesized that even if a person is not conscious of his underlying "private" motivational pattern, these tendencies may find relatively obvious expression in some select aspects of the "public" behavior of the individual and could then be inferred from observation by others well acquainted with him.

---

[24] Frenkel-Brunswik, E., "Mechanisms of Self-deception," *Jour. of Social Psychol.*, 1939, 10, 409-420.

A number of discrepancies between self-images and actual conduct, remindful of discrepancies produced by certain "mechanisms" described in psychoanalysis, were objectively ascertained in this manner. It was further found that the distortion of an individual's self-perception tends to be the greater the more shortcomings he possesses or the weaker his ego. The strong and mature person can afford to face his shortcomings squarely and is, in fact, more concerned with them and with modifying them than he is with his virtues. In addition, not only the self-descriptions of our subjects but also their ethical ideologies as expressed in the alleged "guiding principles" of their behavior were found to be closely related to their personality dynamics.

Thus the ostentatious stress which the authoritarian person tends to place upon sincerity and honesty, as well as his tendency toward self-glorification, must be evaluated in the light of these earlier results involving types of direct behavioral observation not provided in *The Authoritarian Personality*. In particular, these earlier results demonstrate that emphasis on such traits as honesty and sincerity in one's "official" self-image tends to go with objective weakness rather than strength in the particular area concerned.

Still another result of the study on mechanisms of self-deception was the establishment of a number of "formal" criteria to help us discern whether a certain social facade or verbal statement is directly representative of the behavioral or motivational realities involved, or whether on the contrary it serves to compensate for a defect in these same realities and thus constitutes a self-deception about them. Before listing these formal criteria we should like to mention that we were led to the impression that formal elements of personality style, by virtue of their seemingly indifferent, nonthreatening nature, are not subject to censorship in the same manner as is content and that they therefore are potentially powerful tools in diagnostic procedures.

Some of these formal criteria are linguistic while others are more purely cognitive; some of them are crude while others are rather subtle or "minimal." Among the specific formal cues found useful in the differential diagnosis of self-deception were the following: the tendency to make unqualified statement; use of superlatives and exaggerations; absoluteness of emphasis; intolerance of ambiguity; the predominant reference to the extreme values of what actually are continua (dichotomizing); inconsistency between general as contrasted with specific features of behavior or of verbal statement, or inconsistency revealed by verbal responses to indirect questions; the occasional breaking through of a pattern of denial; stereotypy and the use of clichés; small range of variability of response and lack of shading; repetition.

Self-descriptions of various kinds—the only material directly available in *The Authoritarian Personality*—were deliberately kept very detailed in the interviews of both adult and adolescent subjects, and furnished a broad matrix of statements. Attention to the total context and to formal cues—gross as well as minimal—allowed us to infer differentiations between the face value of the statements and the hypothesized underlying motivations. Some of the formal variables listed above were utilized in the analysis of the self-descriptions in *The Authoritarian Personality*, and several of them were fruitful in the process of interpretation. Exaggeration, and inconsistency between the responses to general questions and to specific questions, proved especially useful in revealing the presence of hidden tendencies. Thus the glorification of the parents which is a characteristic of the ethnocentric person is usually confined to initial broad statements, that is, to a verbal generality in a certain context, while in the further, long-range course of questioning the forthcoming specific episodes relate almost exclusively to acts of victimization and injustice on the part of the parents. Over and above this, the initial statements of admiration tend to be stereotyped and filled with clichés, making use of a small range of expression, and showing exaggeration of feelings through the use of superlatives and through the development of positive or negative haloes. In this manner, formal criteria of expression help to highlight distortions in self perception and in the perception of others[25] and of social institutions.

In being able to draw our inferences from a greater variety of verbal utterances, we could further proceed to utilize insights concerning the relation between the latent and the manifest which are directly obtainable only by a longitudinal study.

Over and above this, a linguistic analysis of protocols given in response to the Thematic Apperception Test has been started in

---

[25] Related to this is the finding by R. Christie that subjects scoring high on authoritarianism tend to evaluate less correctly the preferences of their peers as measured by a sociometric test. (Unpublished report given at the Meetings of the Eastern Psychological Association, 1952.)

the framework of the California Study on ethnocentrism in children. With an eye on possible utilization as formal criteria for motivation, we are counting such variables as the verb-adjective quotient, expressions of certainty and uncertainty, qualifications, derivations, use of present, past or future tenses and their sequences, ratio of active over passive verbs, the number of meanings differentiated in the Thematic Apperception Test pictures, and so forth. More directly interpretative are such further categories of classification as consistency and organization, originality, relation to picture, and realism.

It is obvious that the evaluation of these characteristics must be done in an equally many-sided manner. Thus, we may find in the stories of unprejudiced children imaginative fairy tales which still show understanding and penetration of real relationships although on a symbolic level. On the other hand, we may also find very realistic stories which do reveal differentiated understanding of reality. Or we may find, as we did in some of our prejudiced children, an unrealistic story which is full of ruminative repetitions which do not add up to any organized sequence of events; and we may find this uncontrolled, undisciplined, and unimaginative flow of free associations combined—as it often is—with infantile preoccupations such as feeding and being fed. The analyses of the formal criteria in our subjects' productions are made not only for diagnostic purposes, that is, to help us discern the representational statement from the compensatory statement, but also to throw further light on the creativity and the cognitive penetration of our subjects.

One of the most significant findings in *The Authoritarian Personality* was that individuals scoring high on prejudice have an explicit image of themselves which is in contradiction to the one revealed by a more searching evaluation of the interviews and projective materials. This is in line with the studies reported above which had shown the significance of the discrepancy between conscious self-perceptions and the actual dynamics of conduct as seen by detached observers; the greater this discrepancy, the more we could expect actual maladjustments, insecurity, self-deception, and projection. Inconsistencies of this kind between the manifest and the latent layers are at the root of the authoritarian personality pattern. Here there is surface glorification of parents and authorities combined with an underlying resentment and even hatred of such authorities which is only thinly disguised; there is stress on virility going hand

Further Explorations by a Contributor

in hand with an underlying passivity and receptivity which leads to the wish to follow a strong leader; overt emphasis on conventional values is paralleled by a leaning toward destruction and chaos. The avoidance of ambiguity and the need for absolutes is but an attempt to counteract the internal chaos and lack of social and personality identity.

The lack of integration and the resultant break between the conscious and unconscious layers in the authoritarian personality, and the greater flexibility of transition and of intercommunication between the different personality strata in the more liberal individual, appear to have considerable implications for the respective personality patterns. The shutting out of certain aspects of feeling and inner reality in general must be seen as the underpinnings of the distorted perceptions and judgments of outer reality shown by the ethnocentric group. Whereas in the liberal group there tends to be a conscious coexistence of the conflicting trends, the ethnocentric group tends more toward a strict layering effect with one set of attitudes screened off from the others, so to speak.

The answer to the question as to whether a certain tendency is manifest or latent is not a purely academic matter. It may have far-reaching social repercussions. From all we know, it is unaccepted, repressed or latent tendencies, in short, those with respect to which there is self-deception, rather than the conscious or accepted ones which are likely to be projected onto the social and political scene. Thus, it is repressed fear of one's own weakness and lack of masculinity which prevents the development of pity for the weak in the ethnocentric. Ego-alien, immoral tendencies, when repressed in oneself, are the more readily perceived in others and ascribed to groups which seem to be not fully assimilated or else altogether alien. Repressed hostility toward the really powerful groups will be displaced onto outgroups whose weakness makes them suitable scapegoats. It must be stressed that not only the id but also the super-ego may be imbued with unconscious sadistic and primitive tendencies which must be resolved and replaced with the more reasonable judgments of the ego to insure genuinely democratic balance.

Since the essence of the latent tendencies is that they are often expressed in a variety of devious or subtle manifestations, the differentiation between the latent and the manifest is conceptually related to the principle of alternative manifestations. The relatively incidental "choice" between different alternative manifestations of the same underlying tendency is most crucial for the development of personality. Thus, whether a person is ethnocentric or liberal is closely related to whether his underlying aggression is accepted or not, ego-integrated or not, manifested in intensive rages or in a mild, day-to-day form of expression, directed against the powerful or against the weak, against other people or against violation of a principle. This puts an emphasis on manifest "behavior" as an equal partner to latent "motivation" so far as total personality makeup is concerned.

To give a more specific example of this multi-layer determination of personality we may refer to alternative manifestations of the so-called "anal" syndrome. While the ethnocentric variety of the anal person tends to be rigidly moralistic and to show preoccupation with such issues as money, neatness and a "good clean life and hard work," liberal anal personalities tend on the functional level toward constructive planning and systematic procedure as especially needed in scientific work, or else exhibit reaction formation to their anality by extreme denial of retentiveness and an overly carefree attitude.

In making our plea for inclusion of the manifest behavior aspect along with the depth aspect, we must not forget that the preoccupation of psychoanalysis with the discovery of the dynamic importance of the unorganized, primitive, pleasure-seeking system of instinctual drives did not preclude Freud from being the first to point out some important aspects of the intimate interaction of these biological with the social factors in the individual,[26] even if this recognition was largely confined to childhood situations. Such processes as sucking, bowel movement, and masturbation, considered as purely instinctual phenomena before the advent of the dynamic approach to personality, have been woven by psychoanalysis into the fabric of social interaction. However, the way in which Freud and present-day orthodox Freudians deal with social problems undoubtedly does not tell the full story. Very little is said about the satisfactions which may be derived from successfully adopted social roles and identities. The environment, and behavioral adjustment to this environment, enters the scope of traditional psychoanalytic investigation insofar as it permits a repetition of childhood reactions

---

[26] Freud, S., *Totem and Taboo* (Collected Papers, Hogarth Press), London.

to father, mother and other persons in the past social environment of the child.

From the position just described psychoanalysis has moved somewhat toward recognition of the neglected aspects by stressing "ego-psychology." Though Freud recognizes the fact that the ego "has the task of bringing the influence of the external world to bear upon the id," the development of the ego is ascribed mainly to the necessity of delaying gratification. Thus ego development is seen as occurring under the supremacy of the id; or, as Fenichel has put it, the ego is the "differentiated surface layer of the id."[27] The so-called "defense mechanisms," such as repression, reaction formation, projection, and so forth, give the rules of the transformations of the instincts, thus connecting human behavior not only to its internal sources but also to external realities.

Yet, while it is true that the variety of isolated manifestations is too diverse for scientific presentation, it is also true that integration in terms of id dynamics alone is too universal an integration. It is not enough to know the various ways of defense against the instincts; we need also to know the various ways of positive gratification to be gained from our environment. To my knowledge, Hartmann[28] was the first "orthodox" psychoanalyst to stress explicitly the relative independence of perception, learning, and thinking from the instinctual processes. This is a second step in the development of psychoanalysis away from the id and toward problems of adaptation to the environment. The latter type of problems has for a long time been the major concern of academic psychology to such an extent that it often prevented the acknowledgment of the dynamic factors introduced by psychoanalysis.

Although stressed at the theoretical level, the actual development of ego psychology has remained more programmatic than real within psychoanalysis. Such development could have been especially fruitful had it been accompanied by an explicit attempt toward an interaction of psychoanalysis and psychology.

After this short sketch of the developments, the strengths, and

---

[27] Fenichel, O., *Psychoanalytic Theory of Neurosis*, Norton, New York, 1945, p. 57.

[28] Hartmann, H., "Ego-psychology and the problem of adaptation." (Translated from a paper published in 1939.) In: *Organization and Pathology of Thought*, ed. by Rapaport, D., Columbia Univ. Press, New York, 1951.

the limitations of psychoanalytic thinking, we now turn to the problem of the influence of this thinking on the studies of the authoritarian personality. Much of our effort represents an attempt to recognize the irrational, archaic, primitive or deep layer which genetically precedes rational, reality-oriented behavior, and to follow the influences of this stratum upon the surface manifestations and observable effects of behavior. Another relationship to psychoanalysis is given by our assumption that the liberal personality represents a generally higher level of psycho-sexual maturity as envisaged by psychoanalysis than does the authoritarian personality. This hypothesis may also be called upon to account for the greater variability of the liberal group which to a certain extent spreads over various stages of maturity, whereas the ethnocentric group is more strictly limited to certain earlier maturational levels. Aside from the more general developmental approach to this point made at the end of the first section, we further explored the major conflicts of our two groups in terms of the psycho-sexual scheme offered by psychoanalysis by establishing the content of conflicts coming to light in Thematic Apperception Test stories. In the project on children we are in the process of ascertaining what kinds of aggression and what kinds of dynamic conflicts, in terms of orality, anality, etc., are manifested in our "Highs" and "Lows" and what types of formal characteristics go with greater psycho-sexual maturity. The evidence so far seems to indicate that advanced psycho-sexual development, e.g., the prominence of the oedipal conflict, tends to go with realism, originality, and an absence of ethnocentrism, and that the coloring of the personality structure in terms of orality or anality is a further determinant of the formal quality of the productions. Thus, for example, one of our unprejudiced children who showed evidence of having reached the oedipal stage and who at the same time exhibited oral traits displayed striking imagination and creativity in the sense of a true penetration of reality whereas the more purely infantile orality displayed by the boy subject mentioned earlier in this paper was accompanied by a sterile type of rumination about the topic of food. In these and other cases the intrinsic connectedness of the various coexistent features seemed rather evident.

Generally in the description of the authoritarian personality, the categories dealing with the handling of such basic tendencies as sex, aggression, and dependence are among the ones which most effectively discriminate the ethnocentric group from the liberal. Moreover, it is not so much the degree or strength of these tendencies, as the fact of their repression or displacement as contrasted with their acceptance which seems essential.

This latter matter would still seem to fall under the consideration of defense mechanisms and thus to be within the general province of psychoanalytic thought. However, there are several points in the studies on the authoritarian personality and on ethnocentrism in children in which we found ourselves compelled to go beyond these considerations. First, the "manifest personality" had to be taken more seriously in the execution of the program, as witness our exploration of certain rather minute phenomenological shades in our subjects' political and social ideology. Our investigation included attitudes toward vocation, school, friendships, over and above the more obvious clinical topics such as family and sex. We had realized from the outset that a complete picture of personality must refer to both the pattern of basic motivations and to the manner of manifestation of the tendencies involved. Although differences in defense mechanisms may be partly responsible for the formation of sub-varieties within the authoritarian pattern, it would have been very difficult if not impossible to describe, say, the socially constructive and cognitively creative activities of our liberal-minded subjects in terms of defense mechanisms alone.

We may sum up by saying that while psychoanalysis has been first in seeing the necessity of a distinction between the manifest and the latent, its conceptual apparatus has been inadequate in dealing with the manifest layer in its own right. Most of Freud's considerations concentrate on the innate instinctual development while the discussion of their modification under the restrictions and the disapproval of the environment take secondary place. The regrouping of manifest observable facts in latent terms as undertaken by Freud has stressed common "cause" to the exclusion of stress on common "effect." It is the latter that takes the limelight in recent purposive behaviorism and psychology in general. "Whereas psychoanalysis has been asking, 'Which drive?' and general psychology has been asking, 'Which effect?,' a unified psychology should ask, 'Which effect out of which drive?' "[29]

---

[29] Frenkel-Brunswik, E., "Psychoanalysis and personality research." (In *Symposium on psychoanalysis by analyzed experimental psychologists.*) *Jour. of Abnorm. & Social Psychol.*, 1940, 35, 176-197.

THE PROBLEM OF BIAS AND VALUES IN SOCIAL RESEARCH

In conclusion, value-orientations of an over-all kind must be brought into the picture. The two aspects of this problem to be discussed here are, first, the influence such orientation, when held by us as the researchers, may have had upon the results of our investigation and, second, the development of value-orientation in the individual subject.

We may agree with the logical empiricists about the selective and, to a certain degree, subjective nature of value-judgments.[30] But I would stress even more than they do the role facts play in the formation of such values. For this reason, the accumulated knowledge in the social sciences may help us to make a choice between alternative value systems. In giving up a metaphysical or absolute position, we do not need to go to the other extreme of utter relativism. Although the social scientist, as a scientist, cannot make the ultimate choice for mankind, his function is to throw as much light as possible on the implications involved in existing value systems, and to make explicit all the ramifications inherent in the options.

The social psychologist is just as much a child of his period with its varying climates of conceptualization as is the experimental psychologist or the psychological theorist. Over and beyond this, however, as was pointed out by Mannheim and other sociologists, there is probably no way for the social scientist to fully escape infiltration of his outlook by the socio-political climate of opinion in which he lives, no matter how hard he may try. The very labeling of one's topic may reveal the existence of a pre-scientific bias. We may think of the use of such valuative terms as "ethnic prejudice," "health," or "progress" in publication titles and similar ostensive contexts. The use of such terms is justified only if it can be empirically shown that the characteristics or social attitudes concerned have detrimental consequences for their target or for their holder, say, by rendering the latter less suited for coping with the complexities of social and cognitive problems. This is what we have set out to do at the psychological level.

---

[30] See especially M. Schlick, *Problems of Ethics* (transl. New York: Prentice-Hall), and C. L. Stevenson, *Ethics and Language* (Yale Univ. Press, 1944).

Compensation for the researcher's bias may be possible by making explicit, and by tracing the potential or real influences of, the biases inherent in declared or tacit allegiance to any of the competing "points of view." This we have attempted in the manner of a self-corrective. Tracing of bias is one of the foremost tasks facing the history and the sociology of knowledge. A further check consists of investigators of varying standpoints doing parallel research, choosing their own problem-conceptions and tools of investigation. In this way fewer aspects of the problem will be overlooked, and we will be the better equipped to ultimately choose between alternative value systems.

Let us discuss the second of these remedies first. From the argumentative point of view it is unfortunate that research concerning war and prejudice is engaged in predominantly by those who do not like war or prejudice. From this angle we must welcome the fact that E. R. Jaensch has given us articulate description of the ideal personality type from the standpoint of Nazi ideology. The studies of Jaensch, reported in some detail above in discussing cognitive patterns and unity of style, have thus certainly been conducted under a bias opposite to ours; yet they were found to lead to the recognition of similar patterns albeit with a different evaluative slant. All this is over and beyond the variegated corroboration received from investigators who share our orientation and to which little reference is made in this paper.

We may now turn to the question as to whether the authors of *The Authoritarian Personality* held a value-bias incisive enough to invalidate the procedures and results of the book in its own right. If this were true, serious objections could indeed be raised since relationships presented as empirically established would in fact be no more than the expression of a prejudice on our part. We should like to list several arguments against such strictures.

First, although our results are partially based on such interpretative procedures as the evaluation of the interview, we tried to reduce bias to a minimum by the procedure of "blind" scoring as effected by an attempt to conceal from the rater the standing of the subject on ethnocentrism *per se* and by the employment of independent raters for the same protocols.

Second, the quantitative results obtained with the F scale measuring personality syndromes associated with ethnocentrism were in accordance with the more interpretative analysis derived from the interview and projective material.

Third, another bias may have resulted from our emphasis on subjects scoring at either of the extremes on the ethnocentrism questionnaires. Actually, emphasis on extremes was more prominent in the hypothesis-forming stages of our work than it was in the final efforts of proving our hypotheses. While much of the stimulus for the development of the scale-items comes from part of our preliminary interview and projective material which is drawn predominantly from extreme "highs" or "lows," all our findings based on scales, including the F scale, are computed from the total sample. Further support for the generalizability of our results may be found in a questionnaire study of Allport and Kramer[31] which yielded relationships between personality and prejudice very similar to ours. While our concentration, in certain parts of the book, on the two extremes allows them to stand out in clearer relief for conceptualization, it apparently has not distorted the final picture.

Fourth, it must be reiterated that even on the basis of the extreme samples as used for the interviews none of the objectionable "dichotomous types" seemed to suggest themselves. To remove possible misunderstandings on this point we quote the following passages from *The Authoritarian Personality*.

> "These differences are based on an analysis of group trends within statistical samples and do not imply that every individual will exhibit most or even a large proportion of the features belonging to either the 'high' or the 'low' syndrome, as the case may be. . . . Certain individuals seem to possess a relatively large number of either 'high' or 'low' features while others seem to have features of both patterns, with a relatively slight prevalence of one or the other. . . . It should thus be kept in mind that the summary which follows deals with composite pictures of these patterns, abstracted from the study of groups, rather than with individual cases. Were we to lay greater stress on concrete personalities, the most frequent syndromes or combinations of trends within single individuals would have to be determined as an intermediate step, leading to the definition of subtypes within the prejudiced and the unprejudiced patterns . . . which will be taken up more systematically in Chapter XIX" (p. 473).

Fifth, another line of argument against the possibility of error through bias may be derived from the separate California study on

---

[31] Allport, G. W. and Kramer, B. M., "Some roots of prejudice," *Jour. of Psychology*, 1946, 22, 3-39.

children, mentioned above. The reactions of prejudiced children to such clearly defined stimuli as perceptual configurations, stories or cognitive problem-solving tasks show tendencies toward rigidity, distortion of reality and intolerance of ambiguity similar to those frequent in the social and emotional area in ethnocentric children and adults. But whereas in the social-emotional field ascertainment of such tendencies as distortion of reality may be controversial, they can be more definitely pinned down in perceptual reactions where there can be no doubt whether the reaction in question is adequate or inadequate to the stimulus.

Sixth, it may be pointed out that the general immaturity of the authoritarian personality makeup as derived from our quantitative evaluation of the interviews has also been corroborated by the direct approach with the California children. It was demonstrated that many of the tendencies established in both adults and children as accompaniments of ethnic prejudice—such as superstition, intolerance of ambiguity, tendency to dichotomize, admiration of strength—are more frequent in chronologically earlier stages. In other words, the direction of the difference between the prejudiced and the unprejudiced child or adult is the same as that between the younger and the older child. In this sense, the statement of the greater immaturity of the authoritarian personality is a strictly descriptive rather than an evaluative one.

Seventh, a few words concerning our choice of the verbal over a more purely behavioral approach should be appended to this discussion of possible sources of research bias. We may point to the fact that comparing individuals of such diverse kind as our subjects has in a very real sense provided situational variation; the results of such inquiry overlap more with results gained from a direct sampling of situations than "situationalists" may expect. Furthermore, direct observation of interaction between members of majority and minority groups does not *a priori* guarantee greater predictability to other situations than could be furnished by "mere" verbal reports. In any quest for direct observation there is the tacit assumption that motor behavior in general, and behavior exhibited directly in the interaction situation in particular, possess something approaching absolute validity. But in taking such a point of view no attention is paid to mechanisms of conscious or unconscious distortions and to the possibility that such distortions may be even more serious in a direct than in an indirect situation. Thus many of our highly prejudiced subjects who at the same time are conformists would very likely be quite polite when facing a member of a minority group in a concrete situation, yet would otherwise take every opportunity to propagate discriminatory policies. In all such cases the behavior in crucial situations would be more closely approximated by the verbal report than it would be by isolated behavior segments observable in an experimental contact situation. As has been pointed out by the writer in greater detail elsewhere,[32] there may in this manner be more "lying" in some forms of behavior than there is in certain verbal utterances.

Let us now turn to our last topic, that of values as a field of social-psychological investigation in its own right. This problem calls, perhaps more than any other, on the resources of both psychoanalysis and the social sciences for adequate handling. Only by a combination of a genetic, motivational, latent approach with that of an overt social face-value approach can we hope to be led successfully through all its vicissitudes. In *The Authoritarian Personality* there was considerable reference to the ethical ideology of our subjects, such as to their ego ideals and their conception of evil and virtue. A somewhat more detailed study of moral values has been made in the study on prejudice in children. Thus, the question of what they considered "right" or "wrong" was brought up in addition to an inquiry into their conceptions of the ideal father, mother, teacher, the "perfect boy" and "perfect girl" and so forth as mentioned above. Thus we tried to trace the origin of the authoritarian conscience.

An example may be given from the interview protocol of one of our prejudiced boys. This boy, who considers his father to be strict and inconsistent, thinks that anything he himself does is all right as long as he is not caught by his father; only then does it become "wrong." There is a wavering between submission to his father and fantasies of becoming stronger than his father, and this conflict carries over to his dealings with life in general. Sometimes he feels that life is full of challenges which he cannot meet, and that he must be satisfied with a very modest niche. At other times he develops megalomaniacal fantasies of becoming a strong leader and having everyone submit to him. Again, formal criteria such as the

---

[32] Frenkel-Brunswik, E., "Dynamic and cognitive categorization of quantitative material. I: General problems and the Thematic Apperception Test," *Jour. of Psychology*, 1948, 25, 253-260.

tendency toward absolutizing, exaggeration and dichotomizing are being applied in this analysis.

In exploring the value systems of these children, special attention is being given to the way in which they incorporate the contradictory trends presented in their education. The desirability of helping the weak is stressed in our civilization along with the values of justice, liberty and freedom; at the same time a kind of tough realism and the necessity of being successful in a competitive game is also emphasized. Adults often handle these conflicts by relegating one of these two aspects to the field of rationalization and ideology while realizing the other in their behavior. Children, on the other hand, tend to take all the aspects at the same serious level; it may well be that in this dilemma ethnic prejudice has the important function of locating and concretizing the negative images and at the same time strongly differentiating them from the positive. Thus an arbitrary reality is created to take care of contradictions which otherwise would be too difficult to integrate into a common picture. There may be, furthermore, a general discrepancy between the child's real experiences and his stereotypical means of expressing them which could be, but not always is, counteracted by education.

In this same study of social discrimination in children we tried to relate ethical ideologies to the personality structure of the children and to the sociopsychological background of their families. Ethnocentric children and their homes emerge as tending toward over-simplified moralism, a stress on prohibitions and on a negative phrasing of norms, and severity coupled with license; in brief, there is a tendency toward coexistence, or alternation, of absolutism with extreme relativism and cynicism in the realm of values. The same approach could be applied to authors who have formulated ethical ideologies, especially when these ideologies are deviant from accepted belief as in the case of Jaensch. A detailed analysis of the value systems espoused by different individuals and in different cultures, and of the relatedness of these systems to psychological and social realities, appears to be one of the more pressing requirements for future research.

INDEX

Abstract reasoning, 248
Ackerman, N. W., 157, 161, 202
Adorno, T. W., 11, 28, 168
Aichhorn, A., 205
Allport Ascendence-Submission Scale, 66
Allport, F. H., 150, 153
Allport, G. W., 272
Almond, G. A., 62, 63, 69, 212
Alternative manifestations of drives, 265-266
American Jewish Committee, 94
Anal syndrome, 266
Analysis of data, critique of, 96-98
Anomie, relationship to authoritarianism, 90
Anti-Defamation League of B'nai B'rith, 94
Anti-type, 252-256
Arno, P., 101
Aron, B., 11
Attitude scale construction, 14-15, 70-79, 126-140
Authoritarian submission: similarity of fascist and communist, 34-36; subcultural factors, 136-137
Authoritarianism: and behavior, 140-149; and early environment, 173-175, 182-183, 188-189; and ethnocentrism, 154-156, 167; and education, 91-96, 169-171; and the F scale, 125-140; and high school activities, 147-148; hypothetical and empirical clusters in, 133-140; and intelligence, 168-169, 171; and political behavior, 145-149; and presidential preference, 145-146; of "Right" and "Left"; similarities in, 38-42; situational factors and changes in, 190-192; and social class differences, 234-235; and social judgments, 143-144; and volunteering, 142; and voting, 147
Autokinetic phenomena, 248

Bailey, S. K., 204
Baker, G., 200
Barron, F. X., 249
Behavior, general and specific, 260-261
Berelson, B., 114
Benedict, R., 220
Bettelheim, B., 197, 214
Bloch, D. A., 219
Block, Jack, 247
Block, Jeanne, 247
Bogardus, E. S.: 14, 150
Bolshevism, see Communism
Brown, R., 250

Catholics, 48
Campbell, D. T., 151, 152, 155
Centers, R., 118
Christie, R., 16, 22, 134, 135, 138, 139, 143, 157, 168, 169, 191, 248, 263
Cleckley, H., 206
Closeness of opposites, 256-258
Coding, see Interviews
Cogan, E. A., 156, 157
Comfort, A., 220
Communism, analysis of, 30-38
Communists, scores on the F scale, 130-133
Constancy hypothesis, 253
Cook, S. W., 133

276

Index

Correlations, inter-sample fluctuations, 57-60
Coughlin, Father, 48
Counselors, authoritarian and equalitarian, 140-142

Davis, A., 118
De Grazia, S., 213
Depression and anti-Semitism, 158-160
Deprivation and political values, 210-216
de Tarde, G., 200
Dickens, C., 200
Dicks, H. V., 128
Dombrose, L. A., 148, 251
Durkheim, E., 19, 174

Eager, J., 78, 140
Education and attitudes, 64
Education and authoritarianism and ethnocentrism, 91-96, 169-171
Education and interrelatedness of attitudes, 58-60, 171-172, 174
Edwards, A. L., 16, 128, 225
Edwards, M., 245
Ego-psychology, 267
Ehle, Emily, 62
Engle, B., 221
Engels, F., 36
Ericson, M. C., 118, 173
Ethnocentrism: and abstract reasoning, 248; and child rearing practices, 236-245; correlation with authoritarianism, 154-156, 167; definition of, 149-150; education, relation to, 91-96; and memory, 249; and occupation, 233-234; and personality, 157-167; and sex roles, 240-242; and social relations in children, 243-244
Ewing, C. A. M., 203
Extreme cases, use of in research, 65-67, 272

Fascism—26, 27; in the United States, 43
Fascist ideology and the F scale, 127-130
F scale, see authoritarianism and fascist ideology
Fenichel, O., 267
Fisher, J., 249
Frank, J., 212

French, T. M., 221
French, V. V., 101
Ford, G. S., 198
Forthal, S., 199
Frenkel-Brunswik, E., 11, 17, 22, 31, 36, 39, 41, 42, 173, 204, 226, 230, 260, 261, 269, 274
Freud, S., 16, 18, 266, 267, 269
Fromm, E., 13, 228

Garceau, O., 200
Garcia, J., 134, 135, 138, 139, 157
Gaudet, H., 114
Glueck, E., 209
Glueck, S., 209
Gosnell, H. F., 199
Gough, H. G., 147, 158, 159, 160, 242, 245
Groups: characteristics of members, 62-63; membership in and authoritarianism, 178-182; membership in and ideology, 112-115
Guttman, L., 15, 139

Haddow, A., 201
Haimowitz, M. L., 251
Haimowitz, N. R., 251
Harding, J. S., 169
Harper, M. H., 15-16
Harris, D. B., 242, 245
Hartley, E. L., 59, 109, 118
Hartley, R. E., 109
Hartmann, H., 267
Hatt, P., 60
Havel, J., 237
Haveman, E., 105
Heidenhain, A., 221
Herring, E. P., Jr., 200
High school activities, 147-148
Hill, D. S., 95
Himmelhoch, J., 129, 162, 163
Hitler, A., 35
Horkheimer, M., 13, 20
Horowitz, E. L., 58, 109
Horowitz, R. E., 58
Howells, T. H., 17
Huffman, P. E., 242
Hyman, H., 21, 67, 78, 124

Institut für Sozialforschung, 13-14
Intelligence and authoritarianism and ethocentrism, 168-169, 171
Intelligence testing and Nazi psychology, 254-255

Intelligence test scores, 168-169, 171
Interviews: coding of, 80-86; construction of codes, 87-89; qualitative interpretation of, 101-107; quality of, 79-81; ratings of and questionnaire scores, 164-165; ratings of and bias, 184-188; ratings of and blind scoring, 271; psychiatric, 188-189
Intolerance of ambiguity, 245-248
Irrationality and prejudice, 107-112

Jacques, E., 210
Jaeger, W. 198
Jaensch, E. R., 252, 253, 254, 255, 256, 258, 271, 275
Jahoda, M., 157, 161, 202
Janowitz, M., 197, 214
Jarvik, M. E., 237

Kaplan, A., 197
Kardiner, A., 235
Katz, D., 67
Kendall, P. L., 100
Key, V. O., Jr., 200
Kingsley, J. D., 203
Kitt, A. S., 115
Kligerman, C., 221
Kornhauser, A. W., 118
Kramer, B. M., 272
Kris, E., 200
Krugman, H., 130
Kutner, B., 248

Laird Personality Inventory, 66
"Larry", 31, 89, 111, 180
Laswell, H. D., 16, 18, 22, 197, 210, 215, 228
Lazarsfeld, P. F., 11, 15, 93, 102, 114
LeBon, G., 200
Leites, N., 33
Lenin, N., 33, 36
Leninism: see Communism
Lerner, D., 222
Levinson, D. J., 11, 28, 29, 31, 59, 148, 181, 190, 242, 251
Levinson, M. H., 11
Lewin, K., 230
Likert, R., 15, 118
Lindner, R. M., 210
Linebarger, P. M. A., 198
Long, H., 48
Lowell, A. L., 198

"Mack", 31, 89, 111, 180
Macmahon, A. W., 200
Martin, E. M., 200
Martin, W. E., 242, 245
Maslow, A. H., 13
Maslow Security-Insecurity scale, 161
Marx, K., 36
McCandless, B. R., 151, 152, 155
McConaughy, J. B., 224, 225
McDougal, M. S., 211
Memory, 249
Merriam, C. E., 199, 212
Merton, R. K., 11, 115
Michels, R., 198
Millett, J. D., 200
Milton, O., 145
Minnesota Multi-phasic, 144, 158-161
Money-Kyrle, R. E., 210
Moore, H. T., 17
Morrow, W., 11, 234
Morse, N. C., 150, 153
Motivation and behavior, 259-269
Munro, W. B., 199
Murphy, G., 15, 16, 17, 58, 118, 179, 199
Murphy, Lois B., 15, 16, 17, 58, 179, 199
Mussen, P. H., 144, 146

Nativist political groups, 45-48
Nazism, see Fascism
Newcomb, T. M., 15, 16, 17, 58, 176, 179, 199
Neumann, S., 222
Norms, national in opinions, 67-69
North, R., 222

Occupation, 233-234
Oedipal phase, 207-208, 210, 268
Older, H. J., 126
Ostrogowski, M., 198

Parental roles, attitudes toward, 238-239
Patriotism and prejudice, 153-154
PEC scale, See Radicalism-conservatism
Peel, R. V., 199
Personality and political roles, 43-49
Personality centered research, 227-232
Pimlott, J. A. R., 200
Political: behavior, 145-149; move-

ments, development of, 227-228; roles, 198-201; roles and personality, 222-224; science and the study of political participation, 199-202
Politics, functional and conventional definitions, 203-204
Power: centered personality, 202, 206-224; preoccupation with, 37-38; relationships, 197-198
Prejudice, generality of: 57-60, 150-154; See also, Ethnocentrism
Presidential preferences, 145-146
Prothro, E. T., 152
Psychoanalysis and social factors, 266-269
Psychopaths and politics, 205-206

Racism, 255
Radicalism-Conservatism, 17, 24-30, 66-67, 72-74
Raskin, E., 133
Read, I., 62
Redl, F., 205
Rees, J. R., 220
Reichard, S., 161, 162
Riesman, D., 213
Rigidity, 60-61, 247, 248, 250
"Rigid Lows," discussion of, 39-42, 251, 258
Rokeach, M., 17, 60, 61, 96, 97, 169, 237, 247, 251
Roles, political, 198-201
Rorschach scores and authoritarianism, 161-163
Rosen, E., 142
Ross, N. F. S., 203
Rosten, L. C., 200

Salter, J. A., 199
Sampling, limitations, 54-69
Sanford, F. H., 95, 126, 147
Sanford, R. N., 11, 28, 31
Schermerhorn, R. A., 59, 181, 190
Schick, M., 270
Scodel, A., 144
Self-deception, 261-63, 265
Sex roles, 240-242
Sheatsley, P. B., 21, 124, 169
Shils, E. A., 16, 20, 131
Smith, G. L. K., 47
Smith, M. B., 63, 78, 123, 140

Smith, H. L., 78
Social judgements, 143-144
Social marginality, 232-233
Social reality, 107-109, 175
Social relations among children, 243-244
Sociological indices, 232
Sorel, G., 27
South Carolina legislature, study of, 224-225
Sperling, O., 222
Srole, L., 64, 90, 96, 156, 169, 171, 172, 174, 175
Stagner, R., 16, 127, 128, 133, 150
Stalin, J. V., 33, 35, 36
Statistical procedures, 115-117
St. Augustine, 140
Stein, H., 204
Stevenson, C. L., 270
S-type see Anti-type
Sullivan, P. L., 61
Sumner, W. G., 149
Synesthesia, 253

Taft, D. R., 56
Tertullian, 12
Thurstone, L. L., 15
Truman, D. M., 204
Typology, 258, 272

Unity of Style, 252

Vagts, A., 201
Values and bias in research, 270-75
Values and institutions, 213-221
Values, as a subject for research, 274-75
Vetter, G. B., 66
Volunteering for experiments, 142
von Hartmann, E., 200
Voting behavior, 147

Wallace, H., 29, 30, 115
War, attitudes toward, 69
Welsh, G. S., 249
West, P. S., 105
West, R., 213
Whitehead, A. N., 14
Wineman, D., 205
Wolf, K., 100
Wyszynski, A. B., 146